And So Be It

And So Be It

CONVERSATION WITH ANGELS

~ VOLUME II ~

Dror B. Ashuah

EPIGRAPH
A DIVISION OF MONKFISH BOOK PUBLISHING COMPANY
RHINEBECK ~ NEW YORK

AND SO BE IT: CONVERSATION WITH ANGELS © 2010
by Dror B. Ashuah

ISBN 978-0-9825255-2-4

Book and cover design by Georgia Dent

Library of Congress Control Number: 2009939033

Bulk purchase discounts for educational or promotional purposes are available.

First Edition

First Impression

10 9 8 7 6 5 4 3 2 1

To continue the conversation: WWW.ANDSOBEIT.COM

Epigraph
An Alternative Publishing Imprint of
Monkfish Book Publishing Company
27 Lamoree Road
Rhinebeck, New York 12572
www.epigraphps.com

Contents

Dedication

*I wish to dedicate this book to those who give intent
to turn on their light and discover their own divinity.*

A Foreword from the Author

MY FAMILY AND I were traveling to Rajasthan, Northern India in April, 2008. We stayed in an ashram situated on top of a beautiful scenic mountain near the border with Pakistan.

For four days, I found a comfortable routine. After the daily 4 am meditation, I went to the common dining hall to receive the angels' messages. Men and women sipped chai tea and spoke softly about the teachings of the day. It felt safe to do my "work" in the peaceful atmosphere.

But on the fifth day after breakfast my daughter complained that she did not feel well. By lunch she developed a little fever. Unaccustomed to the food, she might have caught one of those strange bacteria or viruses that travelers in India often hear and warn each other about. I feel that I can deal with many stressful situations but when she gets a fever, I forget everything I know and become worried. Her fever was climbing higher and higher, and within four hours she was placed on a bench in the hallway of the infirmary and connected to an IV tube.

The infirmary had no room for her. I sat beside her very worried.

As the hours passed by, I felt angst climbing up my throat constricting my breathing which quickly turned into full-blown fear. My daughter seemed to be getting weaker and weaker by the hour and she was not responding to the medicine given through the IV tube. That night she finally was moved to a room. I remember watching the drips from the IV tube and feeling as if time had slowed to a halt. I felt helpless.

I sat beside my daughter on a crooked chair in a dim, neon lit room as two kind Indian nurses adjusted her IV and administered again a yellow-hued medicine. My fear elevated to near panic.

Later that night, my daughter went to the bathroom and when she returned she fainted in her mother's arms. I jumped up, picked her up and carried her back to bed in my arms. I realized that this was a dream I had weeks before our trip to India began, a dream I did not share with anyone although it remained a vivid memory in my mind.

In the dream, we were in the Ashram and I saw myself pick my daughter up from the floor and carry her in my arms. When I awoke in horror, I wasn't sure if she was alive. Realizing that I was living this dream made me dizzy and nauseated, the fear so overwhelming that I felt like I might faint.

My fear was paralyzing. My body felt cold. This was my daughter lying there! With no hospital nearby, she had become so weak she could not eat. The nurse, in a serious tone, said that my daughter's immune system was not strong because normally people get over these viruses quickly. That was all I needed to hear!

Then it dawned on me. The angels often speak of fear and the havoc it wreaks on our systems. Until this experience, I felt that they were not really talking about me but other people. Now I was experiencing this paralyzing, unbearable fear that stopped my vibration and was so debilitating that I forgot the tools within me. I knew from the deepest place within that I had to surrender, and rediscover my core power. I asked for help. I began, disconnecting from the room and going deeper inside. My hands felt heavy and with effort I placed my right hand over her head to send healing energy. In the beginning my fear did not allow the energy to flow but I kept letting go of my resistance and calming myself down, slowing and deepening my breath. Gradually the energy began to flow more freely. I recalled the angels' teachings and I repeated to myself, *Everything has a purpose and everything comes from love to bring us to our highest learning.*

As I repeated these words to myself, warmth returned to my body. Little by little, I felt more power returning to me. I continued telling myself that all is divine and it is my choice how to see it. The more I surrendered and accepted that I was in the right place and at the right time and whatever happened would be for the highest purpose, the more energy came back to my hands. Soon I felt blessed healing energy flowing through my hands again. I pulled out my pendulum and my healing crystals and began chanting a healing mantra softly.

I have felt comfortable with healing tools and methods as I somehow knew intuitively what to do with them. However, when it was my helpless daughter lying there with 103.5 fever in the middle of nowhere, I forgot everything.

My daughter struggled for three days and nights. On my birthday, after midnight, the fever broke. This was the most precious birthday gift I have ever received.

❧

In a message from *Conversations with Angels: So Be It*, the angels said that I will need to experience many of the things they speak of so the words will come from deep understanding and not theory. The angels told me a few days later in a new message that this experience was indeed a test.

This was one of many tests I have experienced since writing these messages. I have had my own work cut out for me. As a conduit for the angels' messages, I am reminded of my own limitations and the limitless progress I have yet to make. My personal life had become more imbalanced than ever before, and I felt ever more strongly that my mission was to find equilibrium using the "tools" stored in my "tool shed." The messages from the first book foretold where I was going and guided me on in the right direction by illuminating my path when I needed it most. At times, I would hear verses from the book while I was experiencing a challenge. Each challenge pushed me and I, at times reluctantly, grasped the full meaning of this journey.

In the year since finishing the first book of messages, I realized that the writings illuminated the physical, emotional and spiritual journey that we all are facing at this moment as individuals and as a society. These messages are not about blissfully meditating in an ashram. These teachings are not about how much you know and how much of your spiritual teachings and Mantras you retain. The angels' messages are about surrendering and understanding that the only real power we have is love. The way to link to this power of love is by using our tools of intention and trust.

I understood that these messages were not just some abstract nice ideas about life; they were a sacred reminder about how to experience "reality," and how to be "in the moment" despite the challenges that present themselves. They teach us to face our "external reality" while remaining balanced, peaceful and filled with love. These messages are truly about sounding the alarm clock and getting us ready to face the next chapter, so we can do our work and fulfill our missions.

I wanted to share this real life story because it had a powerful impact on my understanding of this journey we are on, and it gave me deeper insight into the meaning and purpose of the messages from the angels. The past year and a half was both intense and gratifying for me on many levels. I feel grateful even for the low moments. Other moment offered astonishingly expansive realizations and experiences. Through my own transformation, I came to understand the meaning of the task ahead of us. It is not just about reaching the end goal of enlightenment, ascension, or even experiencing an epiphany. It is about being the lighthouse in a place of storms, shining light despite the high surge and winds, being fully immersed in life, in an awakened state. It is about true mastery in the deepest sense of the word. It is about facing whatever crosses your path knowing who you are and what your mission is about.

The final chapter in the first book is called "Drinking Nectar." The angels say,

"You did not come here at this time to be sitting in your hammocks and drinking the nectar of heaven. You are the transformers of energy. You are built to bring light to where there is darkness. You are the one who trained for this time and dreamt of the opportunity to be here now when it all happens."

Now I really get it.

Those three days in India and a year's worth of tests have again and again reinforced this point: The messages in these books are not abstractions to comfort us; they are alarm clocks to wake us up so we are ready to face the next chapter and fulfill our mission.

The second book is a continuation of the first. The messages, however, sound a different melody as they become more urgent and in many ways more prescient. In the first book, the angels speak directly and clearly about some of the cultural, political, and economic events that took place after the first book was published.

Now the angels speak of the coming changes in terms of our own responsibility and mission. The angels are not interested in making accurate predictions but in our awakening. They speak of our pending graduation and the acceleration of time as we know it. In the forward from the angels, for the first time, they speak about the transition and how those of you who are on this mission will feel the changes while most of humanity will become aware of them much later. They speak of miracles.

As I read, over and over again, about the alarm clock ringing and that it is time to turn on our light, I can not avoid looking around me and observe the astounding opportunities that present themselves to us every day in our lives to make a choice of love and light.

I feel that these messages are a beautiful, gentle reminder of what we already know and may have forgotten. They remind us with hugs and no judgment of why we came here to this planet at this time and what our mission is about. It is about transforming our thoughts, feelings, and actions and therefore our vibrations, one breath at a time, one heart beat at a time. It is not about reaching a place or a destination, it is about being a fully awakened, activated human beings. They wish us to enjoy the vista and take full benefit from the experience writing the next chapter in human evolution using the three tools of love, intention and trust. They tell us in so many words; "it is all about one thing; a choice, your choice" and so be it.

&

I would like to share one last story.

On July 1st 2009, I was seated at my circular glass table in Woodstock ready to receive a message. I felt my usual excitement wondering what new information will be revealed. I felt light and clear. Outside, a light rain tapped the leaves. Ripples formed on the pond. Frogs occasionally chirped and called. Through the windows I scanned the meadow, pond, trees, and the Catskill Mountains. All seemed so fresh, peaceful, ripe, and open.

I breathed more deeply and asked the angels to join me and read the intention as I do before every message.

The joyful voice came almost immediately and I began to type. When I write, I enter a space without time. I almost lose all sense of my physical body. My fingers just do the work. This particular morning, I was shown a moving image of a giant storm with everything swiveling and turning but they were not asking me to write about it. I tried to figure out where I should incorporate it but they chose just to show me the image. It looked like an image of a hurricane as seen from a satellite. The angels spoke of miracles and of our journey and I felt the hugs and love all around me.

Then suddenly something crashed into the window. I jolted from my seat and glimpsed a bird falling down on our porch. Birds had often mistaken the glass for open space and crashed into this large window. They either die instantly or within a few seconds. I was looking at the special ribbon my daughter had recently purchased at the Woodstock Hardware Store to alert the birds of the glass. It lay on the table, not yet installed. *Too late for that one*, I thought and promised myself to install the ribbon. I felt somewhat sad about this little bird and wondered what message this bird had for me. I know that everything has a meaning especially when I am in the middle of conversing with the angels.

I got up and walked outside. The bird was maybe six inches, black and white checkerboard pattern feathers, and it was lying on the wooden deck quivering and shuddering. The head was twisted and the whole body trembling and twitching, a long tongue sticking out of its bill to the side. Within a few seconds the trembling became weaker and weaker and finally ceased. It was dying in front of my eyes. I kneeled down, and my right hand as if by its own will stretched over the bird and formed a canopy over its little body.

I looked at it and this feeling of love came over me for this little creature. Something inside told me to keep my hand where it was and the longer I kept it the warmer it got. After a couple of minutes an intense heat shot from my hand. My right hand tingled intensely. I stayed with this love and compassion for this tiny body for five minutes or so. By now the bird was on its back and not moving. The head leaned to the side and I felt it died. I gently placed it in a small cardboard box and brought it inside the house. I decided that after I finished writing the message I would give it a proper burial with a short prayer. I was still a bit unsettled about the timing of this crash coming just as I was receiving a message. I then noticed that the rain had stopped and the sun came out for a moment

I sat down and within a few minutes the voice came back and resumed speaking about miracles as if nothing had happened. I wrote for about an hour longer. Once I finished, I rose to give the dead bird a proper burial. As I walked to the box and looked down inside it, I was jolted.

I almost fainted from what I saw.

The birds was on its feet gawking at me. It was standing up. Remembering what I saw earlier and now seeing this bird standing, I knew that I had just witnessed the most extraordinary thing. I felt from the deepest place in my heart that I had seen a miracle. I stared at the bird for a long while as if trying to absorb what has just happened. I know what I had seen. I have been with animals my whole life and I knew that this bird had died. An over-whelming feeling came over me that I can not even describe. It was a sensation of awe in the deepest sense. I felt that I was given this gift to see a miracle unfolding in front of my eyes. I could hear my heart beating faster and I moved away from the bird. I had to sit down. It was almost too much for the mind to accept.

A profound feeling of gratitude came over me and I felt an indescribable sense of expansion and a realization of what the angels are trying to tell us. Some of their words flashed in front of my eyes. This is the age of miracles they said, they spoke of our linear reality and that in their reality one can heal what is considered too late because time has no meaning. They spoke of our messengers from the natural world; they spoke about what the birds are trying to tell us and how miracles could be our reality if we use our tools. Most of all they spoke about the power of love to heal and transform us, the natural world, the planet, and the universe.

Their teaching just seemed to be absorbed into my being like water into sand and all I could say was "*Wow, I get it, thank you.*"

The rain started again. I decided to check on the bird again fearing that maybe it expired by now while I am digesting the event, and sure enough, the bird came closer, flapping its wings and trying to climb out of the box. I put my finger in the box and it climbed on it. This is too much I thought. No one will ever believe this. I walked outside, the bird clutching my ring finger. I sat down and we just stared at each other for a few minutes. Then it jumped out of my hand and flew to a small tree near by.

I am reluctant to write of the circumstance by which I receive the messages because I feel that it is not about me. I see my role, acting as a vessel for this information, but this time it was different. It was a manifestation of so much that the messages speak of: the power to heal, the power of love to transform our current reality and the miracles that are all around us, had played out on my front porch.

❧

The next day as I was walking in nature my feeling was confirmed as the angels told me that indeed the bird (female downy Woodpecker) was part of the message and they asked me to find a way to tell it as I experienced it. I feel infinite gratitude for being shown the power of love, and so be it.

A Note from the Angels

IT HAS BEEN A LONG TIME since our messages first appeared, or has it? We are with you and we look at you with awe, celebrating your progress and hugging you with our wings. You have done well and we are grateful for your work. We ask you to keep going, breathe deeply, walk slowly and look around. When you do, you will observe miracles all around you. Even when you sleep, miracles will cross your path. It is the age of miracles and we ask you to open your eyes so you can understand the magnificence of your contribution to writing the next chapter in the story of your journey as angels disguised as humans.

What you have done is to allow us to enter your dimension as vibration and tap on some of the angels' foreheads so they can open their eyes. The angelic vibration is subtle and quiet. We do not shout or place signs on the side of the road. You will not see us on your TV commercials. We work with each one of you as if you were the only one on this planet. Each one plays an essential role in this upcoming chapter. The one candle burning brightly makes a difference for the multitudes. You are the codes in the DNA that create the new blueprint. As you know from your genetic experiments, you do not need to change much in the blueprint to create something that was not there before. "*What will we create?*" you may wonder. You have the potential to create peace on earth is our short answer.

You must experience many levels and steps before you experience peace but you are well on your way to move from one level of awareness to another. "*Will everyone experience this shift*" you may wonder? No, not everyone is our short answer. In fact, most of humanity will not be aware of this shift for years to come. You, however, will be celebrating with your eyes open and in awe. You are the forerunners of this great shift. Like other shifts throughout your history, this shift happens in the physical dimension and it takes time. This up and coming shift requires an immense power to activate the force of inertia. Once the change is in progress, smaller and smaller amounts of energy are needed to continue the unfolding and rolling of that change. Metaphorically, we ask you to imagine a train going one way on rails that reaches a place where there are no longer any rails and yet the train can go anywhere. This train now is at a place where all directions and destinations are available to it. You re-wrote what was to be the final chapter and now you are writing the next one. Now, the power needed to turn that train and start it moving again to the highest path is no small task. Once the train is moving again and on the right track, more and more angels dressed up in human costume will join the ride because it will become obvious that it is the next destination.

This is the story now unfolding on your storyboard. You are the director, actor and composer of the next movie. Is it big enough for you?

"How do you know?" you may wonder.

We are you on the other side, we say with a smile. We love you unconditionally and we wish you to experience the changes taking place around you with your eyes open, with health, vibrancy and joy moving through the next phase paving the road for others to follow. There are many twists and turns on this road and we tell you in no equivocal terms that your physical reality may present itself at times as a horror movie aimed to bring you into fear and paralysis. We ask that you learn to look inside for the truth. Learn to consult your inner knowing. There is a fierce resistance to change as the old energy battles the new. Shifts require immense upstart energy. Your trajectory began shifting over 30 years ago and the shift and speed is accelerating day by day. Joy is the most potent remedy and answer to those who tell you that the end is near and that humanity is on its last chapter. There are many books in the library and when one book ends it is time to choose a new, exciting book.

We are light beings like you and we are part of the consciousness you named God just like you. We are your brothers and sisters and we come to you with love and light to hold your hand and lead you down a path that is glorious. You have asked us to come and we are here with you talking to you in your dream reality, in your daydream reality, and in your waking reality. To some of you we even appear in the physical reality and we do not always introduce ourselves as we are. Spirit works with you 24 hours a day, 365 days a year. You have sequestered us to shine on your path so you will see where you are going and we did just that; you have sequestered us to ring the alarm clock before it is too late and we did just that. Now it is your turn to do the work you came here to do. There are no more excuses or reasons not to do the work. This is why you came here. Your mission is sacred and honored beyond your wildest dreams. You think that the Oscars ceremony is the ultimate honor in your movie industry. What if the experience we speak of is the "Oscars" in the "spirit industry" in which beauty never fades and glory is never forgotten, where looks are eternal and fortunes are never lost.

Your work is awakening and becoming the master that you are. By doing so you are emitting vibratory ripples that change the blueprint and create the energy that will catapult humanity to its new destination. *"I feel that you are not talking about me,"* you may say". *"I am struggling with day-to-day responsibilities, trying to make ends meet, and dealing with my personal relationships and with the chaos all around me. I hardly know anything anymore"*, we hear you thinking to yourself. You see only what is in front of you. There will come a time when you will see more clearly what we speak of. You are now in prep school and very soon you will need to show that you are prepared for the next level of schooling.

"What do we need to do?" you may still wonder. We ask you to give intention to become the master that you are. We ask you to use love in all that you do. We ask you to slow down and connect with the natural world. We ask you to sit quietly and learn to listen to the conversation taking place inside you. We ask you to hug trees and speak to birds. We ask you to take time to learn from your children. Love your partner or spouse even if you get a frown back. We ask you to walk knowing that you are a master-in-training who is learning to direct your own reality. We ask you to love all of yourself all the time even those parts that you do not like as much. Forgive yourself and have compassion for yourself. And when

you do so, love, forgiveness and compassion will naturally be extended to all those around you. We ask you to be in the energy of integrity and follow your own truth as well as honoring the truth of your brothers and sisters. We ask you to not preach your truth but be your truth. Walk in the now, feeling your breath and your heartbeat and know that you asked to be here at this time and this time is upon you. Do not delay your awakening for to-morrow. Start from today. Ascension is not a destination. Each thought, breath and heart beat is a destination. Understand that you are a divine instrument that emits vibrations. The frequencies that you emit create matter and bond the molecules around you creating your reality. We wish you to understand that the music you are creating is the one being played for all to hear. So it is for you to play your best tune at every given moment.

There is never a judgment, only honor and love for the path you have chosen. We came here to shine light on your path so you have the option to see but we cannot do the work for you. You chose a path that is honored above all, walking in blindness and in a dense reality where your divinity is hidden from you. As you walk the walk, know that you are never alone and always loved. We walk beside you, above you, and below you but it is you who must choose light over dark when the choice is presented.

Many of you feel that you do not have the power to make a difference. The time will come when all that was hidden will be revealed and you will know everything that we know. Until then we ask you to trust your inner feelings and follow your heart. You have so much power and this is not the kind of power some of you are exercising over other people. In the realm of spirit a country's president and a farmer carry the same power and each one must play their game within their respective roles. None is more sacred than the other. You chose a role in the movie of your 3-D reality and it is for you to work within that role. You, however, are not the role. You come and go often and you change roles each time so you can learn the many aspects of you. Power to control others is not real power and it is not the power we speak of. The power we speak of is power over your own reality, your own balance, your own thoughts, feelings and actions.

When you change your own reality, you affect all those who come in contact with you. It is that simple. We have given you many messages. These messages can be compared to short melodies. After you listen to them you are left with a feeling. The feeling is the after-effect of the conversation we have with you. The title "Conversation with Angels" is not the author talking to us but it is us talking to you. If you wish to speak to us, sit on the floor, hug yourself and know that we are with you hugging you as well. Know that when you read our messages we are right there with you working on your feeling centers so you may open to the music that is being played. Know that in each message we embed sentences which clear your energetic blocks and allow healing to take place. You are your own healer and the messages act as clearing and cleansing aids to remove your healing blocks.

You have chosen us to come to you. You have asked us to remind you that which you have forgotten. You know all that is written in these messages but you have temporarily forgotten. We are here to remind you that the time is now. Love is your truth and light is your playing field. We ask you to play your game using love and light and so be it.

From the Angels

How To Use This Book

W E L O V E Y O U and we wish to tell you that you are the author and you will know it because it will feel as if you could have written it. It will feel so familiar. We also told you with a hug that these messages are not meant for all of you. If you are not the "author" you will know it as well and there is never a judgment. It does not mean that you are not spiritual enough or divine enough. It only means that you are on a different mission and you may want to keep searching for that which resonates with your mission. You are all angels, all divine and all are on missions. No mission is more honorable or prestigious then the next. You are so dearly loved and we ask you to become that which you are: a master in disguise walking with the knowledge of your own divinity.

The writer, editor and publisher of these messages are simply your messengers as they cater to your intent, bringing you that which you have requested. Do not look at the typeface, the format or the book cover as they are just tools. These messages act as a conveyor of the energy of love which aims to link you with you and to wake you up to your own divinity.

With a hug we wish to impart to you that Love energy acts and harmonizes with your cells facilitating healing in your body when it is appropriate. It is again, not the tools which heal you but it is you who heals yourself through intent. We wish to tell you that these messages do not come from an entity or a channel; they come from you the reader. They come to those of you who requested them. Those who requested them will be guided to these messages and will know instantly that it is for them. Those of you who did not ask for these messages will not be able to finish a single page as it will appear alien or too confusing.

You are magnificent and we see you as geometric patterns moving about; these messages correspondence to your geometry and each message links to a moment in time in the cycle you call human life. We ask you to read this book like a recipe book. When you crave a certain type of food, look through the **Message Guide** and pick the one that seems the most appetizing. Use your feeling and allow the correct message to present itself. Be playful and allow that which comes from the circle to celebrate with you the shifting of you and the planet. Trust that you read what you need to know for this very moment. Read the messages often and each time you read a new layer will be revealed to you. We will be with you each time you pick up the book working and facilitating healing your growth and expansion.. The book has the spirit of the circle and is not meant to be read in a linear fashion. You are changing and the planet is changing. Your vibration is increasing and the molecules around you dance differently then they used to.

It is the grandest time in your history as humans on this planet and nothing you know will stay the same. All must shift with the shifting of your planet. It is your intent that gave the push for this change and we ask you to become peaceful with all that is around you. We ask you to use love in all your interactions and relationships. We ask you to become the master that you are at every moment that you breathe. There are many who await your awakening, and it is your time and so be it.

The Blind

WHEN YOU GIVE US YOUR HAND we take it and walk with you hand in hand. It is you who must ask us first. This is the way of spirit. It is a dimension of free choice where you are in control. We are always ready to take your hand. When you feel our hand you must let go of all the other gadgets which help you navigate. Your campus is no longer necessary and your maps become redundant. You do not need ropes or survival kits. When you give your hand to your support group on the other side of the veil you are marching on the highway and the signs are clear. All you need to do is follow the guidance when you see it.

What do the signs look like? Some of you may wonder.

The signs are embedded in your feeling center. As you approach an intersection you hear in your heart whether to turn left or right. You may choose to listen to your feeling or ignore it , but the feeling, nevertheless, will be present. Often many of you will think that the feeling is illogical and may lead you to the wrong path.

What if this is a mistake, you may ask?

You are loved whether you follow the guidance of spirit or ignore it. You came to this planet because you knew that you must forget all you know and navigate in the dark. The guidance of spirit is your flashlight.

You may say *I do not believe what I see and I wish to follow my logic.*

We wish to remind you of the circle. You operate in a linear reality that confines you to the limited dimensions you can perceive. What you see is what is there. Your logic operates pretty much the same. One thing follows another. One thing needs to happen so the next thing can happen. In your perception one word must follow another to form a sentence and one event must lead to another in order to manifest. We wish to tell you as we hug you that it is not the way of spirit. We exist in the circle and you exist in the line. We see all your potentials and where they lead you. You see only the edge of your nose and that is in the best of circumstances. When you give us a hand you do not need a stick to feel your way around. Like a blind person who wishes to cross a busy intersection, you ask a fellow angel to help take you across. When that angel gives you a hand, you must let go of all the other means of knowing. You may not trust and keep hitting the pavement with your stick but it will only slow you down. Many of you have had your trust shattered and betrayed. Many of you had lives where you trusted and you were led astray. We know who you are and what you have been through. We wish to tell you that all those times when you were led to falsehood and challenge, it was because you did not trust your feelings, as guidance was always present and available.

You are coming to an era in which your logical mind will be challenged and your 3D perception of reality will not be able to explain what it is that you are seeing. We are your brothers and sisters and we have been through it ourselves. It is a challenging time because many of the things you trusted and relied upon will look differently to you. It is an exciting time when you hold the flashlight and a very confusing time when you walk in the dark. Blind people rely on memory and they know the streets by heart. They walk left or right almost automatically because they remember where things are and they know how many steps it takes from this corner of the street to the other. What would happen if one day all the streets were rearranged and all the street corners were different? For a blind person it might seem like a very frightening thing, like the end of the world as they knew it. For the blind, not finding the light post they relied on as a landmark and a place of orientation is a fearful event. When a blind person suddenly does not encounter what he/she expected to find, they may stop walking, terrified, because they may realize that they do not have any idea where they are. That feeling can create almost a paralysis of sorts. We wish to tell you that indeed your streets will be rearranged. That is not necessarily negative. From our perspective, metaphorically speaking, instead of crowded streets you may find a park with beautiful open vistas and no threatening obstacles. However, a blind person will not know it. That is why we ask you with all love to develop the ability to bring light to your path so you can enjoy the open vista. When you see where you are going, you will experience joy, not fear. This is the way of it.

Many of you are blind and it is appropriate and by design. It is part of your test. You were on the original design team. The rules of the test are now changing and you are developing the ability to see. You have chosen to enhance your abilities and the universe is sending you deliveries of tools you can use to see. We ask you to pick up these tools and use them.

Where do we pick up the delivery, some of you may wonder, while others may ask, *how do we use the tools once we get the delivery?*

You pick up the delivery when you open that door inside you. To get the key all you need to do is set up an intention to do so. It is simple and complicated at the same time. Your conviction in the intention will determine the accessibility of the tools. When you ask you will be given as you are the master. The universe must follow your direction as it always has. You are the creator of your reality whether you are conscious of it or not. When you ask with pure intent to be shown the path and given the tools, you will be given the tools and the door will open to you. Now you may wonder how to use the tools. The tools are built inside of you and they are part of your biology. By opening the door you are activating those tools. The next step is to follow the light of the flashlight. For a blind person who has never been exposed to vision, the new sights may be confusing. This is why we ask you to stay in balance when things do not seem like they always have been. You are walking on earth at a special time and you have the potential to begin to "see". Your vision may be greatly enhanced and the veil of duality becomes to some almost transparent. This may be confusing because the visions are in dimensions that are different than yours. It has no time and no space as you know it in your 3-D reality. We ask you to stay open, trusting and balanced throughout this shift. It is magnificent in scope.

How do I begin and what do I need to do, some of you may wonder?

You already did so much by changing your future. You were on the path to end human life on earth and you chose to stay. The next step is to become aware of your mission and turn on your light. Light is information and as you turn on your light you can see where you are going and what you are meant to do. As you turn on your light you will experience our loving hands walking with you through this maze of sights. It is peace that you will experience because you will know inside of you that you are walking the path that is yours. You would know that you are guided with love and light. You are beautiful and there is never a judgment whether you choose to see or to walk blindly. You came here at this time to discover your divinity and to use the tools of a master, so you can stay balanced and peaceful. Your example is what changes the vibration of the planet and gives those who walk in the dark, light so they can see. What you do for yourself is what is changing the planet. You are not asked to evangelize or bring information to those who walk in darkness. You are asked to take care of yourself. You are the one who activates yourself. Your activation is what transforms your reality. When you are transformed, you radiate energy that goes into the soil of the planet. That energy is what circulates and becomes light. This is the light that becomes available to those who walk in the dark.

You must take care of yourself. There are many who believe that they must save humanity by doing service. They help people or donate money. They take care of everyone around them except themselves. Many of the light warriors who signed up for this shift are holding the belief that it is the giving to others that is changing the planet. With all love, we wish to tell you that your work is important and you are making a difference in people's lives. It is, however, not the mission that you have signed for. Those angels who you chose to "save" are their own creators as well. They choose and create that which they experience. Many of the warriors believe that they must save others to bring more light to humanity. We wish to impart to you that you are shining light by taking care of yourself, staying peaceful and balanced. You are shining light by using your tools to understand the vista that you are seeing. There is a purpose and appropriateness for the suffering of humanity and it may get worse before it gets better. It is by design, and it is appropriate and by choice. Many of you believe that by devoting all your energy and time you can avert the destiny of other people and bring prosperity and peace to all. We wish to impart to you that it is indeed a sacred task that you are doing as long as you are taking care of yourself. If you are in a place of balance and peace and you walk hand in hand with spirit, you are indeed living your mission as well as doing good. It is, however, not the case with many of you. We see you giving and giving to the point that your light is so dim that you are no longer living your mission. You gave up your light for the sake of saving others. We wish to tell you with all love that you cannot save anyone with your light dimmed. You are becoming that which you are trying to save. The vibration that you are sending is aligning with the vibration of the victims you are trying help. Your geometry and melody is no longer in a place of balance and you have lost your purpose. We know who you are. Many of you who are in the "service to humanity department" are told that unless you help humanity you are not worthy. You are only helping humanity and the earth when you take care of yourself first and live with your divinity, awaken peaceful and balanced. Then if you chose to do this or do that, it is all sacred. The service is done automatically by you walking in the awareness of inner divinity and love. Walking in your mission means that wherever you step foot you do service. You are a walking service station and you are helping all those who cross your path as well as transforming the soil that you are stepping on. Many of you feel that you need to go to faraway places to do service and help those in need. In the process you join the victims and become one. You are the service station and as you walk and breathe you do service. This is part of the legacy of the masters who walked the earth. They touched anyone who saw them. They were enhanced humans who walked hand in hand with spirit. People came to them and they did not need to go anywhere. They were balanced and peaceful human beings who discovered the divinity inside. We wish to tell you that we see the master potential in you. We wish to tell you that you can be like them. We honor your journey and we wish you to become all that you can be and so be it.

The Fishing Boat

YOU ARE YOUR OWN MASTER. You may feel that you are not, but mastery is running in your veins. It is part of your biology. You are built to ascend. Parts of your biology carry the signature of God. When those parts are activated, it propels you to your highest destination. It is your choice whether to activate those parts or to let them stay dormant.

Why are you telling us about mastery, some of you may ask? *We just want to have a normal life,* others may proclaim.

We are telling you about your potential because there will come a time when the choice of what you call "normal" will not be available. You will no longer have the choice to stay in a place of limbo. You are at a crossroads where new energy and old energy battle each other. The new will eventually replace the old but the old is trying to maintain its stronghold. You are loved and you are never in a place of judgment. What you choose is your sacred right as an angel walking in lesson. We wish to impart to you the choices that you have so you understand where you are standing at this point of time. You come with biology that is being enhanced. "Night vision" is being added to your perception, as well as ultra-sensory components. You are changing and becoming enhanced because you have asked for it. Your glands are being furnished with additional contact points which allow easier communication with vortexes to other dimensions. You are being furnished with abilities that will enable you to become more interdimensional. It is as if you had the body of a baby and you are now being furnished with the body and abilities of an adult in a very short span of time. It will be confusing to you. Your choice is to honor this sacred opportunity and to awaken to your potential or to stay in darkness and to weather what is coming your way. The difference between those two options is the difference between light and dark. As you awaken to whatever storm comes your way you are prepared to know that you are loved and protected. You know where to go and what to do. You are guided to wherever it is that you will serve yourself and others the best. When you choose not to turn on your light you are loved just the same by spirit but you will have no access to the communications that are coming your way. It is as if you are on a fishing boat at sea and you have a radio which can warn you when a storm is coming. Your radio, however, is tuned to the old station and no communication is coming through. When your radio is not tuned to the new station, you do not get the advance warning about upcoming events in your life. You have no idea what direction the storms are coming from and where to hide to avoid them. You have no idea when the surf will start to surge and when it will end. You do not know the best places to seek shelter while the storm is creating havoc all around you. You are constantly surprised and you are standing around, waiting for whatever comes, without the knowledge or guidance to know what to do to protect yourself.

❧

In other words, you are lost at sea. You are loved and communications are being sent to you, like they are to all the angels, but your radio is set to the wrong station. You are tuned to the station of the old energy frequency and that broadcast has been replaced with the new energy frequency. Storms will come as they always have. In actuality, storms will get stronger and more intense as the planet is gearing to move upward in vibration. Many of you were used to facing weather storms with the tools of the old energy; we wish to tell you that these tools will not work as well, if at all. *How do we tune into the new frequency,* some of you may ask? We thought you would never ask. Know that you are loved no matter where you are and what you are going through. You begin tuning in by honoring your body. You are a vessel and you must treat your vessel with the sacredness that it deserves. Communication is facilitated through your vessel. You can begin by saying, 'I know I am loved by spirit and I set the intention to move forward in this new energy and to increase my vibration so I can awaken to my full potential." When you set the intention, your body begins to shift so it can accommodate the new vibration. You must become sensitive to your body as it communicates with you. Your body which was used for one set of biology is getting an upgrade and certain things that you used to ingest may feel very different. It is you who must acknowledge these feelings and follow them.

Do I have to go on a diet, some of you may ask terrified?

We know how much you like your diets. Your book shelves are full of books about diets and you keep changing books without changing yourselves. With all love, we must impart to you that yes, you are facing a sort of a diet but it is not only food that the diet will address. You are vibrating instruments that are meant to play the most beautiful resonance in the universe. You have the melody of God running in your veins. The vibrations that are around you may enhance the new energy frequencies or curtail it. There will be things that you used to do which will not allow the new vibration to take hold. Mainly we are talking about lower vibrational frequencies which keep you at a lower level.

Can you be more specific, some of you may wonder?

There is never a judgment but if you watch pornography on your computers, TV sets or in magazines you are allowing a lower vibrational frequency into your field. When you watch TV indiscriminately, you allow a lower vibrational frequency into you field. When you chose to eat food that is not alive and has a genetically modified component in it, you are keeping your body in a place of lower frequency. When you misuse your sexuality or carry guilt and shame about your sexuality you hold yourself at a lower frequency. Your sexual energy is your engine, and when it is blocked the whole vessel falters. Sexuality is one of your greatest challenges as a society, which holds you at lower vibrations. You make choices and these choices add up and become your intention. As you set an intention to move upward, you must follow through with every action you take in your day to day. In that way, your intention will become your action and not vice versa. When you set an intention, certain things will not smell right anymore, and certain actions will not feel good anymore. We ask you to listen to your feelings and follow them with actions. Your body is an instrument and it is sacred. It communicates with you every second that you are alive on this planet. It tells you when it is hungry or thirsty. Your body tells you when it is tired and when it needs to go to the bathroom. It tells you when it is in pain and out of balance. In your modern, fast pace society you are fed pills and medicines which continuously numb and block your ability to connect your feelings to your body. When you are tired you drink coffee so you can push your body to work harder and longer. When you ache you take pain medicine which numbs your nervous system and removes your awareness of the pain. Many of you are fed numbing agents all day. TV is one of the tools which help your businesses and institutions communicate and transfer numbing agents to you. You are being assaulted in your day to day from all sides and you are so used to it that it does not feel like anything new. For you to awaken you must learn to feel again. You must learn not to numb yourself when things feel uncertain or uncomfortable. Changing your diet is about learning to discriminate among the energies you ingest. We love you and we wish you to know that your choices are honored no matter what. It is essential however to be in touch with your vessel in order for your life force to remain intact and powerful so it can propel you to tune into the frequency of the new energy. Honoring your body means that you listen to its voice and not try to silence or numb it. When you are tired you must go to sleep. When you buy your food, you must choose food that is balanced, nourishing and alive. When you eat you must honor that food and understand that it is a form of energy and vibration. When you choose food that was made with care and love and honors the planet, for example, on your organic farms, your message to your body is that it is loved and nurtured. Your intention is just the first step but it is an important one. Your intention will begin to change your senses and you may lose taste for certain foods, certain habits and yes, certain people in your life.

We wish to speak of those in your life who may be tuned to a frequency which is detrimental to your path. We ask you to pay close attention to these words and try to feel them rather than analyze them. We have told you about the messengers who are all around you. Some of the messages "gifted" to you are not what they seem. We ask that you feel which messages you want to ingest and which you do not. All messages have a vibration that is here to teach you and complete part of the geometry of your puzzle. Some of the messages coming from angels walking in their duality are for testing your resolve, your commitment and your intention. When you begin to move up, you will face many who are used to having you in their cords who now feel threatened. From where we sit your relationships appear like spider webs which connect all of you with all of you. Some cords are connected to your solar plexus and some may connect to your heart center. Your different chakras are used as energy hubs for these cords to meet. As you begin to move and change, those cords will inevitably try to keep you at the same place. They are like anchors and they have power. We wish to tell you that when you begin to awaken, all those who have cords in you will have to face disconnection of a sort, as you must become free of those cords.

Do you mean that we have to leave all the people in our lives, some of you may ask? You do not have to leave anyone but you will have to change the geometry and juxtaposition of those relationships. All those in relationships with you, whether intimate or not, have an idea of who you are. Most would like to keep you frozen at the place because they feel comfortable with you. Some use fear, some use manipulation, and some even use love to keep you at the place where you were. We ask you to learn to decipher when the energy of control is used on you and to become peaceful with it. You are not asked to let go of any relationships in your life, but to let go of any aspect of the relationship that is controlling, anger based, hurtful, manipulative, guilt or shame based. You are asked to leave behind those aspects from your relationships so you can become light enough to move upward in the spiral of ascension. We wish to impart to you that many of your relationships are based on guilt, shame, fear, anger and manipulation of some sort. Your goal as you begin to cut the cords of these relationships is to re-establish them with the energy of pure love. Many of you are fearful of giving up guilt or fear for love. We know who you are. You have been conditioned by your cultures and families to have cords rooted so deep that just the thought of removing them brings up fear in you. Wouldn't you like to have those relationship around you based in love and give up those aspects of relationships that are heavy?

How do we cut the cords, you may ask? Relationships are a movement of energy between two humans. It is in the exchange of energy that the cords draw their power. It is like a game of "tag, you are it," which goes back and forth. When you stop playing the game of drama and manipulation, the other must stop as well. You may expect, however, that they will try to lure you back into the game with many creative strategies. We ask you to remain balanced and peaceful despite their efforts. Your power comes from the area that you call the heart chakra. When you feel that you are being pulled into the game, focus your attention on the heart and remain with that awareness. When you choose to stay in a place of balance and peace, not only do you transform yourself but you elevate your relationship and empower the other as well. Often they will not see it right away and will try to fight it. We ask you to choose, at that moment, whether you want to be tuned in or tuned out. We wish to tell you that there will be those who do not wish to transform the relationship. As you move forward they may lose interest and move away from your life. Honor their choice to stay heavy and celebrate your choice of becoming light. It is your intention which will create a stir in the pot of relationships. If you stay truthful to your intention, when the sand settles at the bottom of the pot it will become golden and there will be letters written in the golden sand which spell

L o v e.

Are you still worried? All aspects of energy that you are now involved with must support your new path. All that you ingest, whether through your stomach, eyes, ears, relationships, and even thoughts, must support your intention. It is in the awareness of your actions and in the honoring of your feelings that the success of your journey lies. You are dearly loved and your choices are always honored. We wish to tell you that the new energy radio station is transmitting beautiful tunes and it can light your path in wondrous ways. We ask you to tune up your vessel so you can hear the melody and enjoy the journey and so be it.

The Spinning Wheel

THE WORDS WE ARE TRANSCRIBING carry a frequency. Every form of communication carries a vibration and a frequency. From where we stand, it is like a melody with graphics. When you go to a bookstore, the melody or the vibration of a book will harmonize with yours and you will pick it up. Some books are sought after because of word-of-mouth and others are picked-up, seemingly, by random. We wish to impart to you that these messages will attract those who are carrying a particular vibration. It is a code of sorts. The writing will be clear and transparent to some and it will look like hieroglyphics to others. Those of you who are of a specific range of frequency will understand these messages in depth and your vibration will resonate with it fully.

How do I know if I am meant to read it or not, some of you may wonder?

You will know because you will feel it in your heart. Your body will also respond. If you are sensitive you will feel the vibration all around. We wish to tell you that the words on these pages will have a dialog with your cells.

The melody carried to you through these messages will transmit a ringing which is aimed to waking up your cells. The melody will act as an alarm clock for those of you who are ready, and you will feel the waking up through vibrations. The receptivity of your cells will increase and your geometry will begin to shift. You are a vibrating angel and like a jigsaw puzzle; when the right piece is inserted into the right place you can move forward. Your cells respond to love and the wake-up call is the transmission of love from family to family and from you to you. It is a circle and you are its center. Words are read in a linear fashion but their energy carries a multidimensional quality which speaks to your feeling centers. When juxtaposed in a specific order, words form a melody. Words also carry a geometric pattern that creates a specific brain wave pattern.

Why are you telling us about books and brain waves, some of you may ask?

Poetry is a highly symbolic juxtaposition of words and it works directly on your feeling centers. There are those of you who resonate with a poem and feel its vibration very deeply and others who do not read much into it. These writings are very much like poetry in the sense that they are calibrated for those of you who are on the path to elevate the vibration of this planet at this time. It is a code of sorts, like your Morse code. There are those who came to earth with a mission and the mission requires them to awaken. This mission was not designed for everyone as there are many paths to your lessons. There is never a judgment and all of you are equally loved by spirit. We are with all of you and you are family. There are those of you, whose intention was to move up the spiral and discover your own divinity. These writings will be handed to you as part of the manifestation of your intention. There are those of you who have been on special training missions for eons waiting for this time to arrive. We wish to tell you that the code embedded in these words will feel strangely familiar. As if you had heard these words before. In all truth and as we hug you, we wish to tell you that indeed you have heard them before. These words were given to you as a potential before you came down and began your new journey. You come with contracts. The contracts are about your potentials. Some are part of your karma and others are waiting for you if you choose to move away from karma. We wish to tell you that your geometry changes and your melody changes, when you begin to vibrate higher. As you ascend, you drop old contracts that were waiting for you at the lower vibration and you pick up new ones which are potential in the higher vibration. When you do that, we hold an all night party because it means that you have awakened. We wish to tell you that often when you begin vibrating higher you do not have a very deep sleep. You also awake

at night wondering where you are. With a smile we want
to whisper to you that we are the ones who are keeping
you awake. It is all these celebrations that we are having
in your honor. We are in love with you and we sit by your
side day after day loving you and waiting for you to make
a move. When you finally make the move, you can trust
that we are there, aware and in celebratory mode. In your
day-to-day, we see many of you who are moving as if you
are on a spinning wheel. The faster you run the faster
the wheel spins. We wish to tell you in all love that even
when you spin very fast you are still at the same place you
were when you spun slow. Only when you get off the
spinning wheel and walk beside it, do you know that you
are progressing.

You have many tests that are designed to distract you
from your mission. The tests are your spinning wheel
and though you may spin as fast as you want the wheel
itself will not move forward, only in circles. It is by design and it is part of the test. When you set an intention
to discover the divinity within and begin the search you
have stepped off the spinning wheel. The test is built in
such a way that unless you begin to search, you will not
move forward. You will live your life in the groove that
you set for yourself which is the grove of karma. There is
no judgment for those of you who follow that groove as
your choice is sacred and honored. But there are those of

you, who were determined, prior to their arrival, to wake up to the mastery in their veins.

Most of you who came to do the work of light warriors have been here before. There are many of you who have trained in the different mystery schools. There are many of you who have had many lives as spiritual humans. There are those amongst you who were shamans and witches. Many of you have experienced lives in which you were persecuted, chased and yes, even killed by stoning or burning at the stake. The powers of divinity that you intuitively carried in those lifetimes were suppressed by those in the dominant religious institutions of the time. They knew of your powers and were fearful of it.

Many of you still carry the seeds of fear and you'd rather stay asleep then awaken.

Do we have a reason not to fear this time, you may ask?

You came at this time to light your light. All the other lives were a preparation for this one. You have been here before but this time is different. You are the one carrying the torch and all the rest will follow. The energy is shifting and those who were in hiding when the earth was in darkness will be the ones at the forefront of the new energy. You are coming to a crossroads and you can no longer hide your light. You must wake up to your true purpose. You must discover the love which flows in your veins. Your fear is part of the test and we must tell you not to fear. When you hold your light up, there is no power in this universe that can harm you. You carry the knowledge of all those lives in your cellular structure. All the knowledge you have accumulated on herbs, medicine, the language of animals, the language of plants, the language of the body and its energy points, the language of tantra and sexual energy are all part of you and are waiting to be rediscovered. Spinning the wheel will not get you there. The wheel must slow down so you can safely step down and begin your search.

Where do I look once I step off the wheel, some of you may wonder?

As we hold your hand, we wish to tell you that it is all inside of you. In you is where you begin the search.

We are looking but we don't see anything, some of you may say, frustrated.

You are so conditioned to get quick results that when you look and do not see what you expect, you become impatient. We wish to tell you that we have been very patient waiting for you to begin the search. As you begin, all the answers are right in front of you but you are unable to see them because they are subtle. It is as if you move from the light into a darkened room. You have to give your eyes some time to adjust to the new conditions. Here, however, you move from dark to the light, but your eyes are so used to the old vista that the new one does not register. All the answers are there, in you, as they have always been. It is you who must choose to bring yourself to a place where you can see them through your feeling center. You are unique and you are very powerful. The thoughts that you project can make the difference for the whole. Peaceful thoughts manifest peace and fearful thought manifest a reality of fear. You are the selected ones who must remove your shoes and honor the sacredness of your mission. Much of humanity at this time is struggling for survival. Many are fighting daily for their basic portion of food. There are those who still are on a journey of understanding about themselves through acts of violence and terror. There are many others who go about their lives oblivious to their true identity and purpose. There is never a judgment and all angels walking in lessons are family and are loved the same. We wish to impart to you, however, that there are only a few of you in comparison to the many angels walking in duality that have the potential and the mission to awaken. We wish to tell you that out of all of those who agreed to be the lighthouses, many have remained spinning their wheels, feeling empty and never waking up to their true purpose. That is why there are just the few of you who can and are moving upward. As we celebrate you we wish to tell you that you are the forerunners of the new energy of this planet. You are the ones that through your actions, are paving the road for humanity. You are the ones who are catapulting peace on earth to the horizon. We wish to tell you that you are doing it one step at a time by discovering your own divinity. The transformation happens one thought at a time and one action at a time. It is not easy to move away from the spinning wheel. We know who you are. We know your challenges and we know of your fears. We know your doubts and we honor you so much for your path. You can walk this path and never awaken and we will love you as family does. It is you, however, who asked to be where you can make a difference. You are warriors and you know it inside of you. It does not matter how old you are or how frail you think you may be. You are a powerhouse and we ask you to allow that power to carry you where you want to be. Your journey is to discover who you really are and, as you carry the light of divinity in you, to light the way for all those who are searching. We ask you to celebrate your path, honor the challenges and know that you are loved no matter what. We wish to tell you that you are on a glorious path and the vista at the top of the mountain is breathtaking. We wish you to get off the spinning wheel and allow your wings to grow so you can become the angel that you are.

From above, the vista is luminous and it is you who created it. You are so dearly loved, and so be it.

The Dance

W E WISH YOU TO STEP FORWARD. It is your turn and there are legions of us in support of you.

Where do you want us to step, some of you may ask?

You have two options, we say as we hold your hands, backward or forward.

What does it means to step backward, you may wonder?

It is like in a dance; you move back and forth while stepping on the dance floor. When you move backward, later you must move forward. This is the way of it. You are eternal and you are always moving.

Why do you wish us to move forward then, some may wonder?

Forward is the energy of now. It is where the planet and you meet. Forward is the place where dimensions collide. . When you move forward you meet that which you yourself set up.. When you step backward, you meet not yourself but the old energy that is behind you.

There is a box and it is called human perception. All your ideas about yourself are contained in that box. The box is square and it is 3-D. When things do not fit in your box, you try to make them fit. You push here and there to make them fit. Many of you drop those things which do not fit your boxes. Many of you say to yourselves, this just doesn't fit, it is just too circular. We often smile to ourselves when you discard that which does not fit your reality because it has no corners and no beginning and end. You need something to hold onto and many of the things we talk about have no traction. They are transparent and smooth. They have no scent that you can recognize, they have no melody that you have heard before, and they have no lines, only circles which keep folding into themselves.

We see some of you scratching your heads as if talking to yourself, *"There is just nothing to hold on to."*

We are above you and we are also under you. There are some of us who are part of you and there are some of us who have been with you from the beginning and will be with you forever.

Then you say to yourself, *well, that is a long time.*

And we say to you, no, it is forever. There is no time.

And you scratch your heads and say, *how can it be that we are not getting what it is that you are saying.*

We wish to tell you that you are in the box and we are in the circle. In fact we are both in the circle but you are pretending not to notice because that is part of your test. We wish to speak with you about our relationships. What does it mean to have a relationship with your angels? Who they are? What do they look like?

There are those of you who say *do we have proof that indeed we are not crazy?*

We know who you are and we know what some of you think to yourselves before going to sleep. You look at the mirror and say *I am talking to invisible angels and I hear invisible angels talking to me without sound. I can hear their melody without music, and I can hear their laugh although it is totally quiet. I have probably gone mad and should check myself into a clinic.*

We know who you are and you are so loved for trying to create this bridge of communication. We are so close to you that it would make you laugh if you saw us. You would think that it is a joke.

Why are these twenty angels floating all around me, you may ask?

Our answer is, because they are all in love with you. Angels and humans are on the same continuum. You are on the only planet of free choice and you are going through your lesson. You are an angel but you are not aware of your divinity. When you are back with us, you are the same angel but you are fully aware of your divinity. All the mysteries that we speak of are known to all of you. There are no secrets that we know that you do not. Everything that we speak of, you already know. We are just nudging you a little so you will remember and wake up to your purpose. How do angels speak to humans? Angels may speak through other angels who we call messengers. Angels also communicate directly with humans.

How does this communication work, some of you may ask?

With your permission of the highest order an angel may breach dimensions so they can meet you. It is a sacred event and when it happens, all of us know about it. When a human reaches across the veil of duality and visits our realm, we celebrate. When an angel from the other side goes through the crack in the veil and meets a human, we celebrate that as well. It is the most sacred union and it happens more often than you think.

When does it happen, some of you may wonder? We are here with you all the time and we meet you when you summon us. We are there in an instant. There are no delays and you do not have to ask twice. Many of you are used to praying every day for the same thing. Do you think we didn't hear you the first time you asked for it? We wish to tell you that you don't even need to ask as we already know that which you want. Does it tell you a little about spirit? Communication with the other side happens through thoughts. You can whisper or speak loud; it does not matter as we see your wishes through the drawing that you make with your geometry. We can see it in your colors. When we see you we become aware of all of the energy that is you. It is not in three or four dimensions, it is in all dimensions and it is an awesome sight.

There are those of us who are assigned to you throughout your physical journey and they are the translators. They translate the energy of the human and turn it into a language that is understood by spirit.

Does spirit need translation, some may wonder?

Spirit is you and you are spirit. Spirit is a part of you that is shielded from you. The translator is also a part of you which builds the bridge of communication between the box and the circle. The translation is energetic because the frequencies cannot harmonize. When one communicates in the key of C and the other in D, the resonance is in different keys and can cause a disconnection in the communication between you and the higher part of yourself. The translator is subtle and creates bridges of communication. When there is no translation you have no access to the information that is coming from the other side. The other side is aware of you but cannot bring you messages. The translator is therefore essential for you to communicate with your angels. In the past many of you would go to a psychic, a reader, a shaman or a holy person. They would act as your translators connecting you with you. We wish to tell you that things have changed and your traditional translators are no longer needed to understand the messages. You are developing a two-way radio and it is biological. Your radio is in your pineal gland. It has always been there but now it is growing. The changes taking place in the magnetic fields are changing your biology. Some of the biology changes are visible and some are in the realm of the circle which means that they are interdimensional and invisible to you.

What does it mean to us, some of you may wonder?

It means that you now can become aware of your group. It means that you never have to feel that you are alone again. It means that you are connected at all times to those who love you. It means that you can be, if you choose, with family walking both in the square box and in the circular arena simultaneously.

How does it affect us, some of you may still wonder? *We still can't see the angels nor can we feel them.*

We wish to tell you with all love that you can see them and feel them.

How do we get to experience that, you ask? You close your eyes and hug yourself. As you shut your vision, you begin to see; as you quiet the noise around you, you begin to hear, and as you slow your mind you begin to feel.

❧

Nothing is what it seems, and we ask you to step forward to a place you have never been to before. It is a place where there is duality but it is so thin that you can see through it.

What would I see through the veil, you may ask?

You would see yourself with wings, is our answer. You have lived in a box for so long that many of you feel the longing to open the box and see what is out there. We are out there and where we are there is love and there is peace. Where we are there is a deep understanding of your lessons as a human. Where we are there is a library that you call the akashic records and it tells you the story of every relationship you have ever had in this life and in any of the lives you have lived on earth. Your body responds to you. The pineal gland responds to you. Your pituitary and the hypothalamus respond to you. You are the master of your vessel and when you choose to build that bridge between your box and our circle, those parts and pieces of you that are responsible for the communication will begin to change. This is how powerful you are. We can only love you from a distance if you choose to not let us in. We are limited by your free choice and we cannot give you what you want unless you learn to ask for it. There is no greater privilege for an angel to be summoned by a human. We wish you to acknowledge who you are. We wish you to realize that you are the masters of your reality. If you choose to stay in a box, your choice will be honored and if you choose to bridge to the circle there will be parties to celebrate and honor that choice.

What is it all about, some of you may ask? *Why should we create that bridge and connect with the angels on the other side?*

As we hug you we wish to tell you that it is not the other side that you are connecting to; you are connecting with that part of yourself that you call God. It is the mission and the purpose of your test and you are nearing graduation. Your test was about light and dark, and finding divinity inside. Your test is about discovering your true identity. Creating that bridge is how you pass the test. There is never a judgment as to whom, why or when you pass the test. All of you are en route and each route is honored and as sacred as the next. You were coming to the end of human life on earth. It was recorded by your prophets and it was on schedule. It was you who chose to move on to a higher vibration and to avoid Armageddon. It is you who have chosen to create the bridge and tip the balance of light and dark. We are just messengers reminding you of what you already know. We are here to remind you that you are indeed loved, that you are family, and to remind you that there is never a judgment on how far you reach. You are light and you are eternal. We wish you to realize that all that is around you was created for you so you can move to where you are standing now. We wish you to take one more step forward so you can remember who you are and remind others who they are. We wish you to know that you are a part of God, and so be it.

Snowflakes

YOU ARE ONE.

What do you mean? I thought you said we are a group.

You are a group within a group within a group. From where we stand you are one with all of your brothers and sisters.

Isn't each one of us different, some may ask?

You are one consciousness exploring your own mystery. Each and every one of you is taking part in this experiment of the one consciousness learning, understanding and creating its own boundaries. Each one of you represents an aspect of the one. You are all different and so you must be. There are no two of you alike but each of you reflects a different aspect of that grand consciousness. You are like snowflakes falling on a mountain. You say; "look, there is snow on the ground," yet each flake of snow is different. There are no two that are exactly alike. All are white like you and reflecting light like you. When we see you together, you are like snow covering the earth. However, we can also see your parts as each of you holds an attribute of the whole. Each of you has a shape and geometry like a snowflake and is white like the snow. When we see you from a distance, you are one. Humanity is one aspect of the entity you call the great consciousness. Each of you has your own unique task within that great whiteness. Like snowflakes, each of you reflect an aspect of the One from a different angle. Each of you is essential to complete the picture of the whole. There is no human walking in lesson that is less important then another walking in lesson. Each has its own story to tell and its own puzzle to fulfill to complete the picture. We wish to tell you about your oneness because so many of you find your identity in separation from others. We see those of you who classify their brothers and sisters based on their skin color. Others classify their brothers and sisters based on religion. Many of you measure each other based on looks or what they wear. We wish to tell you that when you use these judgments to classify your brothers and sisters who cross your path, you are walking in the opposite direction from spirit. As you put those who cross your path into your box based on color, religion, or cultural/ financial condition, you are separating you from you. There is never a judgment from us. Your choices are honored, but when you use thoughts to measure others, you are creating the energy of separation. As you think about others based on judgments, it manifests in your life in the form of a test and a lesson. It is as if the white snow flake says, "I do not want to be with these other snowflakes because their shape is not to my liking." You are eternal and you come and go very quickly. You are continuously shifting and changing so you can learn about yourself. As you come and go, you contribute to the learning of the whole. When you came to the planet of free choice this time around, you agreed to shine your light and bring your individual energy to the whole, so the whole can see that it is all part of One. We wish you to understand that it is your light that is showing all the other snowflakes the bigger picture. When all the flakes begin to see the vastness of the snow-peaked mountains and valley, they will understand that they are contributing to the magnificence of the vista, and they are part of the whole. The universe is vast and it is teaming with life. Conscious life is everywhere whether your scientists see it or not. Life in all systems is fueled and created by consciousness. We wish to tell you that you are part of that consciousness which created all the universes in all dimensions and realities. We know who you are, and to many of you, from your place of duality, it is unfathomable that you are the creator, but you are. Not only are you the creator, but you are part of the one system. This system would not be complete even with one of you not a part of it. This is why you are eternal. You are part of this great puzzle and the picture is incomplete without your piece.

Why are you telling us about the oneness, some may still wonder?

We wish to shed light on an aspect of "you" learning about "you" which holds many of you back from moving forward. When you see a homeless person begging for money on the street, you form a thought which we can see. It is often a thought of judgment. When you see a celebrity crossing your path, you form a thought and a judgment. From where we are sitting, hugging all of you, we wish to tell you that this homeless person and this celebrity are one and the same in a span of two cycles. This is the way of it. It is the same angel learning about different aspects of being human.

One aspect your society adores, and the other your society condemns. We ask you then, the next time you see the homeless person or the celebrity, try to reverse their roles in your mind. Try to see the homeless person as the celebrity and the celebrity as the homeless person. When you do, you will align your thoughts within the circle, moving away from the linearity of your perception, and creating a higher vibration. If you apply this exercise to your relationships, you will begin to understand the multi-dimensionality of your test.

As you walk in your world day-to-day, you pass many impressions of humans who are experiencing highs and lows. Can you see all as equally loved? Can you see the one who hit someone as just a different aspect of the same energy as the one who was hit? We love you and you are our brothers and sisters. We come from a place that had similar challenges. We know the pitfalls of the journey you call ascension. One of the biggest challenges on this journey is to maintain neutrality and love toward those who appear different from you. In actuality, all angels walking on this planet of free choice represent different aspects of the oneness. When you send the vibration of oneness while walking in your duality, you add to the energy of unity on your planet. Your thoughts create so much luminosity that they could light the entire street you are walking on. When you do not feel sorry for the poor and you do not get jealous or adore the rich and famous, then you are radiating what we call the frequency of oneness to the planet.

How can we see our enemies and our criminals as equal and one with us? This is too much to ask, some of you may complain.

We ask you to move away from your box and join us in the circle for a moment. We wish to take you by the hand and for you to look at the one who became your arch-enemy. He was your friend in another life. He may even have been a family member. He was in the life selection screening room with you and both of you thought that it may be a grand lesson to be born on the opposite side of the fence this time around. You chose to be born in the one life as "left side" and the next life as the opposite or "right side". You wanted to learn all aspects of you by experiencing both sides. Now, as you experience being the arch-enemy of yourself, you may be ripe to change perspective and to become peaceful on both sides. From our porch we see you and your arch-enemy in this life, planning this lesson with the understanding that it would add to the magnificence of the test and learning about the consciousness of oneness. You both hugged each other before coming to the lesson of free choice agreeing to meet again soon. You and your "enemy/friend/brother" said, "maybe this time we will be able to bridge our differences and see the oneness through it all. Let's give it a try." The next thing you know, you are adults, and you have forgotten your agreement. Now, you have to decide how you will treat your enemy. We wish to tell you that your enemy is your brother with different customs. We ask you to become peaceful with those who are different from you. Your thought is what brings closer, or pushes away peace on earth. We know who you are. We know your fears and we know your pain. We see the traumas that were created between you and your other aspect you call your enemy. You feel that you must fight and protect yourself. Many of you feel that unless you do something, the evil on the other side will hurt you. With all love we wish to tell you that the fear creates that which you experience. Your belief in the need to be protected actually manufactures the test in which you will, indeed, need to be attacked. We love you and we know that it isn't easy. When you are back home there is only love. There is no darkness as every corner is very well lit. We ask you to wake up to your magnificence so you can feel the oneness of all of you. When you walk on your streets without judgment you glow because you have activated the mastery in your veins. Your frequency then spills over to your brothers and sisters and it illuminates their path as well. You do not even know that you are doing it because your vision is linear. You can only see what is in front of you. We wish to tell you that as you walk in love and no-judgment, you emanate compassion and your compassion creates a ripple which starts on your planet and moves through all dimensions propelling the shift of consciousness on earth, as well as in the far reaches of the universe. This is your power and it is why we love you so much and wish you to wake up to your true purpose.

Can you hug your partner and love her like she is you and you are her? Can you forgive family who hurt you and become neutral with them, loving them as part of you? All around you is the oneness expressing itself through different reflections. Those of you who carry that awareness are those who shine this awareness to the others in darkness. We wish to impart to you that when enough of you walk with the awareness of the oneness, the planet will shift to a higher dimension and peace on earth will become its flag. We love you and from our perspective we are you and you are us, as we are all a part of the consciousness you call God. No part of it is valued less or more than the other. We wish you to be one who wears the attribute of oneness, and so be it.

Transparency

WHO YOU ARE has little to do with who you think you are. We see you as a vibrant swirling energy which has unique color, geometry and melody. The way you spin and the colors that reflect off of you tell us your story. You carry your experiences as badges and symbols of your life. You are transparent to us and that transparency is what we wish to speak of.

We see you from above and we are around you all the time. There are those of us who are called the "designers." They work with your geometry and they are technologically savvy. They keep your shape intact so you will vibrate at the frequency of the planet. You see, you have choices. Your biology is built for mastery. You are able to transcend your body if you so wish and to become a light being and transparent. It means that you walk in your biology on the planet but you are not seen by other humans.

How can that be, some may ask? Where does the body disappear to?

You are made of atoms and molecules that are vibrating at a specific frequency which is aligned with earth's frequency. This vibration keeps you visible on the planet and allows you to be a human in lesson. It is part of your agreement. We wish to speak to you about a new attribute that is being enabled as part of the shift of vibration on this planet. We will call it transparency. We wish to tell you that to us you look like a spinning swirl of stars. The space between the stars is vast. Within you there is more empty space then matter. You are energy walking and commanding a biological vehicle that is mostly empty space. When you come to earth you come to a much denser plane then the one you call home. Many of the societies currently occupying systems that are similar to yours exist on much less dense environments. It is so to the extent that your science cannot see them unless they choose to be seen. Many of those who come to visit you at this time are of a lighter consistency. Their molecules are separated and are not bonded together like yours. If they choose to, they can create shapes to their liking using energy. When you look at water in a glass it is transparent yet it is the most valuable substance on your planet. When you look at air, it is transparent yet without it you cannot survive for more them a few minutes. Many of the attributes of spirit are transparent yet they act as the force behind the force. Those transparent attributes are the engine behind the engine. To you, transparency often equates to non-existence. When you do not see something you have a hard time accepting it. Yet, water, air and gravity which are vital to your survival are transparent.

This is different some of you may say. *Our science can measure air and water therefore it is physical.*

We wish to tell you that all spiritual attributes have a physical aspect. It is true, however, that your modern science has not yet discovered the physical attributes of spiritual essence. Your instruments are not refined enough and often you look in the wrong places. When they finally do find the physical attributes of spiritual essence, they will realize that it is everywhere. Many things that are vital to your survival and are in front of your nose cannot be observed by your modern day technology. Your magnetic properties, which are continuously shifting according to the position of the planets, shape many events in your reality and their outcomes in your daily life, yet you do not see it and cannot measure it. The science of astrology that many of you dismiss as a guessing work or hobby of sorts plays a large part in your daily coming and going and most of you are oblivious to it. The magnetic fields of your planet affects your sleeping patterns, your emotional state, and your ability to receive guidance from other dimensions, or what you call intuition and yet your science does not even have words for it. The web of communication which connects humans with humans through silver cords is not in any of your psychology literature. The ether is teaming with communication and knowledge that is coming from other systems and other dimensions and yet you do not see any of it. Many of the forces which are operating in your daily lives are transparent. When you come back home you are transparent as well. Transparency is an attribute of spirit. When you begin to walk the walk of a spiritual human you must develop that set of eyes that can see that which most of humanity cannot. Those of you who give intention to walk hand in hand with spirit must develop extra-sensory vision. That vision can see in the dark and it can also see the transparent.

Why do we need to see the transparent?, some of you may wonder.

We wish to impart to you that spirit speaks to you through transparency. Transparency is the language by which information is delivered to you and is one of the forces that you cannot see, but it shapes your life. To many, a traumatic event that comes seemingly from nowhere is tagged as "bad luck" or an "accident." Many of you do not see the transparent threads of karmic settlements which create a shift in your lives. You find reasons for disease, and you find reasons for accidents. You form an investigation to look into why this happened and that happened. Then you find out that the brakes were to blame, or the other vehicle was to blame. We wish to tell you that as you are searching for the mechanics of your life, the real forces that shape your life are not mechanical, they are spirit based. Many of you see yourselves as practical. Many of you read only practical books and do practical things. Many of you eat practical food and do what seems to be practical in your life. Many of you also encounter, all of a sudden and by surprised something that throws you off your practical route. We hug you and we love you regardless of your knowledge or your inclinations. It is however those of you are practical who are most surprised when something "traumatic" seemingly comes "from nowhere" and create a shift in your life. From where we sit on our porch, these are the invisible forces that operate in your life. The transparent energy operates whether you acknowledge it or not. Your universe is made of forces of attraction and gravity. Your parts are connected through an electrical attraction of sorts which is magnetically based.

Why are you telling us this confusing stuff? you may wonder.

We wish to tell you that as you vibrate higher your body becomes less dense. The actual attribute of your physical vehicle is changing to accommodate the new enhanced driver. There are those of us who are working with you so you can become more transparent. They are your facilitators. You have the ability to stay on your planet doing your work in a transparent form. There were masters who walked the planet and shifted their energy from dense human form to light beings who were transparent. As you become transparent, you develop the ability to see those transparent forces which operate around you. When we speak of the enhanced human, we speak of the transparent one. Your society at this time reflects the individual human; and, as there is a split between the light and the dense human, there is a split between the light and dense aspects of your society. This split is between the old energy and the new energy. There is never a judgment, and all of your choices are sacred and honored. You are at a place in time that is shifting very rapidly in comparison to your history; your planet is going through an energy shift where the pull of gravity lessens so slightly. Your body particles respond to even the slightest shift in the magnetic pull of the planet. There are those of you who will begin to align with this new attribute and your light bodies will climb and shift as they follow their paths and activate the pieces and parts of their divinity. There will be those, however, who are the "practical ones." They are loved by spirit the same as the others, but they will encounter a certain attribute that you may call a pattern of coincidences that they will not be able to explain through your logic or science. It is the practical ones who will face a dilemma, whether to force explanations and logic onto events that shape their lives, or move forward and discover the transparent forces that operate their physical reality. We wish to impart to you that light and heavy, dense and transparent are the choices that will face each and every one of you in the near future. We love you and we are always with you waiting for you to give us your hand so we can shine light on your path. We wish to tell you that the transparent forces in your lives will become more powerful and more prevalent as the earth shifts. It is a magnificent sight to see such grand transformation. From the denser human to the lightest human you are all loved equally. However, denser humans will have a more difficult time feeling the threads of love around them as they are continuously challenged to understand the forces that shape their lives. The lighter, less dense human will be more aligned with what happens in their lives. The signs, symbols and messages will come in a form that they can see, feel, and follow because it will match their vibration. There is never a judgment but it is an exciting time to awaken to the transparent forces in your life. It is an exciting time to become transparent yourself. It is the time when all the knowledge you obtain through ages past is available to you, so you can ascend. You are at a place in time that is confusing, and all those things that are dense will be exposed as part of the energy of transparency. There are those who hide in the denser realms of society and use practicality as their weapon. That which is not transparent must be exposed and transformed. You will experience it on all levels of existence whether personal, social, political, or spiritual. We live in a dimension where all is transparent. As the veil becomes thinner you come closer to our reality. We hug you and welcome you. You are your own master in this sacred planet of free choice. We wish you to acknowledge and follow the transparent forces in your life and become one yourself, and so be it.

The Drama Class

WILL THERE ALWAYS BE DRAMA *in our lives*, some of you may wonder?

Drama is your class. It is how you learn.

Why can't we learn without drama, you may wonder?

You can and that is your goal but to get there you must first experience drama. The cycle of your life is built on change. Inevitably, drama is a potential attribute of change. The drama in your life is your choice. If every time there is a change in your life you respond to it with drama, it is your choice. The change is there and your lesson is there for your benefit.

How do we move away from drama, some may wonder?

You move away by going inside and acknowledging your divinity. When you begin to link yourself to your own divinity, you link to the thread of love which is woven throughout your life. You may say, "The pain that I suffered cannot be coming from love, and the pitfall that

I experienced could only come from the darkness." We wish to tell you that the only darkness that is falling upon you is that which is already inside of you. There is no evil anything that is trying to hurt you for the sake of hurting you. There is no evil mastermind that is lurking at the corner to toy with angels on this planet. There is you and your karma. There are choices that you made and contracts that you signed in order to bring you closer to your true divinity. You choose to put plus or minus signs on your experiences. You choose to attach labels such as negative or positive. From the perspective of spirit, there is no negative. There is, however, your perception of what feels good at the moment and what feels uncomfortable or painful. Some of your biggest leaps catapulting inner growth result from experiences you tag as negative. As we hug you, we wish to tell you that some of you are having a hard time with the concept of choice. Some of you may say, "We would never choose an event that is so traumatic and painful." We know who you are and we are with you as you go through your lessons. We know the hardships that you had to endure. With love we wish to impart to you that indeed it is the choice of your higher self to move beyond mere existence in order for your light to expand. It is your purpose and your mission to move away from drama and to discover the thread of love in all events in your life. We see you crying at times at night asking "Why me?" And "What did I do to deserve it?"

We wish to tell you that you are so loved and that all that appears difficult and challenging is a stepping stone for you to move higher in your journey. It is your choice, however, whether or not you accept that the challenge is an opportunity to move higher. It is your choice whether you see yourself as a victim or not. It is your choice to paint your experiences with the colors of drama, or to become peaceful with them. Whatever is happening in your life is appropriate and by design. It is so because you are the creator and you set your experiences up for yourself. Even events that seem to be out of your control and overwhelming in proportion are a choice. All of you knew all the potentials of your life journey before you came down to this planet of free choice. Events that seemed to be negative or positive from your linear and limited perspective did not appear that way before you came back as a human. When you are an angel back home, all events are seen and designed with the big picture in mind. All events are planned with love and with your mission and lesson in mind and always with your permission. There is a great design team working on paving your path and you are the head of that team.

What is the purpose of suffering, you may ask?

When you are looking at the potentials of your life, you are aware of all the lifetimes you have lived, and the lessons that you learned and those you still need to work on. You do not judge yourself and there is no one else who judges you. As you look at your life, you may say to your design team and your teachers; "I feel that I need to go through this test again, so I will become stronger." Then you may say, "I feel that it will serve my higher purpose if I experience it this way because it will allow me the option of transforming myself and moving closer to my divinity." Then you are hugged and you make your way through the various vortexes to the birth canal and out into the world of duality. Within a short few years you no longer have a trace of memory of the contracts you signed and the challenges you designed for yourself. Now you are in the dark, but those things you set up are there waiting for you as you created them. When the time comes, these events will manifest in your life. If you are in darkness, you will say to yourself, "Why me? What did I do to deserve this?" There is never a judgment and your choices are sacred. The drama in your life, however, can be gone when you choose to turn on your light and to expose that thread of love that carries you through your journey as a human in lesson. We know how things appear to you from your perspective. We see your colors, geometry and melody. We wish to tell you that you have the power to change those appointments you set up for yourself, if you wish to do so. You can change appointments that you perceive as negative and you can manifest harmony and peace in places where a challenge was set in order for you to learn about harmony and peace.

How do we do that, some may wonder?

When you set up the intention to turn on your light and discover your divinity, it is as if you gave your hand to spirit and asked to be shown the way. It is then that many of the appointments which were designed to wake you up will disappear.

Why would they, you ask?

They will disappear because they are no longer necessary.

But I thought I designed it, and it is set to happen no matter what, some of you may ask.

Your design team never rests. . There are those of us who are part of your group and they are the coordinators of synchronicity. They are responsible for keeping your appointments. The coordinators from your group work closely with coordinators of other angels to manifest the appropriate lesson for each of you. When the group receives the transmission that you give them a hug and say, "Thank you for your dedication and work but I no longer need that appointment," they hold one of those all night parties in your honor. Nothing is set in your life and planning never stops. Your emotions and your reactions to events in your life are the set of instructions that you transmit to your design team. We see many of you who experience a specific type of drama over and over again. It is like one of your television re-runs. You watch it and you already know the outcome because you have watched it many times before. We know who you are and you are never judged. There are some of you who go into relationships knowing and already expecting the outcome. It is one of those re-runs, and sure enough the scenario plays itself out precisely as it did in the previous one. Some of you attribute these relationships to "bad luck, or bad karma". We wish to tell you as we hug you that there is neither bad luck nor bad karma.

What is it then, some of you may wonder?

It is you trying to give yourself opportunity after opportunity to graduate from a lesson that was not learnt. It is the attempt of the higher part of you to coordinate opportunities so you can finally understand your tendencies and realize who you are and what it is that you are doing to create such relationships. It is "you" trying to teach "you" about "you." It is you calling and coordinating event after event so you will have plenty of openings to transform yourself.

I am tired, you say to us. *I want it to stop,* others say.

You are the driver and if you wish it to stop, ask to be guided and shown what it is you need to learn.

How do I do that, you may ask?

You need to tune into the radio station inside you that transmits messages to you. When you get those messages through your feeling center, you must follow them and not ignore them.

All of you get messages from your angels and your group. We hear many of you saying to yourself,

I know that I have been there before and it feels familiar, and I know that last time it was a disaster, but maybe this time it will be different.

We wish to tell you with all love that it will not be different. You are the one who must change for the lesson to change. The work is internal and the lesson is your mirror which allows "you" to see "you." As long as you have not changed yourself, it does not matter which mirror you choose to experience, it would still reflect you. The drama in your life reflects you. It is your mirror and it shows you the different aspects of you that need polishing. You are the creator and you have designed events and people around your lessons so they will reflect who you are back to you. You are a beautiful angel, and you are dearly loved for just walking the walk. We wish you to give your higher-self a hand so you can move away from the spinning wheels and reruns, and let go of the drama. When you have moved away from the aspects of drama in your life, you get closer to an attribute in your life that we call bliss. It is a feeling of love mixed with pleasure about all you encounter. The energy of bliss when carried by enough angels is the torch of humanity, transforming the darkness and healing the planet. Your mission at this time is to live in bliss. When you do, you are in service for all of your brothers and sisters and the dirt that you are stepping on. We wish you to awaken to the experience of bliss and to move away from the drama in your life, and so be it.

The Radio Station

WE ARE WITH YOU when you call us. We must be. You are the one who is in control of your guides and entourage. We are in a waiting mode and when you call us we are already there. There is no delay. We see you at times calling and calling and you do not realize that we have been waiting for you to open your eyes so you can see us sitting in front of you, hugging you. You are so used to not getting what you want that when you ask spirit for help, you assume that there will be a delay. There is no delay in our reality.

Those of you who call out to spirit your requests are always answered. Some of you decorate your requests with prayers from holy books, or in chants and hymns given to you by gurus, lamas, priests' rabbis or muftis in order to connect with spirit. Many of those forms of "spiritual" communication were given to you as a way to channel your energy in a specific way so you can connect to a specific belief system. We wish to tell you that it is not necessary to connect with spirit through any given text or ritual. You do not even need to speak. You do not need a temple, a book, an icon, a prayer shawl, or beads.

In fact all you need to connect is your intention. Your intention can be expressed in one thought: "Dear Spirit, I wish to connect to the divinity inside me." That's who spirit is. It is not outside of you and you do not need tools to connect to yourself. All you are doing is tuning into a radio station that is playing the frequency of divinity inside of you. Many of you believe that spirit comes from above or from some entity that carries a special energy which facilitates their life. With all love, we wish to tell you that spirit is in your biology. It is part of you. It is embedded in every single cell of your body.

How can that be, some of you may wonder? Aren't our bodies renewing all the time?

Yes, your bodies are renewing but just as your DNA remains intact regardless of your constant renewing, so does the attribute of spirit in your cells. Your cells are alive because of the consciousness embedded in them. Many of you think that first you have life then you have consciousness. You have it in reverse. The thought came first and it manifested into a vessel which you call the human body. You are spirit walking oblivious and in forgetfulness. That is your test and that is your agreement. You are a walking spirit and you do not need anything except your intention to connect with that which you carry inside you. When you use someone else's prayerful method to connect with yourself you are one step removed from pure intention. Pure intention is your most powerful tool. Knowing who you are, knowing that you are it, and that your mission to dig out and reveal what is buried inside you, is your birthright. There are many who choose to be part of this one or another tradition and who feel that using this or that mantra helps them to connect. This is honored and sacred. This is a unique place where the connection with spirit is by choice and if you choose to use tools, that is sacred, as well.

We see many of you who use facilitators to get in touch with their emotions, for example, psychologists or mediums. We wish to tell you that in most cases it is not the facilitator who helps "you" connect to "you" but your pure intention which brings "you" closer to yourself. Your biggest challenge at this time is to connect with your body and through this vessel to connect to your divinity. Once you connect to your divinity it is your mission to activate the divinity within your cells so that your vibration will increase. Your mission is to vibrate higher and higher, in your vessel so you awakes completely to your sacred purpose and shines your light without filters. We wish to tell you as we hug you that we are in love with humanity. We see that your modern society encourages "you" to be separated from "you" so you will need to purchase and buy things to replace and reintegrate what you feel you have lost. We are here to tell you that you never have lost anything. Many of you are being led to believe that you need something or someone to become whole. There is never a judgment and all your paths are sacred and honored. Many of you are being manipulated daily to consume and purchase things that make you feel connected to yourself. Every time you buy into one of those aspects of your culture, you energize the idea that you are not connected to yourself. Your body is like an antenna and it listens to your messages. It is not what you say but the intention behind the words that your body "hears." When you overuse scaffolding to support yourself, your body "hears" the message that you are weak and it cannot heal itself. In your culture medicine is big business because it perpetually sends the message that you need to take this or that to be healthy. Much effort is invested in your modern medicine to distance you from your vessel. By doing so, you become weaker and need more and more support. Your companies make profits from selling you drugs to numb your feelings. Your body is a natural healer and does not require any numbing agent which only prolongs the healing process. Your body, in many ways, is more intelligent than your conscious mind.

How can that be, some of you may wonder? *My toes cannot write poetry.*

Your body knows of your challenges, it is also aware of your past lives and the challenges you have been through in your various life expressions. It knows your intentions and it knows whether you are truthful to yourself. When your body gives you a sign of imbalance, many in your culture run to the doctor or take a magic pill so that the imbalance will disappear. We wish to tell you that all you are doing is worsening the imbalance. All physical manifestation of imbalance is between matter and spirit. Your consciousness is the link. When your body gives you a message of imbalance you try to disconnect from your body so you will not feel the pain. This approach has been spoon- fed to you since early age, and it is the reason why so many modern-day angels carry diseases in them. It is the expression of imbalance that is perpetually ignored until spirit is so disconnected from the vessel that it manifests as a major disease. Aches and pains are the gift of spirit which says to you, in every way possible, to stay with your body and remain connected to yourself so you can rediscover your equilibrium and live in balance and health. There is never a judgment. All of you are loved whether you are balanced or unbalanced. It is your choice and it is sacred. We wish to tell you that those of you who are reading this message are here at this time to manifest the biggest leap of consciousness humanity has ever seen. Therefore, you must be in a place of health and vibrancy. The new energy coming from your sun and other systems enables you to live longer and to heal yourself. Your power lies in your belief. If you choose to believe that you have no power and every time there is flu going around you will catch it, your wish and your fear will manifest as well. You are powerful to heal yourself and also to bring disease on yourself. There is no judgment and you are in control of your body in both directions. We wish to tell you that many forces in your modern day society are set up to separate you from your divinity. This spectrum of forces includes your religions, political institutions, financial institutions, schools, and your health care system. From an early age you were taught that you need crutches because you cannot walk without support. You are being told that you are not enough as you are.

We wish to impart to you that it serves your economy when you are weak, and it also serves your political, financial and religious institutions. The weaker you are the more controllable you are, and the more your energy can be channeled to where it serves others.

You are renegades and you came here at this time to be the light which shines in the dark and warns the ships where the danger lies. You are lighthouses and your mission is to wake up to your power. You do not need to preach or evangelize. You must be that which you are. You must walk on this planet with your light on and your divinity intact. It is the vibration you radiate that will wake your fellow angels from their deep sleep. You are the forerunners of what was named the new sun. You are on the edge of a potential for a huge leap in consciousness. There are trillions of us who are excitingly waiting to see how you handle your opportunities. We love you and we know your challenges. We wish to tell you that it is by design. The fear is also by design. It is time to let go of the fear of survival. You cannot learn to ride a bicycle if you keep your training wheels on. You must let go of all your safety nets in order to allow your divinity and miracles to carry you forward. It is trust in the process that brings the process to you. It is a process of connecting you with you to walk as the powerhouse that you are.

It is a dangerous, scary world and we must be careful, many of you say. Others ask; *do you wish us to ignore all the warnings and be irresponsible?*

We wish you to know that you have no idea how powerful you are. There is no disease that can attach itself to you without your permission, no accident that can come to you without your permission, and no danger that can come to you without your permission. You are fed fear day and night so you will believe that you have no power. You are fed fear and powerlessness so you will consume the things which seemingly give you power. It is that consumption which sends a message of not trusting your divinity and power. The less powerful you feel, the more you must rely on sources outside of yourself, and the more you feed the machine of consumption and greed.

We wish you to awaken to your full power as nothing can touch you when you are fully connected to yourself. We are in love with you and wish you to walk the walk in Joy and bliss. We wish you to know that you are a powerhouse whose mission is lighting the path for those who are in the dark and so be it.

Walk in the Park

You CAN WALK IN YOUR DAILY LIFE as if you have no idea what is going on around you. The fact is that you do know. When you wake up to the knowledge that is hidden in you that knowledge gives you power to chart your own path. When you walk blindfolded you just follow the path that karma has paved for you. It is your responsibility and privilege to be here at this time and know your purpose. When you know it, you do not fear anymore. It is the knowing that ignites the light in you so you can transform the dark. Everything we have said so far in all of our messages is known to you. There are no surprises and no new revelations, just remembering and waking up from a deep sleep. You have been walking blindfolded and we are helping you, through our messages, to take off the cloth that is wrapped around your eyes. When you begin to see where you are going, you no longer hesitate. Just as you trust your vision to guide you in your day- to-day lives, in the realm of spirit it is the same. As you remove the cloth over your eyes you and begin to see the interdimensionality of your existence and the interconnectedness of all things, you begin to see and understand where you are and where you are going. This knowing gives you immense power.

Why are you telling us about seeing, you may ask? Many will say *we do see and our eyes are open.*

We wish to tell you that you are coming into a time when the truth will be exposed both in its ugliness and splendor. As the light shines brighter, more and more of what was hidden will be transformed. Before it can be transformed it must be exposed. We ask you to be prepared and know who you are and what your purpose is when you hear in the news things which may be most disturbing to you. There are many who are trying to manipulate you into fear. They know that by incorporating fear into your daily life you will be weaker and more easily manipulated. Your reality is built on layers. There is no reality per se that is one for all. Your reality is created by angels walking in duality. Your combined thoughts create the general reality which you live by in your daily lives. Each of you creates their own individual reality based on their personal idea of who they are. There are those who benefit from you being in a reality where you experience fear and control. They benefit because they channel your emotional energy in a way that feeds their greed and power. It is time to wake up and filter many of those ways by which your reality is delivered to you. You must use your own feelings and your own knowing to decipher every situation you encounter. We see you walking in a park on a sunny day and the birds are chirping. It is a beautiful day and your reality seems to be in a wonderful state, yet when we look at you, you are surrounded by fear and your energy is not flowing. When we look at your melody, thought and shape, we see the cords of the financial news in your energetic body. We see you thinking of what will happen if the stock market collapses and your money loses its value. This is what we mean by you creating your own reality. It is not your walk in the park that is challenging, it is the thought that something is threatening you outside of yourself and it is imminent, and you have no control over it and it can hurt you. We wish to impart to you with love that when you walk in the park in fear you help manifest that which brings you fear. Moreover, you feed that mechanism that is trying to manipulate you into being fearful. Fear paralyzes your energetic bodies and creates blocks. When fear is present, communication with spirit become cryptic or blocked altogether. You are a vibrating instrument and like a tuning fork, your music and tunes are heard when you are vibrating at a certain frequency. If you hit the tuning fork and then grab it with your hand the melody will abruptly stop. This is a metaphor for how fear affects your psychic and energetic bodies. You are used to being fearful. You have been taught to fear and worry from early on. We love you and we know who you are. We see your challenges and we see your worries. We wish to tell you that there is nothing in your life that you need to fear except fear itself as it holds you from discovering your path. Reality as you know it is changing and things are not going to add up like they used to. When dimensions begin to shift, that which appeared linear will be exposed in all its various dimensions. From where we stand, your reality will be coming to you in a way that is not linear.

What do you mean by that, some may wonder? We wish to tell you that when an event takes place around you which is magnificent in scope and which reverberates throughout the world, we ask you to form your own feelings about it and stay balanced. Do not allow fear to take over. The coming changes are necessary for your planet to move up in vibration. There are those who try to keep you anchored in the old energy and the battle is raging now at this time. You are light warriors who came to hold the energy of balance at this time. You are the anchors who keep things balanced when everything seems to be so unbalanced and wobbly. We wish to tell you with all love that your reality is just a play and it is an illusion created to teach you about you. You are here now to wake up and see through this illusion. When you understand that the game of creation is created inside you before it is expressed in your reality, you begin to awaken to the immense responsibility that each one of you carries as you walk in your daily lives. There is never a judgment and your journey is honored whether you use your power and awaken to your mission or not. It is however our intention to hug you and shake you a little so you will remember who you are and what your purpose is at this time. Each one of you is an important part in the creation of the new reality on this planet. Your awakening is setting the stage for the new crystalline grid to be established.

This grid holds humanity vibrational level. It is now awakening because of you.

As you walk in balance in a chaotic world you hold the balance for all those are around you. You are masters and most of you do not know it. Many of you say that you are barely making it through the day. We see many of you burdened by your thoughts, fears and worries. It is by design and there are those who give you the "gifts" of fear and worry so you will stay in your wheel spinning faster and faster and never step aside. There are those who wish you to stay asleep so they can continue their manipulation in the dark. They are loved like you but they represent the dark aspects of humanity at this time. It is by choice and they believe that they benefit from being in the dark. There is never a judgment but we wish to tell you that darkness is just lack of light. Light represents information, truth and love. When those in the dark are exposed to light, inevitably they transform and greatly benefit from their own transformation. All you are doing is allowing them the option to choose. You are bringing light to where there wasn't any. When those in the dark see the light they can step into it and be transformed or run away. It is their choice and you need not worry about it. You are the one who carries the torch and you must carry it regardless of what others do around you.

There is an attribute of knowing that we wish to speak of. It is the knowing which is beyond doubt. It is the deepest knowing, the kind of knowing that when you see the sun rise and light the earth, you know it is day, and when the sun sets and it is dark you know it is night. This knowing is only available to you when you look inside. Your senses, which are the way you used to have your reality delivered to you, will not serve you as well in the coming transition. We wish you to get used to consulting your inner feelings as they will lead you to this knowing. Your inner knowing is your source of power. As we see it, inner knowing is governed by your feminine aspects. Many of you who chose a female body at this time have some advantage as your biology is linked to that aspect of inner knowing more so then your male counterparts. We wish to speak to the ones who chose a male body in this life. We wish you to get in touch with that aspect of "you" that is feminine because it will serve you and the planet well. We wish you to become open to the frequency of communication that is being delivered from your female counterparts. We see many of you dismiss the communication as not cohesive or too emotional. We ask you to use your "non-cohesive" ear to listen carefully to these communications because it will serve you well. Emotional and non-cohesive communication is closer to the reality that you will face in the near future. Your planet is shifting from predominantly masculine aspects of creation to feminine aspect of creation. That is appropriate so humanity can align its energy with the planet. The energy of the planet is represented predominantly by the feminine. Your transition from masculine to feminine is a natural evolution which brings you closer to your true nature. Being in touch with your feeling is being in touch with the self and the planet. To many of you this concept is difficult. You have been taught to hide the emotional self. We wish to tell you that it is time to reintroduce yourself to that aspect of yourself. Climbing upward in the spiral of ascension depends on "you" balancing the aspects of your feminine and masculine sides within "you."

How do we do that, some of you may wonder?

All of you have been in male bodies as well as in female bodies. In your cellular memory lies dormant the essence you carried as a female. We ask you to give intention for these memories to awaken so you will have a firsthand experience of what it is like. This remembering is now enabled and it will serve you well. You are greatly loved and your female and male sides are just different aspects of your interdimensional self. There is no negative or positive as they both represent parts of the whole and are sacred. We wish you to embrace yourself from all sides. We hug you day after day asking you to remember. We wish to remind you that none of our messages are new to you and all is known to you, and so be it.

Golden Bridge

I F W E C O M E T O Y O U, it is because you asked us to. We are always around you and part of you, but we do not appear before you if you do not ask us to.

Why are you repeating this over and over again, some of you may wonder?

It is because we are patiently waiting for you to ask us for our hands.

Who are "we," you may wonder?

We are angels that are part of the angelic group that makes up who you are. You are a group and part of you is on our side and part of you is walking on earth in duality. In order to give a hand to spirit you must create a golden bridge. The golden bridge is our term for an interdimensional communication which links the dimension of spirit with the dimension of physical matter and time. We exist both in your dimension and in ours. You also exist in both dimensions but you are aware of only one. You are aware of the dimension that you can perceive with your senses.

How can we become aware of the other part of us, you may wonder?

You must create that golden bridge. You build it one golden brick at a time. The bridge is built through two attributes: intention and trust. Without one the other will not create the glue to hold the bricks together. The bridge is built with invisible hands and every time you give intention and trust to the process these invisible hands put more bricks into the structure.

When is this bridge to be completed, some may wonder?

We know of your competitive nature and your result-oriented thinking. This, however, is a different type of bridge.

How different, you may wonder? As you build the bridge, what you wish to bridge becomes vaster so the building of the bridge never really ends. The larger the bridge becomes, the closer you get to the realm of spirit. The stronger the bridge is, the clearer the communication is between you and the other part of you.

How can we cross to the other side if the bridge is never complete, some may wonder?

You can never cross to the other side until such time that you shed your body and come back home. The bridge brings you closer to the realm of spirit although you can never jump off the bridge and be in the realm of spirit altogether. Part of you must remain in the realm of the physical. This is a limitation that you put on yourself as the temptation to cross is great, especially for those of you who have been on this planet for many cycles. You are spirit and the part of you which is physical is the manifestation of a desire of spirit to create and express. You are spirit walking in a human body unaware of your divinity. Many of you give your power to others, who you are told, possess the power of bringing you closer to spirit. Those "others" may be spiritual gurus, rabbis or priests. We wish to impart to you that all pathways are sacred and when you search you find what works in your reality and for your level of development. We see you and we know your past. You have been part of an organization in many of your past lives and in this life you carry the attraction to join and be part of that which you recall in your cellular memory. You are coming into a time that is different than any other time humanity has seen and experienced before. You are actually changing the molecules and atoms which create your physical world. You are manifesting interdimensional DNA that has been dormant for eons. You are creating links in the neurons of your brain that have been inactive since the time of Lemuria. We wish to tell you with love that you are becoming the golden bridge and your biology is responding to your intent. We ask you to honor what is unfolding and not resist it. As you create the bridge, you begin to experience new vistas that are not in your dictionaries and encyclopedias. We ask you to trust as these vistas are your new reality and a result of your intention to vibrate higher. Like a blind person who, through a medical procedure, has her vision restored, you cannot say, "I want to be blind again so I will not have to experience the painful sights which I did not know existed." The painful sights are just your interpretation of what you sense. From our perspective all is magnificent and leads you to a higher place then you ever visited before in your current biology. We ask you to stay trusting and balanced. The energy that is coming from the center of your universe and is delivered by your sun is potent and glorious in scope. The sun delivers to you energy that changes your biology enabling you to vibrate higher. You have asked for it and we ask you to prepare to trust that which you begin to see. It will look and feel different then the sights you have been used to but it is your reality merging with other dimensions.

Should we be concerned, some of you may wonder?

You are loved and never judged. We are in awe of your willingness to walk the walk and manifest the miracles that you have. There is a great interest in the universe and many are here watching you as you choose and create your new path. You have asked to continue this journey and we are your facilitators. We are part of you and others who are the forerunners of the new energy we have named the "New Sun." The attribute of this new energy is light and lots of it. Through your actions and thoughts you are channeling through you more light so the planet can increase its vibration. A chain of events begin to unfold as the planet changes. Many of those angels who walk in duality begin to awaken to the purpose of their lives. This is your mission. Through your light, others begin to awaken like the flower that awakens in response to the longer daylight after a long winter. You are the one who must awaken first and the others will follow. There are those of you who know that it is time. The others are waiting for you to shine your light so they can use it to awaken as well. The waking of humanity at this time has a geometric shape and its own melody. It is written in the sky and foretold by the book written in the stars that you call astrology. Knowing who you are creates beautiful resonance and when you walk, you awaken the dirt under your feet. Your resonance and frequency activates parts and pieces of Gaia. It is a true ripple. That is why we ask you to take care of yourself. When you do, the ripple will grow in concentric circles to include the part of humanity that gave intention for this change.

What do we need to do, you may wonder?

We ask you to love yourself first. We ask you to honor the body that you carry and we ask you to honor all that is around you. When you walk in lesson with the understanding of the sacredness of all that is around you, you are awakened and the earth shifts under your footsteps. This is how it works. We wish you not to preach or evangelize that which you experience. Each of you carries a version of reality that is true for you and it is sacred. No version of reality is regarded more then another. We ask you to walk in the reality of a master. Your approach may be very different from your fellow angel's approach but both of you will carry the same light at the end of the day. We ask you to embrace the process of activation but not the "how to." It is the individual responsibility of each one of you to find your unique path. It is by design and part of the initiation process leading to mastery. That is why this path is not for everyone. There are neither manuals nor sacred books nor gurus who can lead you where you need to go. That is why we ask you to awaken because the knowing comes from within. We wish you to know that as you move away from aspects of your society that are channeling your spiritual energy into their own structure you begin to unravel the truth that is in you. You must walk without your "training wheels." Some may feel fearful walking alone. We wish to hug you and let you know that you are never alone and you are always loved. The only set of instructions that you may carry with you are three words long. These instructions have three pages and each page has one word inscribed on it. The first spells "intent", the second spells "love" and the third spells "trust". This is all you need as the path of truth is in you. It is not the "how to get there" which defines truth. It is the process in which you search that defines the truth. Truth is a triangle of the three attributes "intent," "love" and "trust." One cannot be used without the other. Many of the ailments of your culture use intent and trust without love. Love is your true essence, and all which resonates with the universal energy of love will take you higher in vibration. That which does not carry the love vibration will bring you lower. You are at a place where few have visited. Many of them are known to you because they carry the names of masters from your past. We ask you to awaken to the mastery that runs in your veins and activate your divinity. You are the creator and you create that which you intend. We ask you to awaken to your awesome power and feel the sacredness of every moment you walk in biology on this planet. You are the bringers of light and we ask you to let that light show through you. You are a walking lighthouse and when you turn your light on, you show the path to those who are in the dark, and so be it.

The Universal Symphony

*Y*OU ARE ONE. Even when you experience a conflict with an angel that plays a role as your partner, lover, child, or friend, you are still one. The separation that you may experience at times when interacting with a fellow angel is separation within you. When you experience anger it is a separation of sorts from the link that you have with your inner divinity. When you experience an emotion that you deem negative, you are moving away from your own center and becoming vulnerable to energies that are not balanced. As you move away from your center, you become a magnet which switches polarities and instead of repelling negative energies, attracts them. This process happens automatically and it is part of your geometric blueprint. As you turn the triangle of your geometry, that which was balanced becomes unbalanced. It therefore attracts those shapes that are unbalanced. All geometric forms attract those shapes which complete them therefore attempting to balance those aspects that are unbalanced. As an angel in lesson, you become aware of the negative and positive implication of your emotion. From our perspective they are all valid lessons and move you toward growth. When you experience anger, you become a target of all the negative energies around you. When you are balanced you become an anchor which holds steady all the energies around you. You are a vibration manifested in physical form. While walking in your daily life you vibrate a melody and radiate colors. When we see you moving about, we see a magnificent display of light, colors, and melody swirling and moving. Your emotions are the most powerful tools you carry and as you experience your emotions, your whole form, melody and colors change. When you experience love your colors intensify and harmonize with the pulse of the universe. As you vibrate with love, you become a member of the universal symphony. When you feel anger or hate, jealousy or fear, your vibration and melody moves away from the universal frequency of love and you are in discord with the universal vibration. There is never a judgment on how you feel. You are built having the capacity to experience heaven and hell, light and darkness, joy and anger. They are all in you as potentials. It is your choice to play the tune in line with the universal accord or play the tune of discord. You are the musician and your musical tools are neutral. Each one of you comes with the capacity to play the tunes of the entire spectrum. Your karma is just a set-up for you to have a context in which to play your tune. Like a musician who needs an orchestra or a stage to perform, yours is earth and your karma is the melody you choose to express it through. When you are interacting with another and you choose anger, you are not only expressing your own anger but you are becoming a lightning rod for all the negative energy that surrounds you. Like an electromagnetic tool, you are attracting that which is similar. When you experience hate, the molecules and the atoms around you change as they become literally heavy. When you experience the feeling of love, those molecules and atoms become neutral and your experience becomes one of lightness. From our perspective your aim is to become a player in the universal orchestra. You can become one, when you become aware of your emotions and redirect that which you feel, to be aligned with the universal harmony of love. The energy that you emit through your emotions affects all that is around you and is recorded in your geometry and melody. When you experience hate, you are like a violinist who breaks a string in the middle of a concert. The concert is your life and we wish you to play the most divine music that you are capable of playing. Your angel guides are your conductors and although they cannot play for you they are able to direct you through their invisible magic conductor's wand. You, however, must raise your gaze from the instrument and search for guidance. What happens when you and a fellow angel express anger? It is as if there is a battle between you, where you attempt to pull energy from the energetic body of each other. The other is a mirror of you, so when you are draining them you are consequently draining yourself. You may think that you have expressed your anger and, therefore, you feel more empowered. We wish to tell you that this is the temporary feeling of a drug addict that experiences the high of the moment. Inevitably that high will end in a low.

Why are you telling us about anger, some may wonder?

Anger is the most challenging of all emotions at this time. Most of the interactions you have that you perceive as negative are variations of anger. Anger always comes when your idea about yourself is being challenged. In your culture it is called ego.

What do we do about it, some may ask?

It is a choice whether to play the divine tune and be aligned with the universal energy or to be in discord. The energies outside of you are an expression of your inner world manifested. We know that to some it appears to be that all the elements are there to test you and to push you towards anger and that you have no part in it. Many of you believe that you are just reacting to what was done to you. We must tell you that it is not so. Anger is a choice and a choice that many of you select as a short cut for relieving that which is heavy. When your idea about yourself is challenged, your ego becomes charged and therefore heavy. The easiest way for the ego to discharge and unload the weight is through anger. This, however, creates an imbalance that needs to be balanced later on, making it a short-lived relief. When you express anger, the geometry around you must be balanced at some point as it always strives to be resonant with the universal frequency of love. It is then that you will face an additional opportunity to be challenged with anger as your geometry will keep creating that reality. It is not until you transform that which you feel and experience, that your geometry and melody will change. You are the musician and you choose the types of melodies which give you the opportunity to practice and grow. Many of these pieces of music are those that you left unfinished from previous cycles. Many of them are an expression of unfinished harmonies and they are manifested and brought forth by your lovers, siblings, children, parents and those who you call your friends. They are the transmitters of the unfinished melodies that need to be balanced. If you choose to replace those transmitters, others with the same unfinished melody will come to you as you attract the magnetic resonance of those who complete your geometry. There is no avoiding or going around the transmitters because it is not the name or the face that is bringing you the challenge. The transmitters respond to your yearning to be complete and they help you by presenting a situation where you will need to choose your music. You are one and all those who are around you reflect to you parts of yourself. They are the ones who play the role of your partner for awhile. They may show you a part of yourself that you do not like. They may bring out the worst in you. With all love we wish to tell you that it is by design and it is your choice. We know who you are and we see your challenges.

Do you want to tell us that we need to stay with those who bring out the worst in us, some of you may wonder?

You need to acknowledge that the worst part is within you and it is your partner who volunteered to bring it out for you to see and relieve. When you release that part of you, you may also release that partner as he or she has fulfilled their mission. We see you attached to those who bring out the worst in you long after you have relieved those emotions. Many of you believe that it is your fate and that you do not deserve better. It is your choice and it is honored, but we wish to tell you that you are capable of being with another in harmony when you are in harmony within yourself. When you have mastered yourself, you will see that on the face of those who you interact with. We see those of you who choose to remain with a partner who brought them to a place of anger long after they have learnt their lesson. We wish to hug you and impart to you that it may be time to move on. You are the painter and you paint your reality. Your awareness is your canvas and intention is your paint. When you set the intention to move forward, you must be ready to make changes in your life. Those changes may include those who are around you as they no longer reflect your new intention. We ask you to look at the cords that are surrounding you and decipher which cords anchor you in balance and which ones are pulling you off balance; which cords are heavy and draining you and which are light, infusing you with energy? Look at your relationships through the filter of your intention. We ask you to examine your relationships as they represent you, at the moment. We ask you to see if those who are around you reflect your intention. You must be honest with yourself as the realm of spirit is transparent and without judgment. If you wish to vibrate higher you must embrace the subtle. Honesty with self and self-love is your metaphoric vehicle that you use to move forward. We see those of you who fear that if they let go of someone they will suffer a worse situation. We do not ask you to let go of your relationship but to change the intention by which you hold on to the relationship. As you change your intention those who do not serve the new intention will move aside and allow you to grow. We know who you are and we are aware of your emotions of attachment and how they keep you from moving forward. We wish to tell you that when you move forward you are helping the other to move forward as well. There is never a situation where the one who moves forward is doing a disservice to

Your Children

WE WISH TO SPEAK to you about your children. You are your children and yet you are separated. They are an energetic progression of your own lesson and they also carry the blueprint for their own. Your children therefore carry the responsibility for your growth and their own as well. When you were a child you held the same task and you did it well. We ask you to look at yourself from the perspective of your child. Your children in their early years are a pure conduit to spirit and through them you may link to spirit as well. They represent a key doorway to the vibration of love out of the many doorways open for you on your journey. You must however be connected to them. When you really listen to their messages, you have one of the most profound fountains of wisdom on earth coming out of a seemingly blabbering mouth of a three year old. Your children are your teachers and they chose you so they could teach you about you. They teach you by asking you to teach them. When you teach them you learn about you. Again it is the circle. That is how spirit works and the dynamic of your interaction with your child is one of the most sacred contracts that you carry.

Your children are angels like you, but they are in a costume of a young body. Many of them at this time have been on earth for millennia and are from the "old soul's tribe." They were here when earth was formed and they have come back to see it through graduation. Your children are the ones who carry the burden of teaching you about you. Many of them get frustrated with you because you do not listen. With much love we wish to impart to you that some of you are in such a hurry to use your treadmills that you dismiss the jewels that your children shower you with. Some of you tag it as a waste of time and pretend that you are listening while thinking of your grocery shopping list. We know who you are and you are never judged. You were once a child and some of your parents did the same to you.

It is a new energy on this planet and part of the awakening is coming through your children. They are the facilitators of the new energy and they carry new attributes some of you term Indigo. They come with the attribute of consciously knowing their responsibility and lineage. They know why they are here and often they get angry at you, the adult, for not "getting it." Your children stood in line to be here at this time so they could carry the new energy in their biology. They have what it takes to ascend and they do not need to learn it. They remember it and they wish to take you, the parent, with them. When they talk to you about their book of fairies or their imaginary friend, they are asking you to open up. They are pleading with you to see your reality from a perspective of spirit. They invite you into the circle. Many of you spend little time really listening to your children. You spend a short time conversing with them and most of that time you are thinking about other things. We see many of you try to turn your children off by sitting them in front of the TV or computer to keep them busy. With all love we wish to tell you that you are doing a disservice for yourself, your child and the planet. You have asked them to come and teach you and they are here ready and willing. When they begin, you ask them to stop talking and place them in front of a numbing device. Many of them will become imbalanced as a result of your resistance. We wish to impart to you that each and every child alive today that is under the age of 12 is one of the new children. We call them new because they have a list of attributes that most of you do not. They began arriving over 50 years ago in small numbers paving the energy of the planet and preparing it for this time. It is a grand time indeed and those children are ready to teach. They are masters and they know it. They know that they do not have much time so they are intense. They know that adults are stubborn so they are more stubborn. They know about eternity so they do not fear mortality. They know of the connection with the planet so they vibrate with the natural world.

Many of them are being fed with technology which separates them from the natural world. Many of them devour computer games and are wasting their time on TV. This is by design and this is part of the battle of the old energy trying to keep the new energy at bay. We ask you to filter the food that these kids eat, we ask you to filter the programs that they watch, and we ask you to limit their time with technology. These children are built to connect to the natural world and the technology of today is creating a fence which blocks much of the communication. These young ones are old souls and when they do not get the sustenance that they know they should get, they become imbalanced and angry. These are children who were meant to deliver the new frequency of love to this planet and yet they are fed violent computer games and mind numbing TV programs. We know of your time constraints and we know of your pressures. You are alive at a time of earth initiation and those children are the ones who are designed to lead you towards the "New Sun." They are the ones who carry the seed for peace on earth. Don't you want to take the time to feed them with the right nutrients so they can blossom?

How do we know which children are the special ones, some of you may ask?

We ask you to move out of your linearity into the circle. They are all special and they are all carrying the seeds of enlightenment just like you. Your children, however, were born with an attribute that you do not have. They remember their contracts. They cannot be fooled. They know when you lie. They know because they have an extra-special sensory attribute that is called intuition which is activated and it is connected to the other dimension. It sees through your walls and barriers. These children cannot be fooled because they know who you are and they know your faults. They remember. Most of them will not mention that because they are old souls. The do not want to get in trouble. They will let you know, however, if you listen. If you take the time and listen they can lead you to new heights of awareness.

These children communicate using signs and symbols. They are subtle, not in their talking but in their symbols. They will let you know when you are off. They will let you know when you are not in balance with yourself. They feel responsible for you and they love you. These children are the ones who we call angels' messengers. They come to you and they bring challenges. They need you to wake up and they do not have all day to sit and wait for you to make a move. They will drag you to where you need to be and for many of you it will not be easy. They want you to be present. They want you to be in the "now" because it is the only time that really exists for them and they want to teach you about it. They know of the adult obsession with past and future. They know about illusions and they know about your fears. All they need is for you to be present, so they can teach you what they know. They are here to teach you about unconditional love, they come to teach you about compassion and about acceptance. They wish to teach you patience and they want to teach you to hug. Yes, we are imparting to you that they need to be hugged all the time because that is how they know that you are present.

How are we supposed to do all the things that we need to do and still spend so much time with our children, some of you may wonder?

It is not the amount of time but the quality of time that we are speaking of. We ask you to be in your body and present and not to think of your office "to do" list when you play with them. Do not sneak a cell call while you are engaged with them. We know who you are and we know how you feel. It is a time where the subtle is the force that dictates the mechanics of your evolution. You can have all in order in the office but yet miss the signs that tell you that you are in the wrong job. Your children have the larger perspective and they will deliver it to you through signs and symbols. We ask you to pay attention and be present. Spirit often speaks through children as they are open to this kind of communication. When they speak, do not dismiss their words as "nonsense" or "child's talk," as they have wisdom for you and they will not let go until you wake up to their messages. Many of your children are feisty and stubborn. They are like that because many of you do not live up to your promise; the promise to awaken and be ready to receive guidance from them. Your children naturally exist in the realm of the circle. It is you who teach them to think linear. We ask you at this time to learn from them. The circle can be your reality and it is full of magic and child's play. It is a fantastic reality that you must be part of in order to experience. We ask you to play and be a child so your child sees that you are getting it. You are loved and you are never judged. We know of the intensity of the time and we ask you to remove your watches and turn off your phones when you play with your children. Be with them and look in their eyes. It is their eyes that will communicate to you their remembering. We impart to you that the lessons your children have in store for you are priceless and cannot be taught by another but them. They carry the textbook to teach you about the next step. We ask you to love and honor your journey by understanding the sacredness of this communication. When you are present and in your body when you play with your child, you are allowing spirit to take you by the hand and show you the next step. We ask you to see the love that goes into the challenges that your child offers. Love the challenge as it is your gift. We ask you to allow your child to be the parent as they are your true teachers and so be it.

Child Named Ego

WE HAVE BEEN WAITING for this moment to tell you something about yourself that many of you are challenged by. We wish to tell you with all love that there is never anyone who judges you as you are the highest authority on yourself. When you are on the physical plane you must adhere to the laws of gravity, aging and karma. When you are back home none of these laws apply. You do not age, you do not have a physical mass and you do not carry over the consequences of your actions performed in the physical plane. You are the creator and as part of the energy you call God, you call the shots which relate to your own growth. You are part of a system that is fueled by love and light. Back home you do not adhere to the same game rules of duality and lesson because you are the designer of the game. This game is about "you" learning all aspects of "you" and when we speak of "you" we speak of the collective "you" which is God. We wish to speak to you about an aspect of you that we feel is greatly misunderstood. We wish to speak of what many traditions named Ego. Ego is your duality. It is "you" walking only in a place of forgetfulness. Hence all that you "know" is your physical aspect.

We wish to tell you that your ego is part of you and it is an essential part of you. It allows you to carry with you your lessons and challenges. It offers you a beginning to your path of growth. Ego is your package that you take with you when you go through the cave of creation, where your akashic records are stored, and descend to earth through the birth canal. It gives you the blueprint by which you map your life. Your ego is essential because it is part of your group. When you come to the planet you have to begin somewhere. Ego is that beginning. It brings with it your idea of yourself in this life and from your previous lives. It carries with it your passions to create, your tendencies, you inclinations, your weakness and your strengths.

Ego has its own geometry and its own melody as it is a part of you that is the physical manifestation of your expression on earth. When we tell you that you are a group, we mean that part of you is your ego and another part is what you named your soul. When we tell you that you are one we mean that the soul and the ego are part of the foundation of who you are and therefore they both need to take part in your journey. Like flavored water, although it is made out of hydrogen, oxygen, maybe some sugar, coloring and other ingredients you experience it as flavored water. You do not experience the separate components. It is the same with you and your ego. Ego can never be destroyed as some of your ancient traditions ask you to believe. Ego tells you about you when you look at the mirror. It reflects back to you your face which is not your eternal face but your physical face, in this expression, at this time, on earth. If you wish to destroy that which is your physical expression you must also destroy the physical vehicle which carries the ego. The ego, from where we sit watching and loving you, is part of you and it will always be part of you when you are walking in physical form on this planet. When you move beyond the physical plane you deposit that part of you with its lessons and its residual energy into the belly of Gaia and it is kept there until that time when you choose to come back. It is a physical place buried deep in the mass of earth and it can never be found. When we tell you that you are part of Gaia, this cave is where your energy goes when you are not in lesson. When you come back you pick it up from the cave, deep in the crystalline layers of the inner wonders of your planet and you take it with you as you return to the planet. This cave is what we call the Akashic hall of records and it holds your ego as well as your histories, your karma your challenges and your contracts.

Why are you telling us about ego, some of you may wonder?

We wish to tell you about ego because all of you who have the intention to move upward and ascend in vibration must deal with their ego. It is a part of the process and it is necessary. We wish to tell you that your ego, metaphorically speaking, is like a child. We will even give it an age to make this concept clearer. This "ego" is a child of five years. This is one of the attributes of ego. This "child" never really matures. It is always aged five. Like a child, it needs to be given boundaries, it acts out, and it has temper tantrums. This "child" developmentally is not socially adept so 'it' wants things that others have, and if "it" does not get what "it" wants "it" gets frustrated. This "child" will eat anything she is given because she has yet to develop her own idea of what supports her health and what doesn't. This "child" has fears like any child and many of her fears are self created. When it is dark, she sees monsters and when it is stormy outside and thundering she gets scared. This child has a parent and that parent, metaphorically speaking, is the soul. This "child" needs the parent to direct her like the ego needs the soul to direct it. They are family and they are one and the same but they play a separate role. Ego is designed by you to keep you in a place of duality. Ego represents your lesson and it is your contract to be with your "child" until such time that you come back home.

Why are you telling us about this child, some of you may ask?

We see many of you who try to negate this "child" when you give intent to move forward. Some take this child and put it in a dark closet vowing to never open the door. We wish to give you a few attributes of this "child." Your ego, like the five-year old child, needs to be loved. It needs your attention. This "child" needs to be comforted not punished. This "child" does not mature like the soul. The reason this "child" does not grow up is the same reason that you choose to experience a physical death in every cycle. You designed it that way in order to enrich your lessons and opportunities for growth. Ego is part of the test and it has components which give you contexts to operate from. This "child" like any five-year old, likes to get gifts, she likes to eat what is unhealthy and she likes anything that anyone else gets. This child needs to be directed with love and firmness. We see those of you who go on a regimen of punishing your "child" by resenting it and not honoring it. We see many of you do not acknowledge the sacredness of this "child." This child is part of you and she is here to allow you a personality and a context to act in your physical plane. We see those of you who go against this child as if it were evil or bad. There is never a judgment and your choices are honored but we wish to tell you that when you starve this "child" you starve yourself as well. When you lock this "child" in a dark closet, it will manifest disease and it will show on your body as well. There are those of you who choose to suppress this "child" and to shut its mouth every time it wants to express. If so, this "child" will develop anger and that anger will be bottled up and it will need to be expressed at some point. This repressed expression may manifest through external violent action or through disease choosing to experience implosion or explosion. We hear those of you who say, yes but we know this master and that master and they conquered ego and they became egoless. From our perspective it is not so. When we look at any master that ever lived, we still see the geometry of the ego and it is alive and well. In actuality it is striving and its melody is beautiful and harmonious. These masters did not lock their ego in a dark closet or suppressed its voice. Many of these masters understood that ego is like a child that needs love; so with patience and care they took this "child" by the hand and taught her to walk hand-in-hand. These masters had their egos but they changed its attributes and their relationship to it. Their egos no longer acted like a five-years old. They wrapped it up with the cloth of spirit. The "parent" or the soul walked the elevated path and the "child," which is ego, followed. We wish to tell you that there is not a single person alive today and throughout your history that did not have an ego. Ego is you and it holds your duality intact. It is essential and it is sacred. Ego makes you perform in your physical realm and it gives you the reason to move from one point to another. Ego has its own signature and energy. From our perch we wish to impart to you that you must honor your ego as you honor your own child. You must also love your ego like you love your own child. Like a child you must feed it the right healthy food and lead it to where it can strive and be healthy. When you choose to go against your "child" and you express shame, guilt, pain, suppression, repression or anger towards it, we must tell you that you are changing your own melody because this "child" is part of you. When you do not take care of it and try to ignore it, it will let you know either by rebelling, throwing anger fits, or becoming sick. This child must express and expression is its natural attribute. As you drive on the highway of the journey you call human life, this "child" must always sit in the child's seat in the back of the vehicle. It is also has to be belted and safe. You must not let it drive the car as you wouldn't let a five-year old do that. You carry the attribute of a group and at the same time you are one. Your group includes your higher self that is the "I am" which is all knowing. You also have angels which operate in the subtle realm that is not in your visible dimension. There is your physical "you" that has a body that must adhere to gravity, aging and death. Part of your group is also this child named ego. We see those of you who hate their "child" because she will not go away and she refuses to disappear. We wish to hug you and tell you that if you try to kill your ego you must die with it. Your ego is you and it is here to stay. When your "child" acts out we wish you to acknowledge it, hug it and thank it for being a sacred part of you. We wish you to listen to it and then take it by the hand and with a hug show it the path that is elevated. Show this child the path that comes from the wisdom of the "parent." If you let your five-year old child rule your life we can guarantee you that you will be in a challenging place. The path of ascension requires the parent to be in the driver seat but the child also must be present, belted in the back seat and safe. Your "child" needs constant attention and love, it needs constant guidance and to be set boundaries. When you acknowledge your "child," it will grow to be healthy with self-esteem that is grounded, and it will walk with you rather then rebel against you. We wish to tell those of you who tag their "child" with negative names, that it is not the way of spirit. You are sacred, all parts and pieces of you are divine and were put there by design, your design. We wish you to honor the sacredness of your path and honor all the parts of you that make you whole. When you do, you experience states that we can only describe as bliss. When you go against parts of yourself they manifest as an imbalance that affects your physical vehicle. We wish you to embrace the beauty of your path and experience the state of bliss as you walk hand in hand with your "child," and so be it.

Black Hole

HAVE YOU EVER WALKED ALONE on a path and became fearful?

Why do you ask us about fear again?

It is fear that we wish to speak of. Fear is your biggest obstacle for moving forward at this time. Why fear, some of you ask? Fear is what we consider darkness. Fear represents everything that is not light. Fear represents those aspects of you that are hidden from you. Fear is an energy which negates other energies. It is a form of an electromagnetic neutralizer. When you wish to move forward you must find energy to do so. Fear negates that energy and nullifies it. It is a unique property of fear to transform positive energy and, through a process we call negative alchemy, to neutralize that energy and bring your progress to a halt. It is as if you stepped into a car and after pouring gasoline in the tank and starting the engine, someone took the gasoline out and replaced it with sand. With sand in the gasoline tank, your car cannot move, thus rendering it useless. We wish to tell you that fear has been used since the beginnings of humanity to control its progress. It was the fearless ones who allowed humanity to progress on the spiritual path.

We wish to tell you that fear is the most effective of all methods to absorb light- energy and dim it. Fear can be compared to what your scientists call a black hole. Although their understanding of black holes is incomplete, one of its attributes is that it absorbs light, swallowing and trapping it. It emits practically no light as the gravity of the black hole pulls all energy into itself. With love we wish to tell you that the system of fear was developed to control and channel the energy of humanity so those in power can benefit. Historically, the system of power was developed by your religious institutions, governments and leadership to hold you in a frequency of fear, shame and guilt. Whole campaigns were orchestrated to maneuver large populations into fear. Your religious institutions were used by governments and vice versa in order to justify campaigns of fear.

All fear-based campaigns and systems were based on misinformation which was presented as "truth" and later rendered as "truth." It was then packaged and manipulated in such a way that it could be communicated to many. Large populations were driven and coerced to believe in that "truth". Those who resisted suffered consequences that were punitive, and those who complied reaped "rewards." It is one of the oldest "tricks" in the book as far

back as we can see. We wish to impart to you that fear
is the most prevalent method of the dark to negate light
and it is an effective way if you give yourself permission
to accept fear. We always love you and there is never a
judgment even about those of you who choose to use fear
to control and manipulate others. This is the way of spirit. Free choice is honored and you are allowed to play the
game of free choice while on earth walking in duality. We
wish to tell you, however, that fear has to be invited in to
your energy field. It cannot enter unless you allow it to
enter. Fear is energy by invitation only but once it enters
it can wreak havoc in your energy field and degrade your
vibration rendering you energy-less. It is a system that is
designed to drain spiritual energy and to confront you
with the real choice between light and dark.

*Why are you telling us about inviting fear? No one wants
fear. How can we resist fear?*

We wish to impart to you that all fear-based vistas are
illusions. You are a powerhouse and your own master.
You can only experience that which you allow into your
energy field and it is all a choice. There are events, that
when presented to you, can be fear-generators or not. It
is your choice of interpretation. You have been conditioned to accept fear and survival as natural. It is part
of your duality and it is by design. You come in with a
mechanism that is built to keep you alive. That mecha-

nism is based in the lower energy center of the body and it is governed by what is known as the base chakra. This system holds the core energies of the instinct of survival and sexuality and it is also the energy center which you must use to generate spiritual energy. Your first and second chakras are your batteries for all spiritual movement forward.

We wish to speak to you of one of the methods used to control you and anchor your energy in fear, rendering it weak and malleable. Sexuality is one of the greatest misinformation campaigns used to control and maneuver humanity keeping it at bay and in the frequency of fear. From your religions to your governments, patriarchal structures down to the relationships between males and females, you have been taught that there is something dark and fearful in sexuality. You have been told that it is evil and bad. Sexuality was controlled to such an extent in your history that many of you experienced death and torture as a result of sexual freedom. The fear is ingrained in your cellular memory and it is one of the main reasons that your society today is viewing and practicing a sexuality that is predominantly of a low vibration. Sexuality has been limited to procreation and superficial physical gratification and it has been separated from the spiritual purpose it carries. As we see it, sexuality is one of the greatest challenges that you face today as you move upward in the spiral of ascension. It is one of your greatest obstacles to move forward because you have not come to terms with all the lies, control, deceit and manipulation fed to you by your society, and released them. You must find peace and joy in sexuality bringing this energy back to the forefront of spiritual growth and away from the frequency of fear.

How do we do that, some of you may wonder?

You are at a point where you will need all the energy you can attract in order to stay balanced throughout the process of accelerated time. Your time is literally ticking faster and your initiation into the process of becoming a light-holder is well underway. You must have all your chakras open and functioning. You must have the lower chakras healthy and vibrant. You must take care of your energy system as the energy blueprint that you carry is transferred to the planet and helps the transformation that you are now experiencing. You are a Stradivarius and your instrument is your body. For the Stradivarius to play the most beautiful tunes it must be played with regularly. It cannot be placed in a glass closet and displayed for all to see because it would lose its divine qualities. The same is true with sexual energy. It must be continuously stimulated and brought up through your chakra system to support your spiritual growth. Your batteries must be recharging all the time. Like a car, when you do not drive it for a while the energy from the battery drains as the battery loses its polarity. Your mission is not to just have sexual partners and use sexuality because you are engrained with the blueprint of fear and control. Your journey has to do with moving away from the old idea of sexuality, re-discovering and liberating yourself from the patterns of fear and negativity. In order to do that you must dig inside yourself to discover the hidden patterns that hold painful memories and with love release them one by one. This is a journey that is essential in transforming the pattern of fear inflicted on many of you lighthouses who are at the forefront of the new energy. You are a vibrating spectacular instrument that when played with skill can produce a harmonious tone that shields you from the pull of fear. As you learn to play the new tune, you get in touch with your true center, rediscovering your power and thereby relieving and cutting the cords of control, fear, shame and guilt. Once you sever the cords you are free to ascend to where few have ever visited. This is your time. We see those of you who say to themselves, "Not me, I am too old, I am not attractive, I am afraid of getting AIDS or other STD's. I have no partner or my partner is not into it." We wish to impart to you that all these "reasons" are "gifts" given to you by those who wish to keep you under a leash and manipulate you to believe that sexuality is not for you. It is your choice and it is honored. We wish to promise you that if you set the intention and not allow fear to hold you, those obstacles will be removed. When you are free of the cords of fear, you are at the core of truth where fear cannot come in. Sexuality has been removed so far from its original intention that very few of you are actually enjoying it. It has been portrayed as something that is so artificial that many of you began to believe that you were doing something wrong. Your media and your industry of pornography and sex-trade are all tools used to separate you from yourself. We wish to tell you that for the most part the campaign of manipulation of the dark with sexuality has been effective. You are the ones who one by one must find a way to remove the layers of misinformation and find that which works for you. You can play your own instrument or find someone with like-vibration to rediscover with you what it means to vibrate higher using sexual energy. You must practice it as this exploration is at the core of your movement forward.

How do we know if we are doing the right thing or with the right person?

As we hug you we wish to remind you that you are powerful and you are the creator of your reality and universe. Like all creation you must begin with an intention. That intention must be of the highest order and you must repeat it before you mix with another and when you begin to look for another. If you wish to move on your own you also must use an intention. Your intention will lead you down the right path. You may discover what you need to know in the resources of yogic tantra or other sacred texts. Your journey is an individual one and there is no truth or falsehood. Your path is to fear not and walk, and as you walk, your truth will be revealed to you and you will begin to experience freedom. Your truth is your truth and your brother or sister's truth may be different. You must find your own truth, and when you seek it with pure intention you will find it. We wish to let you know that sexuality is in the core of the split between dark and light. Using your energy with integrity, with love and with the highest intention, is what can tilt the light/dark ratio. Light is energy and dark is just lack of light. We ask you to turn your light on. You are at the forefront of a battle between the old energy of control, fear and misinformation, and the new energy of transparency, integrity and love-based interactions. When you choose to free yourself, many of those in your circles will resist your journey as it will threaten the very core of all that you have been led to believe by the same institutions that marry you, divorce you and control your marital affairs. We wish to tell you with all love that you are renegades and you are responsible for yourself first.

When you are vibrating at a high level only then are you fully on your mission and shining your light at the highest luminosity. You do not need to evangelize or preach your views. This journey is not for everyone and most of your society is in the dark. It is for you to find a way. We know who you are and the planet can feel your footsteps. We ask you to give intention to find the path to remove the cords of fear and control from your sexual centers. Your path is sacred whether you choose to be free or controlled. The time, however, is now as the planet's vibration increases. You are at a point at which you have only dreamt of being and you now have the opportunity to fulfill what you were trained for in your many expressions on this planet. We ask you not to fear as you are eternal and your journey is honored no matter what. We know who you are and we know of your fear. You have been so conditioned to be removed from yourself that many of you fear that you cannot distinguish between right and wrong. We wish to tell you that there is no wrong if you set the right intention with integrity and follow the signs coming from your feeling centers. Your intention will bring you hand in hand with your angles and together you will discover that which has been in front of you all along. You will discover your divinity, your power, and your mission. You are so dearly loved, and so be it.

Favorite Song

IT IS ABOUT GRATITUDE that we wish to begin our message. As the story has it you are an angel walking in duality and the things that happen in your life are your stepping stones to moving forward.

Why is that, you may ask?

There is a bigger picture out there than any of you angels walking in lesson can see. The picture stretches out over the horizon and you can only see what is in front of you. It is therefore necessary for you to use trust. Some of you call it faith. When you begin to move forward those things that happen in your life have a direction. The direction is following your intent. This is why we always hug you and ask you to give intent. Without intent there is no clear direction and you are just moving about. As you begin to remember who you are the picture becomes clearer but even for the masters who walked on earth, trust was needed as they also knew that they were limited by their contract to be in 3-D and linear reality. They knew that the bridge of faith must be built in order to get over those things that were beyond the horizon.

The masters knew that the bridge would appear when they needed to cross over a metaphoric river and the river was the "things that happened in their lives". Some of you call them obstacles. We wish to tell you that obstacles are only a limited view of the magnificence of your journey. When you want to buy a car and you find that you do not have enough money, you call it an obstacle. This is not so from the perspective of spirit. That car that you wanted to buy in the time that you wanted to buy it may have served you to move backward. You might have used it to get to work faster but then missed the view of nature and the experience of the one who uses a bicycle. The car was faster, you thought, but the bicycle gave you the opportunity to be in a meditative state where ideas can come and direct you in your day to day life. Spirit has the larger view and your obstacles may be your greatest treasures. Obstacles exist only in one place. Obstacles exist in your mind and they do so because it is a wish or a desire that you have and an expectation of how to fulfill that wish or desire that is then being blocked. When you create the desire and it is not fulfilled you react with frustration. If you see an obstacle it means that you have set up your own idea of the path and you cannot reach from point A to point B the way you have imagined it. Spirit is not linear. Spirit works sometimes from point A directly to Z without needing to stop at each station. We love you and we know who you are as we have been with you from the beginning. There is never a judgment about how you act in your world. You are the creator of your reality. We wish to tell you, however, that the shortest way from point A to point Z is to walk with trust, setting intent and following your feelings. Your linear idea of "the correct path" may take you on a journey that is much longer and at times tainted by limited ideas of who you are. When you are in a place of trust those things do not come into play and you have no obstacles. You walk on a highway and the road is always clear. It is clear because you are walking to where you are guided without using expectations and timetables. You are, therefore, always at the right place at the right time.

We see you from above and from below and it is time to speak with you about a structure that you named "religion." We wish to speak with you about your religion as most humans walking on earth at this time subscribe to one form of faith or another. Your religion is sacred and honored as it is your free choice to create that which propels you forward to discover your own divinity. It is sacred and honored to search and your religions are one of the paths that angels, like you, created to look into the nature of themselves in relation to God. You created religions so the search would have a structure around it. We wish to tell you that all religions have the same basic intent. The intent is to bring humans closer to God and to do it in a way that is built upon traditions, doctrines, mechanics, structures, rituals and ceremonies, all which are sacred and honored, as they all represent free choice. We wish to speak to you about these sacred institutions from our perspective. We are you, not in duality, and we know who you are because we are with you every single day of your life on earth. All religions and faith-based structures, large or small, have a specific vibration. More so, they carry specific frequencies that have a specific geometry and specific melody and even colors connected to it. The geometry of a religion can be compared to the geometry of an angel walking in duality. It is the macro and the micro of your humanness and your quest to find out who you are. All religions and faith structures have a linear beginning and they have a path just like the human which involve karma and moving higher. All religions have come at a certain point in time to play a part in human spiritual evolution and to allow those who seek to find a bridge to move beyond the river of drama to find peace and divinity.

Many of you are looking for the truth and subscribe to one faith or another. You try to justify yourselves by saying that your faith is the ultimate truth and other beliefs are not. We wish to hug you and tell you that it is not so from the perspective of spirit. There are those amongst you who are trying to find historical facts which support the stories in your sacred texts. There are those of you who dig the earth in search of artifacts to support the stories that are told in your sacred books. We wish to impart to you that you are looking in the wrong places. You are looking again from the limited, linear 3-D perspective. Your sacred books are interdimensional vortexes which aim to propel you to a place where you can get closer to discovering who you are. Your sacred books are vibrating instruments just like you. They communicate to you not through words but through geometry. They contain codes that activate your latent memories. Your sacred books are code-activating, multidimensional tools that aim to carry you away from your limited reality. When you try to justify them by digging here and there or looking for support in historical accounts you are missing the point altogether. These sacred texts were meant to be taken on faith like any journey that has divinity written in it. Your sacred texts are a tapestry of sorts. They are written texts composed of a collage of legends, mythologies, and historical events that are colored with a certain world view. Some of them have foundations in actual physical events and some are embedded in stories which have been circulating in human consciousness for millennia. Many of your scriptures have been handed to you in the same manner that these messages given by us are being handed to you. Parts of your sacred books have been given to you from beyond the veil. There are those of us who work with humans-in-lesson delivering messages at a point in time for the purpose of spiritually uplifting a segment of your society. It is not a one-size-fits- all. There are those from behind the veil who connect with angels who act as vessels, via sacred contracts, to be the carriers of spiritual energy to the planet. Some of you named these vessels God's messengers. We wish to tell you that you are God's messenger as much as they. The difference is that those masters who brought you some of these messages were fully activated human beings who vibrated in the frequency of mastery. The delivery of the messages is sometimes called channeling in your culture but in fact it is a meld of sorts between the human and spirit. These texts have been brought to you from beyond the veil by non-incarnating angels like us but with different specialties or interests and have done so by design, and with appropriateness. Some of your sacred texts were delivered to you as images, pulses of visions or thought-packages. It is the human who must interpret the message that they receive based on their own social, cultural and knowledge-based foundation. All sacred texts were written by angels like you for you, and none were written, as some claim, by God. Many times the information was intended one way and interpreted another. That is the way of it. It is up to the individual to discover what resonates with their own internal mechanism. None of your religions have an actual physical story that is truer than the other. They are all colored and tainted and brought to you from a frequency that is connected to the human spiritual journey on this planet. Certain religions began when it was time for a certain tune to be played out so humans could climb the next step towards their understanding of themselves and their relationship to God.

We love you and we wish to impart to you that your journey represents one consciousness exploring its own multi-faceted aspects. Your religions are one way to help you discover who you are. Each religion or faith represents a new frequency introduced to the physical plane at a specific point in time, which answers a need for growth or diversity in the human psyche and its quest for answers. When you say that your religion is truer than another religion it is as if you claimed that the song you like is more beautiful than the song that your brother or sister likes. Your preference for religions has to do with the spiritual geometry that you carry in your interdimensional DNA. Once activated, you resonate with a certain faith similarly to the way some of you resonate with one song and not the other. The geometry and melody of the "search for God" aspect of your DNA has a specific frequency. Your religion has specific frequency. You are attracted to religions that vibrate on a similar frequency as yours in your "spiritual quest department". You carry, as part of your multi-dimensional DNA, a "department" that is dedicated to the spiritual quest and to finding out about your own divinity. When you activate it, you begin to move to where you find the melody most harmonious to your own individual ear. We find it humorous that you embrace one religion while negating the other. Your religions are like the different music stations on your radio. Some of you like rock some like classical and others jazz. None is more sacred then the other. You do not go and persecute the classical listeners because they will not tune in to the rock station.

This is how it appears from the perspective of spirit. All the "different tunes" serve the same purpose and show you the beauty and wonder of your diversity. Your diversity is grand and so is your quest. We wish to tell you that all paths are equally sacred as it is the individual search that is sacred and not the structure around it. Your search therefore is honored, as with free choice, you create the vehicle that propels you to find answers to your spiritual identity questions. Religions are one such path. The structure that you build around your religions is what we wish to speak about. Within the structure that you have built there are humans who subscribe to those structures and act as instruments to bring specific knowledge or ideas to humanity. Within your religious structures each of you has the choice of light and dark. Some of the darkest hours on your planet have been brought on in the name of religion and some of the most luminous, enlightened vistas have been introduced to you by your religions. We wish to impart to you as we hold your hand that it is not the structure that determines the light and dark choice. It is the individual human and what he or she does with the structure. The choice always remains light or dark. Some of those who acted the role of leaders of a faith created some of the most forward movements toward acceptance and distribution of sacred universal laws. On the other hand there were others who introduced to you the darkest concepts and ideas in the history of your planet. It is the human who must choose.

How about God, some of you may wonder? *Isn't it about God*, some of you may ask?

Yes, indeed it is, we say as we smile and hug you. Your search for God is honored whether you do it through this faith or that faith. God does not care about the structure. God is not religious and does not have preferences. God responds to the individual intent. The intent is the vehicle that propels you to activate your own divinity. There are those of you who believe that if they do this ceremony God will listen and if they do another ceremony God will reject them. God responds to your intent because you are part of God and your search has to do with you activating your own divinity. Your own divinity responds to your own intent and it does not matter how you do it. You are the creator and the structures that you have built to help you in your spiritual journey are sacred because it is your free choice that is honored not the structure. What you do is honored because you are honored and your choices are sacred. Religions help many of you connect "you" with "you." Religions created ceremonies and cultures around your divinity to help bring the concept of God to you in a package all dressed up in your individual cultural dresses and with your individual ceremonial rituals. All of that is honored because your search is honored. However, it is the original intent of the organization that determines the level of luminosity delivered by the structure of this or that religion. Some of your religious organizations created doctrines of manipulation to maneuver humans to behave in a certain way so as to empower the structure, gain control and obtain wealth. On the other hand, some faith-based structures were created and maintained their pure original intention to elevate the human and bring them closer to God. Again, it is always the individual's choice that ultimately determines the degree of light or darkness brought forth by the structure of religion. We wish to impart to you, that the light flooding your part of the universe at this time is exposing those who acted in the name of religious structures under the shade of night and without spiritual integrity. These religious structure-based manipulations inevitably will be exposed and those secrets will come to light. There are however, other organizations who kept their intent pure and brought luminosity to the planet through their pure intent. These faith-based spiritual structures are helping to change the vibration of the planet and bring about the "New Sun".

We wish to tell you that you are coming to a new vista where all that was hidden must come to the surface. Much that has to do with your religious structures will not be "pretty." Much of it was hidden for a long time under the shield of secrecy and manipulation. This is no longer possible as all shields become transparent for all to see through. We wish to tell you that all religions are sacred as they represent your quest to move forward and to find your divinity. We ask you to not look at the other music station and claim that your music is better or truer. The truth lies in you and whatever music directs you to discover your own divinity is your truth. As we look at you and love you we wish to tell you that you are coming into a new energy. It is the energy that is marked by your year of 2012. It is the energy of change for the entire planetary consciousness and all of you will have to adjust to the new tune. The tune that is being introduced to you is the one of unity consciousness. It is the tune that delivers to you the frequency of the "New Sun." It is your time to choose as all of you will face the dilemma of light or dark; separation or unity.

We wish to speak now to the light-warriors, as this portion of the message is directed to you. Many of you have been disenchanted with faith-based structures. Many of you have been in one structure or another throughout your many expressions on earth and you know that power corrupts and that the journey is about you and not the ceremony. Many of you intuitively know that you can activate your own divinity sitting at home in front of a candle and you do not need anyone to link you to yourself. We wish to tell you that in the metaphor of the radio stations with the different tunes playing, you are the one who is actually creating your own music. You are the composer and the music you create is already inside of you. You do not need a radio to link you with your own music. All paths are sacred as they are all different landmarks on your journey to discover who you are. Your journey is a grand one and we wish you to honor your journey as much as your brother's and sister's. We wish to impart to you that the different kinds of music each of you are choosing are all equally sacred and honored. You must therefore celebrate your diversity and the beauty of your individual paths as they are all leading you to a place of a breathtaking vista and so be it.

Brush Strokes

WE WISH YOU TO KNOW who you are and what your purpose is. We have come thus far to hold you by the hand and take you to where the sun always shines. We are part of you and yet we have individual identities. You and we are, metaphorically speaking, like the ingredients of a soup. A soup is a soup but it is made out of different ingredients. The soup is you and the ingredients are your group. You cannot say I am only the salt or I am only the pepper. When you see yourself as a group you understand that there are different components to what makes you move forward. When the different components receive intention from the driver, which is your a higher part of yourself self, you are on track to vibrate higher. When the group receives instructions from the part of you that is without higher awareness you are moving neither forward nor back. You are moving in your groove.

As we look at you we see a beautiful galaxy of stars swirling and we see the vibration that you emit. We see the love that fills the gap between each star so we know your capabilities, yet when you are moving around, many of you feel powerless. You feel that you are walking alone without love and without support. You feel fear because you do not see the destination and you do not trust that where you are going is any better than where you are now. We know who you are. You have come so far to complete a mission that has been on the drawing board for so many expressions yet many of you feel that you are moving about without clear direction. We wish to hug you once more so you can feel the love that is all around you and tell you that it is time. It is the time that you have been looking for and there is no other time. We wish you to be aligned with your clock.

What do you mean, some may ask?

Your clock always shows you the now. We ask you to be aware of the clock so you can be in the now.

How about planning for the future, some may wonder?

Your future is built on the now so if you look to the future you are not focusing on the building blocks of the future. The now creates the future. Many of you negate the now for the sake of the future. You say that tomorrow will be so much better so it is OK to feel not as good this moment. The future is the now a second from now and then it becomes the past. When you are in the awareness of the now you are building the future on your own terms. When you are not in the now the future comes and it doesn't look any better than now.

What are you asking us to do?

We ask you to be in the vibration of self-love and gratitude for every moment that you breathe. We wish you to be in gratitude because it is a vibration that resonates with your highest potential and brings you the most elevated blueprint. Gratitude is a vibration that always attracts the highest potential for your life. We see many of you walking in your biology feeling that you have been sidelined by life. We see many of you walking as if your life is pushing and pulling you and you are just trying to stay balanced. You are so focused on the effort to stay on your feet that you are missing the magnificence of your journey altogether. When you are in gratitude, the web of your existence weaves a complete picture that is always appropriate, customized for you and with the most beautiful signature scripted in gold which spells LOVE.

How come we do not see any of it, some of you may wonder?

You do not see it because you are not in the now and you come not from gratitude but from the feeling that you are not in control. When you are in gratitude, you are the driver of your feelings and you attract that which is the most elevated potential to come your way. You are the creator of your reality. When you create your reality it is the gratitude which is the signature on the canvas of your creation. Many of you attach a negative or positive symbol to the various brush strokes that make your painting. From the perspective of spirit, your different brush strokes represent different phases of you and different aspects of your development. None is more valued then the other. The value that is placed on your creation is based on your attitude. When you are in an attitude of gratitude your creation is priceless. When you are in the attitude of victimhood your creation is worthless. It is worthless because you have not put the pieces together so the lesson was not digested. It is as if you went to class but slept through the whole thing. You were present but you were not in the awareness to absorb the lesson and integrate it into your life. We see you and we know your feelings. You cannot hide them because they show up in your melody and your colors. Your geometry is ever changing based on the emotions you emit. The feeling of gratitude creates a beautiful painting.

How can we be in gratitude when we feel bad about certain aspects of our lives?

The answer is always in you and it must be found through looking inside. When you are outside of yourself you only realize that which is in front of you. When you look inside, you begin to see the magic thread which creates the tapestry you call life.

How do we look inside, you may ask?

You look by closing your eyes, you listen by being in silence, and you sense by being still. When things around you feel bad, the part that is bad is your interpretation of what your duality presents to you. Nothing around you is good or bad. You are the one who is putting the plus or minus sign on the events in your life.

There are things that are surely bad, some may say.

Yes, indeed you may see it that way, but when you come from the attitude of gratitude those things that were perceived as bad become one more brush stroke in the masterpiece that you create. As you come from gratitude you begin to see that you cannot name one brush stroke as good and the other bad. It would seem humorous to go to a museum and to look at a painting by a master and to see next to the painting a description which separates the good brush strokes from the bad ones. It is the same with your life. It is the attitude that you bring to the events in your life which determines the light that you emit. When you are in the attitude of being a victim and seeing your canvas as bad, indeed that is the canvas you are creating. You are the creator as well as the art critic and the viewer.

This journey is for "you" to learn about "you". How can one lesson be "good" and the other be "bad?"

Your attitude toward that which you experience determines the amount of light that you shine. Your mission at this time is to shine so brightly that all those in a place of darkness will have the option to see if they wish to. No one can be forced to see if they wish to keep their eyelids shut. When you emit light, you give those around you the option.

Why do we need to know that, some may wonder?

You are at the end of an energy pattern that has been prevalent in your reality for a long time. This energy pattern is now being replaced with a new energy that is much higher in vibration. One attribute of this new energy is that it allows you, if you choose, to change your reality and gain mastery over your life. It is as if earth was going in one trajectory and it changed to a trajectory that has the potential to bring peace on earth. The new trajectory is grand and you collectively asked for it. Now is the time to understand that you are in control of your direction and to be in an attitude that empowers that which you choose. Gratitude is the attitude which always places a positive mark on your experiences, coloring your canvas with the most brilliant colors and creating a future that is made out of brilliant segments of "now". We ask you to celebrate that which comes your way and not judge it as good or bad. We ask you to be in the now so you can bring the future of your choosing. It is the being in the "now' and maintaining the attitude of gratitude which creates the most harmonious melodies and paints the most beautiful canvas that is called your life. When you begin to experience your life in that way you are in mastery mode and you are shining a light that is brilliant. Your canvas is being painted brush stroke by brush stroke and when you see all the brush strokes as part of your masterpiece you are changing the vibration of the planet bringing it to a higher place than ever before. We are sitting all around you watching you with love as you paint on the canvas of your life and we wish you to love it as we do, and so be it.

The Disco Ball

WE ARE GLAD to welcome you back. Indeed it was a test and a test it was. We see you when you are experiencing that which you know. We know that it is part of your journey and we wish to congratulate you on walking the walk. Many of you ask to move forward in your intention but when the actual test comes you sheepishly change your mind and tell yourself that you really did not mean it. It is with love that we wish to hug you and let you know that there is never a judgment and if you change your mind you are loved just the same. As you experience that which we call a test it is all about one thing: choice. You appear to have multiple choices but in fact you have only two: light or dark. It is that simple but yet very complicated when you are actually experiencing it.

How can that be, some may ask?

As you go through tests some of you cannot distinguish between the light and the dark as it all looks like shades of grey.

How do we know what it is that we are choosing, some may wonder?

When it is your time to make a choice use your heart and feel if your choice honors yourself. Does it honor your fellow angel? Does it honor life? Is it coming from love? If the answers are yes, you chose light. We wish to impart to you that in every situation there is a choice that is elevated and that is in harmony with universal laws. You must "feel" the options you have and choose the most elevated path presented to you. You are walking the walk on a journey you call life and the road seems clear. All goes as you planned it and you can see the end destination of your life and you are excited about the prospects of walking in your groove as it all seems to be cut out for you. It is as if you are gliding in the air and there are no serious obstacles.

We wish to speak to those who get surprised when all of a sudden an obstacle appears. This obstacle is not too big and although you are surprised you continue and yet another one appears and another one and soon you encounter only obstacles and you find that all you are doing is putting out fires and trying to survive the day. Your end destination is soon forgotten and you are fighting the battle in the trenches from day to day. Does it sound familiar? We love you and we know who you are. You are not who you think you are and your journey is not about what you think it is about. You came here for a mission and the tests that are around you and present themselves to you at a certain point on your journey are your initiation into the elevated course.

You may say *how come? That cannot be. All I am experiencing is hardship and nothing spiritual.*

We wish to ask you then, if you were only on the course of gliding through your life then when would you have time to land and find spirit? Many of you find spirit only when you must land and face yourselves. It is through limitation that you begin to realize your limitlessness and power. It is through lack that you realize your abundance. It is through darkness that you must realize your light. As we watch you from above, below and around we wish to tell you that your learning always has to do with discovering your inner resources and not looking out. It is so happens that for many of you the only time you begin to look inside is when the outside has been constricted. You may call it obstacles or tests but we call it your initiation. We wish to tell you that the process of awakening for every master who ever walked on earth had to do with a test that was followed by the realization that the outside reality is not what it seems. The realization was then followed by a yearning to discover the "truth" about the journey. The yearning was followed by an intention and then by the search itself.

This is your journey and what you encounter is delivered to you with the highest intention to bring you to your highest path. The spiritual path is where you begin to discover the love connections that are woven through the events of your life. This follows by you discovering your own divinity and your power to create your reality. Next you begin to experience peace as if you have no more obstacles. This is not because everything goes as planned or is easy. It is because you redefined "obstacles" and you now understand that all that crosses your path is there by choice, it has divinity, appropriateness, and a purpose, and it always has the word love in it.

We wish to talk to you about something that many of you focus on and that you name "truth." We see many of you say to yourselves, "that does not sound truthful but this does." Many of you seekers have been advocates of the truth throughout your many expressions and at times you got in trouble for seeking the truth. In your history on this planet, religious institutions, governments and your society has brought much darkness by coercing their constituents to accept their doctrine in the name of truth. There are those of you who pushed the envelope of what you call reality and redefined it in the name of truth. Truth is something many of you are concerned with as you follow the highest spiritual path. We wish to tell you as we hug you that truth is like a disco ball. It is, metaphorically speaking, like a round object with mirrors glued on to it. The disco ball has small mirrors which reflect light or truth from all sides. As you shine the light from one side it reflects to you one truth and as you shine your light from the other side it reflects another truth, both valid and appropriate.

How can that be, some may ask? *How can it be the ultimate truth if it is not one truth?*

We love you and we know of your duality. You again walk on a linear path where in fact the "truth" always resides in the circle. You want to have one simple answer to all that is around you. Many of you find consolation in simplifying the reality around you and thus adhering to the "one truth." But, truth is continuously rewritten as you learn more about yourself and about the world around you. What is true today may be false tomorrow. We wish to tell you that you are so dearly loved and what you call truth from your perspective is not what we call truth. Each mirror reflects the light or truth from the perspective that the light is coming from. The disco ball is swiveling as well which makes the truth change continuously. As you walk on the path of your life and feel that the ground beneath you is solid and hard and then you trip and fall and bruise your knee, your idea of truth is being reinforced. If an angel came to you at that moment and told you that the sidewalk is not more solid than water, and in fact it is made of atoms that are very separated, and that there is more empty space than solid matter, and in actuality, you are made of the same basic material as the sidewalk with slight variations of atomic molecular structure and vibratory rate, you may not be too happy to hear it. As you walk in your daily lives you have an idea of what is truth and what is false. From where we sit, much of what you believe to be truthful is false or an illusion created by you for your learning. From where we sit, nothing of what you know about yourself is our truth. You see yourself as a human and we see you as an angelic light being made out of vibrations which appear to us in a form of colors, geometric shapes, a galaxy of stars, sparkles and melody. You are beautiful and grand. You see yourself as a person that is born and will die. We see you as an angel that was never born and will never die. You see yourself as human and in fact you are not human. Your humanness is a very short lived costume that you put on for a while in order to do the work of God. You are part of that energy and your work and mission is to go into a body to do your work and come back home. You have done it before earth was formed and you will do it well after earth will be no longer. This is how ancient you are. You are eternal.

So how do we know what is truth, some of you may wonder?

Truth is what appears in front of you and feels light and untruth is what comes in front of you and feels heavy, is our short answer. Truth is not universal as each truth holds multiple dimensions. What is truth from one dimension is not truth from the other dimension

There is never one truth. Truth in your history, culture, politics, religion and daily life is always tainted by the color of your limitations and perspectives. There is never one truth. One person's vocabulary, cultural contexts, ideas about life, and place in history determines their ideas of events in their life. When you look at an event from the experiencer's viewpoint, you see one truth but when you see it in the context of history it is another. Truth is a disco ball and we ask you to understand that the reflection of light on the disco floor is all but an illusion. Your truth, as you call it, is but a reflection of your light and as you move along the truth moves with you.

This is confusing, some may say. *Why are you telling us about the truth if there is no such thing?*

We wish you to begin to understand that in all your relationships the one that stands beside you, may it be your partner, friend, child or parent, shines the light from a slightly different angle, therefore their truth will look different to them than to you. We ask you to become multidimensional as you seek the truth. We hug you as we impart to you that there may be two people that love each other, and each one sees their truth and it is different from their partner's yet both may be correct and both truths may be appropriate. Can you get into the circle while walking in duality in your linear reality?

When you feel love for someone and a close member of your family feels hate towards that person, can you honor them and accept that their lesson in relation to your loved one is different than yours, yet it is still sacred. Can you feel that despite the opposite positions you both hold toward that person, both of you may be expressing your truths? Can you live with this kind of unity? We know who you are and we know it is not easy but it is precisely what we wish you to do. We ask you to utilize the same in all your relationships. Your planet is changing and you are moving through an acceleration of time and events to a place of unity consciousness. It is the foundation that will catapult peace on earth. To create that foundation you must begin to see your world from its various dimensions. It is the sign of the new energy and it is the power that you now possess. You can change your idea about things thereby emitting the energy of unity to Gaia. Your energy is the fuel that propels the engine of change. We wish to impart to you that you are coming into time that may stretch your idea of truth. Many of the so-called truths that you have learned to hold dear will no longer hold water. We wish you to use a new method to decipher truth from falsehood. We wish you to redefine what is called true and false.

You are an angel walking in duality and we wish you to hold the idea that you are eternal and that you are the creator of that which you experience. We also wish you to hold the image that all that is around you is glued with the adhesive we call love energy. We ask you to begin with a foundation that does not attach to the details or logic but is connected to feelings. Call upon your feminine intuitive side to filter information as it will serve you well. What feels truthful to you is your truth and you do not need to convince anyone else nor let anyone else convince you. What is truthful is what feels truthful inside you. There is no other source you need to consult because your truth is your truth. Your fellow angel's truth may be very different and we wish you to honor their truth and not try to convince them.

How can we hold a society together where everyone has a different idea of the truth, some may ask?

Your society is composed of individuals and when each individual respects their own truth as well as their fellow angel's, you have brought upon you peace on earth. It is the acknowledgement of the multifaceted, multidimensional attribute of truth which brings harmony into the idea of you learning about you while honoring as sacred the search of another. The "truth" of your spiritual journey to discover your divinity and activate the mastery that runs in your veins is sacred and honored. Each one of you must follow their feelings and we wish to tell you that like the snowflakes no two are the same. Honor your path and hold sacred the path of your brother and sister. You are all brothers and sisters and you are all angels and eternal and, most of all, you are all loved. This is our truth, and so be it.

The Fashion Designer

YOU HAVE TAKEN A LONG TIME to arrive where you are now. You are standing at a crossroads and the traffic moves all around you. It is indeed a confusing time. At times you are wondering,

"Where is the right path, what turn should I take?"

The traffic is buzzing and it seems to be moving faster and faster. Those decisions that you need to make present themselves daily and you are wondering when all this confusion will change. Will it ever slow down?

We wish to tell you that you have been on this path before but never have you experienced the intensity that you are experiencing at this time. The intensity is, in actuality, growing and the need for you to be able to know when to turn and in which direction will become vital to your journey. From our perspective it is a grand time but you may see it as a difficult one. Some of you will feel very unstable as if the world is going to end. With a hug we wish to tell you that the world as you know it is coming to an end but a new world vibrating at a higher frequency is just over the horizon. Some of you will experience the new world and will be part of it and some of you will not. With a smile we wish to impart to you that if you read this text you are surely one of those who have the potential to be part of the new earth. We call it the "New Sun" but in actuality it is you waking up to your interdimensionality and seeing your magnificence. You have signed up to be part of the entourage who facilitates the change and it is your call of duty. Some of you feel that you are the only one who has doubts, thoughts and ideas about the changes that are taking place all around you. Some of you think that everyone is faring better then you are.

If I am supposed to lead why is it that I feel behind the rest of the pack, some of you may wonder?

We see you and we know who you are. In the battlefield, from all the dust and noise, the warriors can't sense their position and advances. They are just responding to what is around them the best they can. We wish to impart to you that it is you who is in the battle and it is precisely what your mission is about. You are limited in your vision. The bigger picture is hidden from you as it is appropriate. It is part of your test. We wish you to trust that you are at the right place at the right time and you are doing what you are supposed to be doing.

I have no idea what I am doing, some of you may wonder out loud. *It is all so chaotic around me that I am not sure where I am at all.*

You are so dearly loved, and we wish to tell you that you have trained for this. You have done it in many other expressions knowing that the day will come when you will need to use all of your inner resources to manifest an energy that is catapulting a change in Gaia and in your part of the universe. Your part of the universe will create a change for the whole universe and that is why so many of us are watching and supporting you. It is you who are doing the work. We are only the ones who can shed light in the dark of battle, letting you know that you are loved and to keep going.

How do we know if we are doing the right thing, some may still wonder?

You will not know but you will feel. You will feel joy bubbling inside of you. Inside of your heart you will know that you are in the right place at the right time and must utilize your training and use your tools.

What are the tools, you may still wonder?

We have told you before that you are enabled but we remind you that your first and most powerful tool is self-love. When you are residing in a sanctuary of self-love, you are creating the energy that is changing the vibration of the planet.

We feel that it is egoistical to love ourselves. Aren't we supposed to be in service for humanity and not focused on ourselves, some of you may wonder?

With all love, we wish to tell you that you do no good to anyone with your service if you do not learn to love yourself first. Those who try to give love to others while not being in love with their own divinity in effect "gift" their own ambiguous feeling about self to others. There are those of you who feel that they are "punished" and "sinful" and the only way to correct these feelings is to help others by giving. We wish to impart to you that there are no concepts such as sin and punishment in the place we come from. Your challenges are not punishments. There is no punishment in the universe of light. There are, however, past actions coming back to be balanced. All are choices of the self. Your pain is self-inflicted, and by self we mean higher self. There is no higher authority over your life other than your higher self. From where we sit, the giving always starts with the self. Who you are shows in your melody and your geometry. You cannot give what you do not have. If you feel bad about yourself that is precisely what you project to others. If you feel guilty about the self it is exactly what you will "donate" as your service. If you feel shameful or anger about the self it will be your contribution to whomever you come in contact with. From the perspective of spirit you are transparent and you cannot hide behind your badges of honor, your certificates and trophies. These concepts do not exist in our realm. You are your vibration. Your contribution to the planet and to your brothers and sisters has to begin at the source which is you. If you try to make up for your guilt by being in service to others, it will not be effective. There is never a judgment and you are loved whether you are effective or ineffective. We wish however to impart to you that you are doing more disservice than service if you have not learnt to love yourself first.

What does it mean to love oneself, some may ask?

We thought you would never ask. Loving yourself means to hold sacred all that you are from all directions. Loving yourself is to accept you and to truly honor the gift of life and all that it entails. To love yourself is to love your body as it is a divine instrument that you have been given to hold your energy while on earth. To love yourself means to not love only your head and to negate the rest of the body. You must be in peace and harmony with all your parts. You must become peaceful with your sexuality and your sex organs and honor those parts that give you pleasure and hold no guilt or shame about your body. Your body is a vibrating instrument and when you hold the energy of shame or guilt it is as if you are trying to play a concerto with a damaged instrument. You must learn to love all that you are. You must learn to forgive yourself for the things that you have done that you deem "negative". Loving yourself is the most powerful attribute of a light warrior. You cannot have compassion for others before you master compassion for the self. You cannot learn to love another before you have learned to love yourself.

This whole aim of this journey is to teach "you" about "you." All that you experience is here to teach you about yourself. When you go out of yourself to give to others while neglecting to clear out the self first, it is as if you were a fashion designer who tried to market their designs while walking dressed up in rugs—neither very convincing nor effective. We see some who feel guilty about loving the self as it is seemingly going against the idea of giving. You were taught to give selflessly. From our perspective it is not the intention of spirit.

What do you mean, "We should only think about the self," some may wonder?

With all love we wish to tell you that your biggest contribution to humanity and to planet earth is when you walk the walk of a master knowing that you are loved and loving yourself as you are. When you do achieve that stage you are giving to all of humanity just by being alive. Naturally people will come to you just to be near your vibration. You will be changing the magnetic fields of the planet and the dirt under your feet will vibrate higher. Many of those who vibrate in self love are in service of humanity because it is where they feel the love. They are so in love with themselves that they are in love with humanity. They have so much compassion for the self that they have compassion for all angels walking as humans on the planet. They give themselves so much that they can give others as much and never lack. This is the true giving from where we stand. We wish to hug you one more time and to tell you as we always do that you are so dearly loved and your journey is sacred and honored beyond your dreams.

We speak to those of you who are in the "service department" helping others. We ask you always to be in the mindset that you are helping yourself to learn about you. When you teach love, teach by example and love yourself first. We see those in your history who were righteous and taught love while feeling no love for the self. Some of the darkest hours that your society has experienced were introduced to you by those who brought "the love of God" to you in the name of this or that religion while having no love for themselves. The message was always delivered in the manner in which those people felt about themselves. Those messages were expressed in brutality, pain, hatred and anger that permeated your cellular memory for many lives as well as your current expression. It is time to move away from those memories. Love for self heals those wounds forever. If we would dare to make a generalization we would say that most of you have experienced one form of torture or another and even painful death in the name of "the love of God" packaged by one religion or another. We know who you are and we love you just for giving it another go. We are in awe of your love for humanity and your commitment to come time after time and to try to change that which is in front of you. This is why we ask you to know that you are loved and to know that you are at the right place at the right time.

We wish to touch upon your question: *"what is it that I am supposed to be doing?"* You are supposed to hold your vibration in peace and balance. You are supposed to know who you are and know that you are loved even if a hundred people tell you to the contrary. You are supposed to feel love for yourself as well as for your worst detractors and have compassion for them as you do for yourself. You are not asked to evangelize, preach, distribute leaflets, convince your friends or start an organization. You mission is to be who you are, to know who you are and to vibrate at your highest potential. When you do, you are the most magnificent lighthouse and even though the storm around you surges and the wind is blowing, your light is making all the difference to those who are seeking. You are in the midst of a change of energy and it is intensifying. Your year of 2012 is the marker for the beginning of the "New Sun." You are one of those who came here at this time to facilitate this transition. From where we sit there will be a split between those who wish to move to the higher planes and those who insist in staying with the old energy. The move higher is what you collectively chose and you are heading that way. There are those who wish to slow you down as they do not wish to be exposed to light. They feel comfortable in the dark as it is all they know. Your light is allowing them to see and to choose light over dark. We ask you to turn on your light by learning to love yourself, and so be it.

Welcome Home

WELCOME HOME. This is what you hear when you come back to us after your cycle of lessons end.

What happens when I return, some of you may ask?

You have been separated from part of your energy, and when you come back you reunite with you and with all that is. Your part that is God was separated from you and hidden from you. You have to search for it in order to feel it when you are in a physical form on earth. When you come back your search ends and you encounter what we call love in its grandest manifestation.

We are with you throughout the transition you call death. When you walk in lesson, there is nothing more terrifying on your journey than the word *death*. For you it signifies the end of all. Many of you fear it so much that you forget to live and become a manifestation of what you consider death to be while still walking alive in duality. We wish to speak to you about death as it is something that from our perspective looks very different than it does to you.

When you come back, there is a celebration in your honor.

Why would that be, some may ask?

It is because we love you, and we missed you. There is a group for each one of the angels walking in duality on earth at this time that is waiting to reunite. We wish to give you a metaphor at this time. When you fell in love – with your partner or your child – and then you had to separate for awhile, how did it feel? Did you feel a longing or yearning to be together? It is the same in our reality. When you are in lesson, there is part of you on the other side that is longing to reunite. It has the love of God in it, and it waits patiently to be one again. When you shed your physical costume, indeed, you meet with your group and the first thing they do is celebrate your return. It is a reunion of twin flame lovers after a brief separation. When you say, "I met my twin flame" it really means you met you.

You fear the transition of death, but this transition from our perspective is the same transition that you experience every night when you go to sleep. You are surrendering your consciousness so it is free to wander in other dimensions and realities, and when you wake up you pick up your consciousness where you left off. Death is very much the same process as going to sleep. Are you fearful of going to sleep? When you go to sleep, you do so in the awareness that another morning is coming where you will be awakened and continue the journey you call life. It is the same with death. When you go to sleep you know that even though you leave your body it is only so that you can wake up in a new body and continue the journey you call life. It is not a fearful event.

We wish to tell you that what you call evolution imprinted on you the fear of death and the desire to survive. It is indeed appropriate, and it is by design, your design. Even the transition you call death is your design. You think that you have to die, but from our perspective it is not so. You think that you have only so many years to be on earth and then you must die. We wish to impart to you that from our perch this process is voluntary. You can live many more years than you are telling yourself. It is the belief in aging that actually manifests aging. When you believe in youth, you actually age more slowly. You can stop the clock of aging if you give intent to do so. It is not easy as your cells know what you really believe in, so you must "believe" in a way that convinces your cells.

In many of your ancient cultures death was celebrated as a transition, and it was understood that the mechanics of that transition are sacred and appropriate. In the ancient culture of Egypt, some of the mystery schools taught you how to move away from physical death and change dimension while still in a body. They understood the mechanics of the KA or the life force. Many of you are those initiates from those times. We see many of you who carry the knowledge of ascension in your veins longing to be activated.

Many of you have walked the walk of the master and know that aging and death are a choice. You are so dearly loved and we wish to tell you that whether you choose to come back earlier or later, the celebration is still taking place.

What is the celebration for, some of you may still wonder? *I lead a very unimportant life and I feel like a failure during most of it,* some may still claim.

We wish to impart to you that from our perspective what you consider a failure is still grand. The celebration is for the walk you call life. You are celebrated for choosing to go to the school you call earth and walk the walk. You are celebrated for walking blindfolded, looking for your divinity in the dark and creating light from within. You are celebrated for being part of God on a mission that is not easy but has everyone in the universe knowing you by name.

What happens to me right after death, some may wonder?

First you have a reunion of sorts. You are reuniting with your group, and some may go through energetic adjustments. From your perspective everything must take time, but as you move from your linear dimension to the circle there is no time and you are at a reality that is very different, and there is a period of adjustment to allow yourself to integrate.

How long may that be, some may wonder?

With a hug we wish to tell you that anywhere between a second and a thousand years. There is no time, and you can be leaving your body at the same time as being reborn as a new baby and those two events which you call the cycle of death and rebirth will happen simultaneously.

What do I do after I die, some may still ask?

We do not know because you never die. You simply go to sleep and awaken in your dream state. In that dream state you are awakened, and you know everything about creation, your life, your journey, your challenges, and the secret of the dimension you call God. You know it because you are part of it and it is part of you. After you move away from your body you are busy.

I do not get to rest, some may ask?

The short answer is no. You do not need to rest because you do not get tired. There are those of us, however, who work with humans whose energy has been damaged to reintegrate them and allow them time to become whole again.

What do I do then if I do not need to rest, some may still ask?

You go back to your specialty and continue in your line of work in the job we call creation. It is a grand scheme and to an angel trapped in 3D reality it is unimaginable in scope, as you are limited by your physical dimension.

Can you give us an example, some may still ask?

With a smile we wish to tell you that there are those of you who work to create life on your planet and others who work on creating celestial bodies; there are those who work on binding molecules together in far away systems, and those who become part of matter in a system so they can learn about an aspect of creation and themselves. There are some who work with humans and other life forms in the millions of conscious systems throughout the universe. You have plenty to do and you are excited to do it.

Why would I want to go back to being on earth then, some may still wonder?

We have so much love for you because we know what it takes to come here and do what it is that you do. It is surely not a short cut or the easy path, but you still do it life after life, and you are so dearly loved for walking the walk. You know that by doing so you are contributing to the grand creation of the system you named God. You are doing your mission, and it is sacred and so honored.

Do I have to come back?

Our answer is no, you do not, but you will as it is your desire and you have been at it for a long time. When you come back home some of you cannot wait to give it another try and go straight back to the birth canal. None of you wish to miss the opportunity of learning what your system is offering at this time.

What happens to us after we celebrate, some may wonder?

You have meetings in which you look at your life. Some call it a "life review." It is your opportunity to learn from the dream you call life on earth. It is as if you went to a school in which you were asked to perform particular tasks and tests. After you have finished those tasks and rests you got together with your teachers and jointly you examined the decisions you made and see what was appropriate and would needed work.

We wish to speak to those of you who came at this time to be the teachers. You chose to be here at a certain time and to be born in specific circumstances which allowed you to become an angel facilitator.

What does it mean, you may wonder?

You are here to ignite the flame of divinity first in yourself and then in others.

How do I do that, you may inquire?

You do that by using yourself as a vessel for the Love vibration you call God and linking it through you to others. We know who you are, and when you are awakening to this mission you will be walking on air as gravity will loosen its grip over your life.

How do I become lighter, you may ask?

By remembering your mission and knowing that you are eternal and that death is just a transition of energy. When you move away from your idea of mortality, you become fearless; when you become fearless remembering truly becomes part of you and you are awakening to your path. With all love we wish to tell you that by not fearing the transition you call death you can live longer. You have the knowledge and you have the tools to do so. We wish you to celebrate every moment that you are alive and to seek the highest potential in every situation. We wish to tell you as we hug you that you came here to shine your light so others can see. That is why we call you facilitators. You must, therefore, remember why you came here in the first place and awaken to your mission. Many of you cling to life and forget to live. We want you to know that you never die and the transition you call death is only a transformation from one dream state to another.

You are consciousness and part of God exploring itself, and as such we wish you to acknowledge the time that you have in this expression and celebrate it. Do not fear and do not hold back. Allow love to be your guide and intention to be your vehicle.

Why do you speak to us about death, you ask?

You are coming into energy in which there will be those who will choose to transition as a path to moving forward. Those who do so do it by choice as they acknowledge that they are unable to shift their vibration to accommodate the new energy that is now coming to your planet. There is never a judgment and they are honored as much as any of the angels walking in duality on your planet. You, however, came here at this time to stay alive and live longer and healthier than ever before. This is part of your mission and your responsibility. We wish you to honor those around you who wish to depart and hold their journey as sacred as they will return soon enough. You, however, who are reading these messages, are here to be in health, vibrancy, and power, and for that you must not be fearful of what you see around you as this is the split that we spoke off. We know who you are as in the circle we can see all of you who will ever read this text.

There are those who will be with the new energy and those who will choose to stay with the old. The old energy will not support their biology as it did in the past and many will choose to transition and come back home. We wish to tell you that you are now at an age that is mature, aware, powerful, and ripe to fulfill your mission. We wish to impart to you that you must adopt the awareness of health so you can fulfill your mission and walk your path. It will not serve you or the planet if you choose to transition and return as a baby while the greatest shift on your planet is taking place. We ask you to be in the awareness that you chose to be a lighthouse and a facilitator and to give intent to your body so it will know that you plan to stay here healthy and powerful for a long time. Do not look at others and feel that if everyone is transitioning you must too. This is not the case; each of you comes here for different reasons. We are in love with you regardless of the choices you make and we wish you to wake up to the path you have chosen and enjoy every moment of it as it is the grandest journey a human in lesson can make, and so be it.

Hot and Cold

E WISH TO SPEAK TO YOU about heat.

Why heat, you may ask?

When you are cold and you ask for heat, heat is good, and yet when you are hot more heat is considered "bad." Heat, however, is energy, and as such it always must be in balance.

Hot or cold is like light and dark. When the energy of heat is absent, you feel cold. It is the same with the planet earth. When the sun is not shining, you feel cold and when it is radiating, you feel the heat. Heat is one way to sense the energy of spirit. Many of you are searching for sensual confirmation for your connection with spirit. We see those of you ask, *but how do we know there is a spirit? Maybe you are just making all of this up.*

It is humorous to us that the reality that you believe in is to us a "make-believe" story and the reality that is real to us you have difficulty accepting.

We wish to give you a physical attribute that allows you to sense when you are connected to the energy of spirit. It is subtle like all things related to spirit but nevertheless it is distinguishable.

You are, from our perspective, a vibrating consciousness expressing itself through physical matter. You have fields around you which are geometric in essence, and you have other fields that are tonal in essence. Yet, you have fields around you that emit specific color spectrums that reflect the energy wavelength you project. You move and operate through these dimensional fields. We see you in all your grandness, which means that we can perceive all the dimensions in which you operate. Your body is not equipped to sense the different dimensions, and your organs are not sensitive enough to process the subtle fields that surround you. However, when you connect with spirit the energetic fields become enhanced, and, therefore, your energy increases.

As you move to a place of higher vibration, you will feel the additional enhancement of energy as heat or inner vibration. It is as if your body acts as a heated tuning-fork. The energy feels like bubbles moving outwardly from within. We wish to impart to you that when you choose to connect and sense coldness, this sensation means from our perspective that you are not connecting to the realm of spirit. When you sense fear or imbalance of any sort, you may be connecting to energy, but that energy may be depleting you rather then enhancing you. Your intent is your direct dial to the realm of spirit, and when you set up that area code you will reach the right place. The higher part of you which is also a part of God is a place of peace and balance. Its attribute of heat is nurturing and never threatening. It is never cold as it has balance and love emanating from it. When you sit in front of your candle and you feel love you know it, and when you feel cold or fear you will know that as well. We wish you to always set up the intent to connect to your own highest vibration of love and light as it will send you down the right path.

Your body is a vibrating instrument and as you act, your melody, colors, and geometry changes. The changes register in the field around you and thus create and attract your experiences. Your inner reality literally brings to you that which you experience in your outer reality. As you think and feel, you create shapes and forms, colors and melody. That which you create has a frequency and a wave-like attribute. You are, in actuality, bringing to you the fields that need to be completed and become whole. You are attracting that which is unbalanced as it is a universal attribute that wishes for all things to be balanced.

When you feel that you are perturbed by something in your outer reality, such as jealousy for example, you may experience that emotion in relation to your partner, child, or friend, and this emotion dominates your awareness. Your learning, therefore, is to balance that which is imbalanced. The emotion of jealousy from our perspective can be seen as the tip of a pyramid. The base of the pyramid is lack of self-love that results in feeling lack of self-worth, which in turn results in fearing the loss of love from an outer source. That fear of losing love from others creates a need to rely on external sources, a fear that then creates anger directed at the self. The anger against self is difficult to digest energetically and is, therefore, projected outwardly as a form of an emotion you call jealousy. This is one version of an emotion expressed in one way, yet its foundation has roots in a much deeper imbalance.

When you walk and you feel in your daily life, you create a pattern and a frequency yearning to be balanced. The reality around you, therefore, rearranges itself to give you opportunity to balance the imbalanced. In other words, you the angel walking in duality and forgetfulness create situations in which you will encounter reasons to be jealous. It is you who through your imbalance create a lesson for yourself. Many of you will say that it is not you creating these situations but your "promiscuous partner" or "too-friendly child." With all love we wish to hug you and tell you that you are so dearly loved and that there is never a judgment whether you acknowledge your part in creating your reality or not. It is, however, you who by design and with appropriateness create situations that will balance that which is imbalanced. This process works counter-intuitively as it is the way by which spirit facilitates your growth.

Many of you will say, *why do I need to be teased? If he or she would not create those situations I will be much more balanced.*

With all love we wish to tell you that everything is your choice. You choose a partner who will allow you to heal, and you create situations that will allow you to heal. These situations irritate that which is imbalanced so you will need to find ways to balance. There are those of you who discard partners just to discover that the next one and the next one after that creates the same exact situation. We wish you to grow and understand that there is no one who creates things around you to hurt you or harm you. All is done with love and for your growth. Those of you who go deeper and understand the patterns of your lives begin to dig in to the pyramid and re-structure the foundation, which is self-love.

We see those of you who feel stuck because you see the same pattern surrounding your life, feeling you are a victim of a scheme managed by none other than darkness. From where we sit this is not so. The love of spirit and of the group that is part of your angelic self has the higher perspective, and they wish you to move forward in each of your expressions. They do not waste time as your life span is brief. You will always encounter situations that irritate those areas in your life that are imbalanced. It is by design and it is your design.

Your thoughts and emotions create your experiences.

Why are you telling us all of that, some may wonder? *We do not feel that we are creating our reality,* others will claim.

With all love we wish to tell you that by acknowledging that your reality is a manifestation of your thoughts and feelings you come to a place in which you take responsibility for your experiences. Only then can you begin to change what you experience. As you connect and link to that portion that is the "I am that I am" you are able to see the pyramid and transform through the process of alchemy the foundation of the emotions that you deem negative from lack of self-worth, anger, and jealousy to self-love. When you experience self-love, all other layers will no longer be necessary, and you will no longer have irritating experiences as your geometry and frequency will not attract those patterns. As you become balanced you will create a reality that supports balance.

You are here now to transform yourself, through the process of alchemy, from lead to gold. It is the realization that your core essence is gold that changes the molecules around you. Many of you carry memories in your cells that are heavy with ideas of shame, guilt, fear, and worthlessness. You are now living an expression that is an accumulation of all your past expressions. It means that you are living in a reality that is a combination of this life as well as all your past lives. Many of you have been on earth many times and you have been embedded with heavy experiences. We wish to tell you that by linking you with that part of you called your higher self, you can begin to cleanse those residues and change your reality.

How do we know that we are connecting to our higher selves, you may ask?

As in the circle, we wish to impart to you that you will feel heat and vibration in your body. When your body is linked, it changes and expands. Your field around you becomes enhanced with the energy of spirit.

Many of you search for physical proof of things before you make a move. We wish to tell you that the realm of spirit operates in the subtle dimension of transparency, but we ask you to pay attention to feelings. Feelings have an attribute of spirit and are not diminished from the world of energy to the dimension of matter. Now we are adding the attribute of heat. As your vibration increases, you will begin to sense that which we speak of.

We wish to tell you that this sensation was not available until recently. Your biology is changing, and the fields of energy around you are becoming enhanced to accommodate the new magnetic grid around the planet. You are in transition, and your physical form is being enhanced. You are living at a time that is both magnificent and grand. It is our intention to hold your hand and lead you to a place where you can understand that which is around you and move to the highest place. We wish to show you how to jump over what you perceive as a pattern of "stuckness" in your lives. You are here to shine your light for all to see. You do so by discovering your divinity and by walking in your divinity you allow others to discover their own divinity. You must, therefore, clear all that which holds you back from experiencing the love for self. As you love yourself you begin to project love to all that is around you. You become the drop in the ripples and you create the concentric circles that are ever widening. You become the lighthouse. We wish you to move to that place as you are enabled at this time.

It is the heat and the feeling of vibration inside your body which will let you know that you are on the path and yes, you are receiving that which you ask for. We ask you to become a manifestation of light and love and bring yourself to a place of balance and peace. Through your balance and peace, peace on earth will manifest, and so be it.

The Sleeping Conductor

T O YOU YOUR PATH IS ONE of ups and downs. As you use your senses to observe your reality you place a value judgment on all that you see, smell, and touch. It is as if you are an interpreter of a holographic movie. We are hovering above you and around you, and what we see is the imprint of your interpretation. We do not see your reality as you do because from our perspective your reality is a result of your construct. We wish to tell you that as the creator you are the one who must acknowledge your role in the movie in front of you.

We see you asking yourself *how did I get here?* Some of you find yourselves in places that you would never want to go to and you wonder how you got there. We wish to hug you now and show you that your path is one of wonder, and the places that you feel are difficult and challenging offer you the opportunity to transform not the reality construct but your inner interpretation of it.

What do you mean, some may ask? We can see that we are in the pits, yet you want us to feel good about it?

We wish you to move above your current situation and get a sense of the circle. In the circle all that you have ever experienced, are experiencing, and will experience is present. When you are in the circle you begin to see the magnificence of what we call the divinity of your path. You begin to sense the magic of all that is in front of you as it allows you to discover the divine. Divinity is not discovered only by you being in a blissful environment with enlightened people who are educated and well-mannered. Divinity is discovered inside of you, and then regardless of the company you are with and the environment you are experiencing you still maintain your sense and identity of divinity.

Some of you have been through a lot of challenges, and we know who you are. We wish to tell you that you are loved and that which you went through, as horrible as it felt, has divinity inside. When you begin to peel away the layers of pain, anger, shame, guilt, and resentment, you discover a little golden ball that shines ever so brightly, and it emanates love. In the presence of that little golden ball, you cannot feel negativity, only love, love for yourself and for all those who are around you. Some of you feel you can never forgive what was done to you, and we know who you are. You feel you were wronged and seek justice by revenge. Some of you feel you deserve all the terrible things that happened because you believe you are sinners, and, thus, all you can feel is anger towards yourself as well as shame and guilt, and we know who you are as well.

You are masters of love, each and every one of you. You are capable of being a master who can shine your light so brightly that all darkness will disappear around you and all who walk beside you will have a clearer path. When you walk your walk, you are honored, and there are legions of us supporting you. You are never alone and you are never led to a place where you are subjected to punishment. There is in actuality no authority over you that can do things to you without your permission.

You are a master and you have the ultimate authority over your life. Whatever experiences you face are the experiences you "cooked" for yourself so you can progress. We see those of you who are at a place you do not like and blame the ones around you for taking you to this place. Do you really think that anyone has the power to bring you anywhere against your will? All is choice. Ultimately, all that you experience is your choice.

I did not choose any of it, you may claim.

There is never a judgment and you may believe in what we tell you or not. You are loved just the same. It is our understanding, however, that you are never taken anywhere without your permission.

Some of you do not recognize your divinity and your self-sovereignty and thereby experience reality as a series of mishaps that just "happened" to you. When we see your geometry, melody, and colors, we see how you interact through your melody with those around you. Ultimately, you are the conductor and you choose which instrument plays when. There are those of you who do not believe or experience your responsibility as conductors and, therefore, allow the musicians in your orchestra to play "freestyle." We see those of you who just allow whatever comes to come and neither take charge nor responsibility for this. Indeed if you vacate the seat of the conductor, either the orchestra members will each play their own tune not in harmony with each other, or a "volunteer" will step in to conduct for you.

There are those in the universe who search for those who do not occupy their body fully and "volunteer" to "help" by filling up the vacancy. It is as if you were driving a car and handed over the steering wheel and the pedals to another so they could drive the car for you. Then you moved to the back seat and faded into the background observing the scenery. From our perspective, although you have made the choice to let go steering the vessel, it is still your ultimate responsibility.

Why would we give up the driving of our vehicle, some may ask?

Some of you feel that giving up the driving frees you from responsibility and difficulty. From our perspective you are not moving forward and you are just delaying your learning. If you choose to not take responsibility for your circumstances you will face similar ones in future expressions. There is no way to avoid your lessons; you can only delay them as your free choice is honored.

What does it feel like when we are not in control of our vessel, some may wonder?

The feeling is one of blurriness as if you were intoxicated or unconscious, not knowing what is right and what is wrong. It is a state of inner confusion; your body is no longer directed by you because you are being directed by a power that is outside of yourself. If you are not in command of your vessel, it may have been taken over by lower vibrational energy that expresses itself through you in your physical reality. You may feel then that you are in a fog and you are hardly aware of what is going on around you. You are just going through the motions, acting without awareness and without intention. From our perspective, you have surrendered your consciousness which is your biggest asset.

The easiest way for this to happen is by ingesting substances that separate your physical vessel from the energy you named soul. When you abuse alcohol, drugs, sedatives, sleeping pills, or allow food addictions or sexual addictions to control you, you are separating yourself from yourself. When you are attaching your energy to pornography, gambling, or abuse sexuality, food or drugs you are risking allowing your light to be locked in a closet so someone else can have a ride on you and you will not be responsible. From where we sit, your responsibility never ends and when you allow someone else to take over, it is still you who are allowing it.

How are we at risk of being taken over when we watch pornography or take drugs, some of you may wonder?

We wish to tell you that your universe is teeming with life, and you are the highest consciousness. As such, when you engage in a continuous exchange with lower vibrations you are in essence giving them permission to move into your vessel. You are a vibration that is expressing itself through matter. When you are engaged on a regular basis with another vibration that is lower than you, you become like it.

There are many entities around you who wish to learn about you. They come from different systems in the universe, and they are puzzled by your power of emotions and your power of love. They do not have such capabilities and they are always waiting for those of you who wish to move away from your own vessels so they can move in and take over. No one can ever take over without your permission. When you choose to engage in low vibrational activity, you invite those of like vibration to interact with you. When you stop making choices and act out of unconsciousness, you in essence allow a different consciousness to move in. This process is not rare, and many of your fellow angels are walking on the planet "taken over" by lower vibrations. They can always choose to take back the vessel, but the longer they are absent the more difficult the struggle is.

Why are you telling us about this struggle? some may wonder.

You are unlikely to be the one who is taken over, but there may be fellow angels you know who are walking in the fogginess of unconsciousness as they have given away their most precious asset. We wish you to be aware of those and know of the process.

What do we do if we encounter those who are 'taken over?'

With all love we wish to tell you that your job remains the same: Shine your light and walk in your divinity. The light that you shine disperses the darkness, and those who are "taken over" represent the darkness. Those who are in the dark will either run away from you, or they will use your light to regain back their consciousness. You, however, just need to be the lighthouse as the rest happens automatically.

What do angels who are "taken over" look like? you may wonder.

There are those who resort to violent expressions, those who resort to self-destruction, and those who just move to the background and allow a different voice to take over and handle things for them. At times you will not notice, but if you know the person well, you may feel that he or she does not have the capacity for compassion and does not react to love. These are the two flags that point to an angel who lost its vessel and was "taken over." The entities that are allowed to move in wish to learn about love and compassion, but they have no capacity to sense these emotions themselves. They are aware of these emotions' power, but they do not possess the ability to feel them. It is a highly prized ability, and they try to learn about it.

At times those who surrender their light and are "taken over" may act with such brutality that it is as if they have no heart. They are capable of doing things that you deem unfathomable. They are capable of inflicting pain on others or animals without feeling anything. In your Christian mythology priests use exorcism and other methods to regain consciousness, and in Jewish mysticism this process of being "taken over" was called a Dybbuk. In the large game of creation that interaction is allowed as part of a reality which exists in a universe of free choice. There are those who are allowed to interact with you as they are part of your lesson. From our perspective it all comes down to your choice of light and dark. If you choose low vibration, you invite darkness, and if you choose high vibration you invite light and love into your life.

How do we tell the difference between those choices, some may still ask?

You are an angel and a part of God, and as such all that you do is guided by love. The lower the energy the more removed it is from the vibration of love. You must be in a place of much darkness and unconsciousness to be replaced and "taken over."

How do we know if we have ever been 'taken over?'

With a smile we wish to tell you that you would not be able to pick up this text and read it if you would not be from the light. Darkness has no power over you, and it cannot do things to you. You can transform darkness. Darkness creeps into places where light moved away. That is the choice of a human whether to be with light or without. If the human chooses to hide her light, she allows darkness to come in. We wish you not to give away this power as it is just another piece in the puzzle of light and dark. Your universe has many forms of life and consciousness. They are all interacting all the time, and we wish you to understand that your light is your most treasured gift. As such we ask you to honor it as sacred and see all that happens in your life from the prism of light.

Do not confuse "bad" things with darkness. Darkness is your inner reaction to your outer reality. When you are in a place of gratitude, love, and compassion, no darkness can get close to you. When you try to cover your reality by using numbing substances or consciousness-altering drugs, you open yourself to lower vibrations and, without realizing it, you may be giving away your treasure. With all love we wish to tell you that there is a battle raging, and it is intensifying by the day.

Your mission is shining light so those who are in darkness transform. It is a magnificent time, and we ask you to shine your light and walk in your divinity. It is you, one at a time, who are tipping the scales toward the light. We wish you not to judge others as all paths are sacred and honored as free choice. Your mission is not to convert anyone or use methods to exorcize those who have been "taken over." Your mission is simply to take care of yourself and shine your light as brightly as you can so those around you can choose to see and transform through your light, and so be it.

The Joy Ride

WE ASK YOU to hold your own higher self's hands and lead yourself through the maze of forgetfulness. You are living in a fog, and as you walk through it you can only see that which is close to you. When you walk in fog, invisible hands can direct you because these hands know the way to the treasure hidden in the center of the maze.

You, however, doubt these hands and insist on relying on your eyes. You often discover that your eyes were short-sighted and your vision only helped you arrive at a dead-end. When you reach that dead end, you must retrace your steps and search for a different route.

Many of you use fear when navigating. In fact, many of you use all means possible except the means offered by the invisible hands of the one who knows the end destination and how to get there. Why is it that you rely on things that get you lost and you do not follow the signs that get you where you want to go?

We do not really know where we want to go, some of you may claim.

This is precisely why you get lost, we answer.

All of you come to earth intending to walk the highest path, yet many of you compromise somewhere near the lowest potentials.

Why, you may ask?

We have the same question in mind.

We wish to tell you that time after time you choose the lowest path when you are offered the option. Your choices are honored, and you are loved when you choose the high path or the low path. You are dearly loved, and we see you when you get lost on the path, and when you make choices that direct you towards your lowest potential and not your highest one. We wish to tell you that in most cases when you choose the low path rather than the high one, we observe the geometric shape of fear around you.

Didn't we cover fear, some may wonder?

We cannot talk about it enough as it is your biggest obstacle to finding your treasure.

We see you asking yourself, *when should I go right or left?*

Right may represent the easier choice and left may represent the harder choice in your opinion. Which do you choose?

Of course we chose the easy one, you respond. *Isn't it all about choosing the light and not the heavy?*

"Yes," is our answer, but you are still choosing the heavy over the light. You take the "easy" path because it is convenient at the moment, but in actuality it takes you away from your end destination and often into dead ends. We wish you to move from your seats and fly above yourselves for just a moment. For you to know what is easy and what is hard you must first discover your lessons and learning. When you go through your lesson, you get closer to where your treasure lies. When you choose a path that is not dealing with your learning, you either get further away or stay where you were.

How do we discover our lessons? you may wonder.

First, you have to walk the walk, and when you get to an intersection you must feel which will serve the highest potential of your path on earth. In order to sense the correct path for you, you must reiterate an intention to yourself at every opportunity. Your intention is to be directed to the highest potential of your life so you let your group know that you aim high. You must set up the intention that you are aiming to the highest spiritual goal which is about discovering your own divinity. The easy path may only seem easy because your intention is not clear or it aims for material comfort.

We see many of you who are not in the mindset that you are the conductors of your spiritual journey. We wish you to know that you must hold your journey sacred and direct your journey at every moment. Instead we see many of you just letting go of the directorship and flowing with whatever comes. You keep making choice after choice of that which comes your way and with every choice you take the easy road. Soon enough you are stuck at one of the maze's dead ends. A dead end is a place where a "major message" is introduced to you.

What do you mean, you may wonder?

You always have the option to learn in harmony with your path or to move so far from your path that you need a "major message" to get back on the high road. It is as if you are asked to slow down and you do not because you do not choose the path of learning and then you encounter a circumstance in which you break a leg so your physical body forces you to slow down. After you recover, you continue the fast speed because the message was not integrated or learned. Finally, you encounter a situation in which you break your back, and only then are you forced to slow down enough so the learning is absorbed. We wish to tell you that "major messages" come from the same source as the "minor messages." They all come from your higher self directing you toward the treasure hidden in the middle of the maze. This is why we ask you to be in tune with your lesson so you will not need to face a "major message."

What should we base our choice on, some of you may wonder?

You are a master and as such you set goals for your learning. Each and every one of you knows inside what tests and trials are set up for your learning. When a test or challenge presents itself, you must choose your direction based on the lesson involved. Do not instantly choose the easy path because it may prove to be the long and hard one. Much of your reality is not what it seems, and we wish you to become sensitive to the message that is coming toward you. The maze is subtle and the messages are subtle.

It is you who must choose to follow or not follow your learning. When you face a message, it always appears heavy at first as it represents a lesson neither learnt nor integrated. As such it carries the heaviness of karma. The heaviness of karma relates to your journey in past expressions in which you did not pass a test. As you face it again, it fills you with fear. You are faced with that fear because your cells remember the last time you attempted to conquer a lesson and failed. The "failure" registered in your geometry. With all love we wish to tell you that from our perspective there is no such thing as failure and all your choices are honored and are additional brush strokes on the canvas you call life. You are creating a masterpiece and every brush stroke is a lesson and learning that is invaluable.

How would you wish us to discern which way to go then, some may ask?

You are loved and that which causes you fear is always an indication that something is up. Fear comes from some place, and it offers you the first sign that a challenge you face has energy that is asking to be cleared. At times you may relieve the fear by turning the other way, at other times you must go through that which causes you to feel fear and release it.

How do we know, you may ask?

You must connect to your lesson and let the lesson lead you.

And how do we do that, some may still wonder?

Knowing comes from a place in your heart.

You must open your heart and ask your heart to guide you. It is your heart which takes the hand of your higher self and your angels and shows you the way. When you set up the intention to walk the highest path, the angels around you blow up balloons in preparation for the party. They know that you are on your way to meet them, and they get very excited.

Once you sit quietly and set the intention, you must go back and recheck the feeling of heaviness or lightness. When you set up your intention to walk the highest path, no matter how fearful the event may seem, the path to the treasure will feel light and the path to the dead end will feel heavy.

The key is pure intention and love. Love is your vehicle and pure intention is your fuel.

The maze was set up by you for you as it represents your choices. Fear is the turn in the maze that leads you away from the center. From our perspective, your five senses are not useful in leading you down the correct corridor. You must quiet the senses so your inner vision, inner hearing, and inner sense of smell can be activated.

We wish to impart to you that you are on a grand joyride, and in the amusement park you call life you face many scary visions. We wish you to find the place in you that is always in equilibrium and which holds the intention for the highest potential in your life. Intention is your light as it illuminates the path that you intend. Intention must be set with your heart and not with your mind. Intention is the key as it creates the reality that you experience and the rest falls into place. Once you set up an intention you must trust that you will be guided.

It is not helpful to go all the way just to turn around at the end, not trusting that you were led correctly. We wish you to climb the train in this amusement park and tell yourself that you want the track that will lead you to the highest spiritual path, then trust the path and enjoy the ride. We see you and your fellow angels building up the most astonishing amusement park and creating your own carts to take you on the tracks of ascension. You are the master and you are enabled to manifest a reality only dreamt of in your past. We wish you to use love and intention when you negotiate left or right in the maze and when you do, you will surely find your treasure and so be it.

The Chicks

*Y*OU WANT PROOF and the proof is already in front of you. The proof lies in those actions that you perform in an awareness that transforms you and others and catapults the situation to its highest potential. You are acting in a world that is limited to 3-D and you wish to see the results of your communication with us in 3-D. We wish to tell you that the results are your feelings and actions while walking in duality in your biology. The results are apparent at every move you make and you wish to see it written on an advertising board or told to you by others. This is not the way of spirit. You are your own alchemist and you transform that which you are. The proof is then in you. The proof is in your feelings and your attitude toward that which you experience. You always have a choice to feel or not to feel, to believe or not to believe, as your intent creates your physical reality. We wish you to know that if you look at yourself from our perspective you are evolving at a tremendous speed and it is a wonder and a joyful event to us that you do. We know of your limitation and we wish to impart to you that you must depart from the "need for proof" in order to fly. When a chick is in the nest and it has not tried to fly yet, it knows that this is its ultimate goal and that its survival depends on it. It must trust its wings to carry it. It always faces the chance of jumping off the tree and crashing to the ground. However the chick has an innate knowledge as to the timing of such an attempt. It will know that it is ready and only then it will attempt to fly. At times it will make its way almost to the ground and at the last moment it will spread its wings and begin its new phase. This is what we are asking from you. Know that you are built to fly. You can flap your wings while sitting in your nest and wait for 3-D signs telling you that you can and are ready to fly. With all love we wish to tell you that this sign will never come. The knowing must come from within and when it comes you must jump.

Nature is your guide as it tells you the story of you. You are part of the birds and the animals, the flowers and the trees. Each and every one of you carries attributes of the "natural world" that is expressed in you. Use the chick as your teacher and observe it. It will teach you by its own action how to learn to fly. You must first learn how to fly and then allow others to observe you. From a student you are becoming a teacher. You do not need to hold gatherings but just to fly. Those who wish to learn will observe you and will gather the necessary tools by watching you. On your path contemplating jumping off the tree and spreading your wings there will be those who will test your resolve. From where we sit, we observe that your tests come mainly from your inner group of family partners, spouses, or close friends. It is your action that may "stir the pot" in those who are close to you. They may feel threatened by you and fear that you are about to learn to fly and thereby leave them. You must know that you will face attempts from those who are close to you to hold your vibration at such a frequency that flying will become impossible. There will be those who will try to tie your wings and keep you anchored to them. We see many of you who choose to cut off your relationships hoping to become free of anchors so you can fly. Many of you, however, discover soon after that you go into new relationships that the same dynamic repeats itself. We also see those of you who just allow your wings to be tied down and give up the idea of flying all together. We hug you and we want to whisper in your ears that we know who you are and what you are going through. We know your challenges and we cry with you when you are in pain. We want to remind you that your mission is grand and the time is now. You are a lighthouse and as such you cannot allow your inner circle to turn off your light. You are meant to show them the light. We spoke to you about heavy and light and how to choose the highest path. Use your tools as your tools are your wings. Give us your hand and ask us for help because we are the air under your wings which pushes you upwards so you can soar to new heights. Every choice you make which is light brings you one step closer to flying.

Why does it have to be so difficult with those who are close to me, some of you may wonder? *We feel misunderstood, and we feel that we chosen the wrong partner,* many of you say to yourselves.

With all love we wish to tell you that a chick flaps its wings and the air acts in resistance to the movement of the wings so the "resistance" actually pushes the body of the chick up thereby assisting it defying the forces of gravity. So it is with you, your close circle acts as the air and their resistance is what helps you to learn to fly. You must use their resistance so you can learn to defy the forces of gravity and take flight. Again it is counter intuitive but it is the way it works. When a chick flaps its wings it is for the purpose of learning the force of the air resistance. It must learn to use the resistance so it can soar above it. This is precisely what we ask you to practice. If you choose to move yourself from relationships because of resistance and seeming incompatibility you are wasting precious time. It is part of your process.

Why can't we find someone like us who have a similar enlightened awareness, some of you ask yourselves? *It would be so much easier.*

We wish to tell you that the resistance will be created even in those partners who are both vibrating at a high level. It will manifest in different forms and it will have different names. If you choose to move away from all relationships that have resistance and surround yourself only with those who support your journey it is as if you light a candle in a very well lit stadium and no one benefits from it. You create light that is not distributed to those who are in the dark. Moreover, when you are around those who are like you, the resistance that you need to learn to fly will not exist and you can flap your wings all you want but the "air" will not carry you. It is as if you place a bird in an environment without air. It will flap its wing but no resistance will be present and the bird's body will not be able to defy the forces of gravity.

Why does it have to be so difficult, some of you may still wonder?

We see those of you who feel tired struggling with those around them who they perceive as lower in vibration. We ask you to go into the circle with us for just a moment. We ask you to remember that you are a part of one consciousness exploring its own magnificence and boundaries. We ask you to understand that you are all brothers and sisters and those who you perceive as the ones who make your life more difficult are your assistants. They come at this time to be the resistance under your wings.

They are necessary for your journey. Do not push them aside because they do not see what you see. They have a different job description then you do. They may come to help you see what you shouldn't do and what needs to be transformed. We never judge you and your free-choice is honored above all. We will never interfere and help you if you do not first ask it of us. We love you regardless of whether you recognize us or not. We see too many of you who choose to discard relationships that they believe are bringing them down, just to find that even those who are considered enlightened offer resistance and challenges of their own. We are in love with you and we wish to tell you that you have a mission that is essential to the evolution of angels walking on earth in forgetfulness. You must be with those who have forgotten so they can remember. We ask you to hold your light even if those who are in the dark call you names and tell you that you are only thinking of yourself. You will be called many names because those who are around you will be threatened by your wish to fly. Remember that they are necessary for your learning and their resistance is the foundation for you conquering gravity. Honor them and hold their presence as sacred. Send them light and continue to do what you feel is your truth. It is your service to them and to humanity at this time. Do not worry about hurting those who are around you. You are hurting them when you believe them and are not living your truth. They count on you to keep your light on no matter what. They signed a contract with you before you came to this planet that you will help them move higher. If you allow their resistance to hold you down you do not fulfill your promise to them and you do not do what you promised to do. Know that you are loved and you are never alone. We wish to tell you that you came here at this time to shine your light and the multitudes around you are counting on your light. You are an angel and you are here to fly. We wish to remind you at every turn that all that you encounter is part of your journey and so you must hold it as sacred. Honor it and know who you are. We wish you to wake up to who you are and know your divinity no matter what others think of you, and so be it.

Fame and Fortune

No matter where you are or what you do you are linked to all that is around you. What you do affects all that is. You are never separated from the universe around you as you are an integral part of it. Your actions reverberate to all that is around you and that is why every action you perform is seen by all of us. Your actions impact the universe and what you do has significance.

I feel so unimportant in the big scheme of things, we hear you say to yourself. *I am so small and insignificant,* we hear others think.

Your actions are not measured by the amount of people who know about them or whether it was reported in the news. The importance of your actions and thoughts are never measured from the human-impact perspective. You are an angel and as such your actions are measured in the realm of heaven not earth. Earth is your stage and heaven is your home. You are an angel who volunteered to come down to play a part that is grand. Part of the role you play is forgetting who you are and trying to rediscover your true identity. We see many of you trying to gain fame and fortune in order to feel more significant and important. We wish to tell you with all love that you do not have to work hard to gain these things. In our realm everyone knows who you are and you are part of the most glorious and grand energy in the universe. Your effort is not only redundant but it is often misdirected. We never judge you and you are free to choose your role. We wish to tap on your forehead if you let us and remind you that your actions are not measured from the temporary fleeting moment you call human life but from the perspective of eternity.

Who you are is not what you see in the mirror. You are beautiful and grand and you are eternal. You appear to us as shapes, melody and colors all swiveling and sparkling. When you act, you create shapes and vibrations which spread to all directions and reach the far corners of the universe in an instant. That is why we ask you to know who you are and know that you are significant. We ask you to understand that as you do what you do as mundane as it appears to you, it has significance. You came to play a role and your mission is to create light and tip the balance of light and darkness on your planet. As such your role is to create and maintain your light at every moment.

How do we do that, some of you may wonder?

It is through the awareness of your actions that you create light. When you walk and act knowing your true identity and act from the source of divinity we call love you are elevating yourself and all that is around you.

How can we create light when all around us there is darkness, others may ask?

With a hug we wish to tell you that your light is allowing those in darkness the option to choose seeing. That is your role and your mission. Most of humanity are in darkness and the job title you were given is light workers or light warriors because your mission is to stay balanced regardless of all the darkness that surrounds you. You were trained for this mission for many expressions and all the knowledge you need is at your fingertips. You are enabled and powerful if you choose to open your eyes and see yourself as you truly are. Those in the dark will want you to be like them. Those in the dark fear light because light automatically transforms darkness and they fear change. Those in the dark will try to get to you by using fear and holding you down so your vibration will not threaten them. Your mission is to keep your light and your vibration and when you do they will run away or transform. The ones of darkness cannot get close to you if you hold your light and if they do their darkness will disappear as they will be illuminated by you.

What is it that you want us to do, some may wonder?

You are to radiate your vibration of love inside of you to those who are trying to tell you that you are hurting them. You are to emit the vibration of love to those around you who will tell you that you are only thinking about yourself and you are inconsiderate. You must project the vibration of love to those who come to you and tell you that if you won't change they will leave you. We ask you to send the vibration of love and stay as you are, doing what you are doing, holding your light and knowing that you are divine and no one can ever make you do or be something else or someone else.

We know of your fears of separation. When you experience fear you cannot emit the vibration of love. We ask you not to fear separation from your fellow angel. When you hold your partner in the highest vibration and wrap them in the energy of love you are opening a door for the highest potential of the relationship to manifest. We know how difficult it is for humans to be together and then separate, we know the challenges of the cords that you develop with your partners and then have to sever. We know the longing of the one who wishes to unite with the other when the roads are blocked. We see you in all your human drama and the fragility of your emotions and we tell you that you are so loved for walking the walk. We wish you to be in a place of love so your partner can use the love vibration you radiate to climb out of their own fears. We ask you to close your eyes and step into the circle where you are always united with all that is. We ask you to feel the hug from us as we surround you and give you our hands. You are walking on earth at a time when the struggle of light and darkness is intensifying as many around you become fearful because the ground under their feet is changing and they feel very insecure. Things do not work as they used to and many do not know what to do.

Know who you are and know that whatever you do in any circumstance has significance and importance. Know that being true to yourself and walking in your divinity is your mission. We ask you to remain the lighthouse regardless of the storm that is coming your way. The lighthouse does not care which storm is coming because its mission is to shine light no matter what. You are that lighthouse and the challenges that you face will increase as the vibration of the earth is moving to the phase we call the initiation of the new energy. This initiation will be marked by your year of 2012 and it will create the potential for peace on earth and a shift of dimensions. Your experiences now are but drills of what is to come. We wish you to know with all love that you are trained for this mission and we ask you to remember who you are and to hold sacred that which you face. We ask you to know that you are built for storms and as painful and threatening as they seem. Know that you can withstand them and come out victorious.

Gaia is creating a vortex for new energy to come in. This new energy is channeled from outer space to support the lighthouses of the planet. Much of this energy is being delivered to you through your sun. We ask you to stay grounded with nature and expose yourself to the sun when you can. Even if you do so for ten minutes a day you may absorb this energy. We wish you to create a sacred space with the sun and nature where you can find your center. We wish you to allow Gaia to support you as it is part of you. It is more important than ever to take the time and connect to the flowers, the trees and the birds. Allow yourself to be part of the energy of the natural world as it has much to teach you. The natural world is you and many of you are separated from it because of your technology and your media. We ask you to search and rediscover that link that you have with the earth under your feet and absorb the love that it has for you. Absorb the love that comes your way from the sun. These are your tools to become powerful. Reconnect with your body and hold a ceremony around it to bless it and give it love. We wish you to love yourself and receive love from the elements. There are many of us who support you as you move forward to meet yourself. You are so dearly loved and we are always with you. We are with you when you doubt us, and we are with you when you are in pain. We see you when you cry and we cry with you. We see your sensitivities and your raw emotions when you are hurt. Know that you are loved and all that you feel is sacred and appropriate for your journey to move forward. Honor that which you face and hold it as sacred. Know that you were meant to be here at this time and that your every action and thought has power. Hold your intention to choose the highest potential in every situation and know that you are divine and that there is never a judgment on what you choose. You are so dearly loved, and so be it.

Angel in Designer Shoes and Tuxedo

W E HAVE BEEN WAITING for this moment when you are ready to receive this message.

Why now, you may ask?

It is in the vibration of the receptivity of your brain that we coordinate our messages accordingly. Your thoughts emit waves and we are riding on your waves and inserting our messages between the polarities of the waves so you will be hearing them clearly. At times we will be ready to deliver a message but as we descend and begin our process of linking with you, our communication gets blocked because your receptivity is not aligned with the frequency of our message. It is then that we must wait for the right moment.

What makes a moment right, you may wonder?

A moment is right when your vocabulary is ready and your inner experiences support the language of the message. It is in your geometry that we can observe your readiness but at times we get ahead of ourselves and we then must slow down and wait for what you already know to be digested. With all love we wish to tell you that it is necessary for you to experience many of the things we speak of so your points of reference will not be theoretical but practical. We also must use your actual vocabulary as our thoughts are vibration and not words so we do not communicate as you do. Your communication is cumbersome and linear as one word must follow another. It takes time and it lacks many multidimensional expressions by which we can describe to you, our reality. It is therefore necessary for us to wait until your vocabulary and experience reach a maturity which supports the vibration of the message. It is then that we hug you and sit all around you to tell you our version of you.

We wish to speak with you about the connection between two angels who come together in a bond of love. We wish to tell you from our perspective how one angel dressed up in designer shoes and a tuxedo falls in love with another angel who wears a long dress at the prom. We wish to speak with you about the mechanics of humans who pair in order to learn about themselves. Each one of you has a pair who is your polarity and it is magnetic, biological, and spiritual combined. You were built to look for a mate as you carry either a masculine or feminine polarity and to find balance you seek the one who balances you and it is by design and appropriate. You may seek the same gender but the polarity still exists. One will represent the male and the other the female. As in your magnets the attraction stems from the tension that is created by each side carrying the opposite charge which then creates electromagnetic polarity. Where there is no polarity the attraction will be weak. Your biology and science tells you that you are attracted to the one who best represents the continuation of your genetic pool and you seek the one who will be most suited to produce babies that will survive and strive. You are told by your scientists that you are like animals looking for a certain set criteria to hook with the one who can continue you gene pool, protect and support you. The lioness will pair with the lion that defeats the other lions, and the female gorilla will pair with the largest and most powerful gorilla that pushes away the competitors and claims its territory. From our perspective this is just a small part of the story. Your story is much larger and much of it is in the circle and not in your biology. You are indeed attracted to the one who can carry your gene pool and bring about the continuation of you. This attraction, however, is not deep as it represents the beginning point of your journey as an angel seeking a partner. From our perspective the biological component is not more than the booster energy that propels you to begin the search. You are a divine being and a part of the energy you call God.

You come to this planet of free choice to learn all aspects of being a human. We love you and we wish to tell you that you are much more than the sum of your parts, biological and otherwise. You can act in your physical world as a walking biology and you can walk in your world as a full-fledged angel. There is never a judgment as to which you choose to be and your choices are sacred and honored. It is our intention, however, to light aspects of you so you will remember your mission and know that the choices you are making are part of your journey. In our realm there is no right or wrong. If you choose a partner and you then realize that it was the "wrong choice", you have learned a lesson and if you made a choice and it lasted a life time you have learned a lesson as well.

Yes, some of you may say, *but by choosing a relationship that broke off I lost much time as well as experienced pain.*

We hug you and we wish to remind you that in our reality you are eternal and time is there to serve your lessons. You have not lost time as time gives you a context through which you can learn and grow. The pain you experienced is your choice as it represents a lesson and by understanding the divinity of your journey you may transform the pain and become peaceful with that which you have experienced. All your relationships are known before you come, through birth, to this planet. It is through contracts that you establish the landmarks of your development as a human. The contracts are based on karma and the lessons that you have not mastered and choose to learn. Before you come you have sessions with those whom you will meet and you align melodies and ways by which you will recognize each other. The melody or frequency of recognition is in the realm that you cannot see but you feel it, as your biology responds to it. When you recognize each other through your melodies you are bridging the realms of spirit with the physical dimension. Some of you call it love at first sight, as if you have seen that person before and you recognized each other. The point of recognition is grand and the process of karmic appointment is magnificent. It is by design, and as you meet someone with whom you have potential of pairing, you will feel it at times as a heat wave flooding you or dizziness. The recognition is often established through the eyes.

Why through the eyes, you may wonder?

Your eyes are a bridge between spirit and matter. They see much more than your brain can interpret and they send you much more information then you can digest. Your eyes see that which is subtle but the brain interprets only that which is biological. It is then that the recognition is registered in the feeling center. Often your heart will beat faster and you may even sweat a little as your body will react with blood overflow.

When you meet someone and it is indeed an appointment an interesting process happens. We can only describe it metaphorically and it will sound funny. In your day-to-day you may experience sending a fax. When you send a fax you may hear a loud beep on the other side. This beep was coined a 'handshake." When this beep is heard it means that a link was created between the sender and the receiver and the fax will go through. If on the other hand there is no fax machine on the other side the sending fax will keep ringing but the fax will not go though as there is no compatible fax on the other side that can "shake the hand" and allow the transmission to pass. It is a similar process in your human pairing process. All of you who are walking in biology have a compatible pairing, someone who can receive your transmission and it is by design. The one who you were meant to meet will meet you because it is by appointment that is always kept. Some of you feel that they need to search through this or that method and often from so much searching you do not realize that the one with the "hand shake" is very close to you and they have been waiting patiently for you to look their way. What we are asking you to do is to open your eyes to the mechanics of your pairing. To us, your pairing process shows up in your geometry. You are multidimensional and as such you have geometric shapes that are all around you. Each one of the geometric shapes in the relationship department represents a potential for learning a lesson. The geometry of a partner that you pair with may be perfectly suited to complement your shape thereby facilitating your lesson. When two meet and the "transmission beep is sounded, the geometric shapes converge perfectly to create a bond that is made in heaven. That is not to say that this bond is easy or peaceful.

What do you mean then, some may ask?

We mean to say that it is an appointment made by you on the other side in order to create a rich environment for your learning and that the appointment was kept and manifested. As you mature you begin to feel the need to find a mate and this need will get stronger and stronger. It has a biological component that you will feel as urge that is both emotional and sexual. The need is based in biology as a catalyst to move you in the direction of mating. It is both to insure the survival of your species and to allow you the most profound environment for spiritual growth. As you search you send sensors out to your environment whether it is at work, at a party or at a social gathering. The sensors are sent both from your energy center we call the solar plexus which is in your third chakra. When you are in the mode of searching, your senses are heightened. Your biological component is looking at the body shapes around you, as well as smelling the scents that are emitted by those whom you deem attractive, but your spiritual component is searching for subtle signs of recognition that you have set up before you came this time around. It as if you are at your fax machine at home dialing all the numbers you were given waiting to hear the beep which represents the "hand shake" on the other side.

How do we know that indeed it is the one for us? Some may wonder.

With all love we wish to tell you that if you are going after your biological component only in an effort to spread your gene pool, your interest will be limited and it will wane rather quickly. It will be as if you are mating with a 2D cartoon figure as the depth of 3-D will not be present. Once the biological component has been satisfied you will lose interest. From where we sit, we see many of you following the dictates of your culture in search for the "right" mate and in doing so you are setting up ideas of what is it that you are looking for. Many of your short-lived relationships are results of you being influenced by what your media, magazines, parents, and culture tells you are appropriate. Once you choose to follow your cultural dictates rather than your heart you will soon realize that the relationship with your chosen mate will unfold as excitingly as your relationship with an animated figure in a video games. You will soon discover that the person you chose is not sounding the "hand shake", so your ringing is going on and on without the transmission going through. You likely will feel then that the learning

or experience you know to exist is not hidden in that relationship so you will either move away or lose interest.

We see those of you who chose their mate based on
color, religion, convenience or just because they are looking and that person is around and available. With all love
we wish to tell you that all relationships offer learning
and all are appropriate. There is never a judgment as to
whom you pair with. You are a divine being and you have
free choice, therefore, your relationships are held as sacred whether they are biological or spiritual in essence.
We wish to impart to you that the relationships that were
written in the heavens are the ones with the spiritual
component in them and they are the one with the "handshake." When you feel the signs of recognition in your
feeling center communicated to you through heat waves,
dizziness, sweating or maybe just rapid heartbeat, at the
moment you met someone, know that your fax just went
through. Those relationships have the potential to offer
you the richest and most rewarding context for learning
as they carry a karmic component and lessons that you
signed up for before coming to this cycle.

*How do we recognize the "handshake," ones with whom
we have contracts, some may still wonder?*

The signs of recognition set before you came to the
planet are complex and vary. To each of you there is a

different sign. The key may be in the voice, gesture, eye contact, even a touch that feels familiar. It may also be buried in your first kiss. There are no rules and we can only impart to you that you yourself may not know where the key lies but you will surely feel that something is happening and your biology is responding to it. You will know when you heard the "hand shake" because your cells will sing a different tune that is aligned with the universal resonance of love.

What happens next, you may ask?

With all love we wish to tell you that your biology kicks in and you will undergo a period of amnesia when the karmic weight is put on hold so you may develop a bond and create a union. It is biological but with spiritual attributes. You may have a period of one to two years when you are in your "in-love" stage. This period is important as it allows you to create the necessary life choices before you get to the "good parts" that are heavy and karmic based. All spiritually based bonds have karmic weight attached to them and learning and a lesson for both angels. Relationships that lack karmic bonds will fizzle rather quickly as your higher part knows that it has little to learn. Some relationships may be peaceful but without the karmic component may also be skin-deep and boring. You are meant to be in relationships that offer challenges and that stretch your limits. You always have the choice of light or darkness as you work through your relationships. You may work your differences out through love or through anger, through drama or through peace but all karmically spiritual bonds offer challenges that are meant to lift both angels, as well as balancing the weight of karma resolving whatever needs to be balanced from previous cycles. Your primary relationships are your richest context for moving higher in your journey. The biological delay imbedded in the term "being in love" is meant to allow you to be at a place of elevated vibration so you will know what you can achieve once the biological euphoria wanes and the karmic learning kicks in. If you had to deal with karma on your first date you might not show up for a second date so this period of being" in-love" gives you time when you can experience that which is the highest flow of love between your partner and yourself. Then you must face karma knowing that you have had this in-love experience and that you can go back to it and be in it with that partner through transforming that which you have to face and moving upward in vibration.

We see some of you who choose to break off your relationships once the "in-love" phase ends and karma begins. With all love we wish to tell you that you are missing the best parts of your learning by doing so. We wish to impart to you that this process will repeat itself in every relationships as it must. You have the potential in your relationships to move from being "in love" to love, honor and respect thereby creating a beautiful melody that is not biologically based but spiritually based and is recorded in your soul and in your akashic records rendering it eternal.

There are some of you however who choose not to engage in intimate relationships. With all love we wish to tell you that your choices are honored and there is never a judgment. We wish to impart to you however that even though you may wish not to engage in intimate relationships you will still seek relationships to grow and learn as relationships act as mirrors for you. It may not be intimate as you may shield yourself from being hurt or touched but you will still have to engage with those who are around you and your lessons will still be there, although it may come to you through family, co- workers and even strangers. You came here to learn about you and you do so by exploring all aspects of you through relationships. Your relationships are your mirror as they reflect you back to you. Metaphorically it is like two musicians who are determined to record a song. They know that they have the potential to create a beautiful melody. First, however, they must learn to harmonize their tunes and create a new melody by using love and compassion where discord and anger existed, and finding peace and balance transforming drama and chaos. Your mission is to find the silver lining of love in all that is offered to you. It is a grand process and one that the universe around you and trillions of entities from all over the cosmos are watching in wonder.

There are still those of you who may ask, *how do we know who is the right person? And is there only one waiting for us?*

With all love we wish to tell you that all the potential relationships exist in the circle and there are many for each of you based on your choices and place of vibration.

How do we know which one to choose then, you may wonder?

The process of choosing the right person to share your life with depends on your intention. When your intention is clear, the prospective relationships that are waiting in the wings will come to the foreground and present themselves.

What if we are not clear, you may ask?

Your lack of clarity will be present in the partner that you choose. It is you who is choosing your lesson and learning. At times the right angel will present themselves to you at a particular time when your intention is not clear and you will feel that you have "missed out." We see those of you who met a person that they know offers the highest potential for growth but for different reasons chose to move away from those relationships only to realize later that they "missed out." With all love we wish to remind you that you are eternal and whatever you "missed out" on, you can revisit in your future cycles. It is however our intention to make you aware that indeed there is one potential relationship who offers the highest potential for your growth.

How do we know who they are, you may wonder?

When you are faced with the potential relationship that offers you the highest path, it may come in a package that is less attractive then what you imagined or have been sold on by your culture or your media. The relationships that hold the highest potential may come with a different skin color, race, language or height. It may come to you without the prerequisite cultural "musts" of diploma and a great job or stable income. We wish to tell you with all love that it is by design and appropriate as it is part of your test.

Your journey is about bridging the reality of 3-D to the reality of spirit. Much of it comes as transparent and without large tags that give you instructions. You must use your inner guidance and knowing to navigate. The choice of a life partner has to come from knowing. The knowing has to come from intention to be with a partner that offers you the highest potential for developing your divinity and releasing your karma. When you are clear, that partner must show up. It is the way spirit works.

What if we missed out, you may ask?

As we hug you we wish to tell you that in the circle you have not missed out. It is part of your lesson and you must become peaceful with that as well. Your missing out was a potential that did not manifest and you should not dwell on that. Your mission is to find divinity and love in whatever crosses your path and become peaceful with those things you rendered painful. From where we seat, there is nothing you missed out on. You have trillions of potentials and the potential you choose to manifest is the one accurate and correct for you based on your vibration and lessons, and it is always appropriate. It is therefore your mission to be in the now and in gratitude no matter what and who you believe you have missed out on. We wish to tell you that the process of finding a partner is eternal and those you have missed will come to you soon enough when you go back home. When you return you may set up yet another potential and that one may indeed manifest. You are never too far from anything as energetically you are connected to all the angels in your physical world and in our dimension. We wish to tell you that you are always loved and never alone. Your choices are always honored and your path is sacred and celebrated by all of us. We love you so and we wish you to always choose light over dark and your highest potential over your lowest potential. We wish you to know that you are beautiful and divine and your biology does not begin to tell the story of your magnificence. We wish you to honor your path and celebrate every moment that you are in physical form, and so be it.

2012 Time Warp

WE WISH TO SPEAK of where you are at this moment. You are living in a time that is warping in front of your eyes. The future mixes with the past and the present is accelerating to the point where you feel you have to chase it. It is as if you have been waiting for a bus and without you noticing it the bus has passed you by and you find yourself chasing after it. That is metaphorically how many of you experience time. There are those of you who feel that you are walking behind your own self and that reality is moving faster than you are. Events are being replaced with events and drama follows drama so much so that you cannot distinguish between one drama and the next. For many of you one day becomes the next and everything seems to be moving except you. Those of you who watch the news and expose yourselves to world's events cannot keep track of all the threats and disasters that are striking all around you. We see many of you getting more confused by the day. It is indeed a confusing time and we wish to hug you and let you know that this is just the beginning. What you see is light exposing that which was hidden. Your world is not darker than it was and in actuality it is becoming lighter.

It is the process of shifting that you are now witnessing. We wish to speak with you about the year 2012 and what it means in the scheme of your daily lives.

There are many speculations and comments written about the Mayan calendar and the significance of 2012. Some called it the end of the world and some called it the end of time as we know it. We wish to tell you how we see your shift from our perspective. You were on track to end your civilization and human life on your planet around your year 1998-9. That was not just a prediction but it was a real potential that all of you knew about before you came to this planet. You knew about it and you still chose to come. Not long ago, a dramatic turn has taken place which directed the energy of the planet to shift from its expected trajectory. The shift brought forth new cosmic energy. That shift marked the beginning of a new era. It was marked by a new infusion of cosmic events which supported your shift. In your year of 1987 an event that was coined the "harmonic convergence" occurred. It marked a delivery of a new paradigm. It was magnificent and it hallmarked the shift of dimensions that you are now experiencing. It reinforced the change in direction from masculine energy back towards the feminine Goddess energy on the planet. The change was already in place but this event accelerated the shift.

Why is it the termination did not take place, some of you may wonder?

It was the balance of light and dark that shifted your potential. The test was about the balance of light and dark created on the only planet of free choice where angels walk disguised as humans. The balance of darkness was dominant for a long time and then something happened that none of us predicted. The balance began to shift to a place of neutrality as more and more light was created on your planet. It was at this point that a cosmic event took place. We can describe it as the "reading" of the balance of light and dark on your planet. It was found that the vibration of the planet increased to such an extent that you could potentially change the trajectory of your journey. It was then that the collective consciousness that you are part of was asked if you want to continue the test or terminate it as scheduled.

Who was asked exactly, you may wonder?

With all love we wish to tell you that you are one consciousness exploring itself as trillions of parts that are all connected to that one consciousness. All those who comprise that consciousness were asked as were those who were part of the Lemurian energy that housed the planet in your past; indeed all consciousness that has ever lived and will live in physical form on the planet were asked.

The reality of the past, present and future is in the circle where there is only now. Those who were asked are those who occupy the circle in the reality of now and are connected energetically to this test on your planet. It was magnificent and the answer was a resounding "yes, we do want to continue." This choice of cosmic proportions resounded in the universe and many of the events you are witnessing in your reality that are coming into being started then.

What events are you talking about, you may wonder?

The world script began to shift and the threat of the extinction of human life on the planet was changed. Some of the players who were part of the doomsday scenario dropped their plans and disseminated peacefully. Within a short period of time you have experienced a new reality in which the players who would have begun the devastation of your species had shifted to where that was no longer necessary or desired. It was then that many of the energies in the universe that are helping you now began their journey toward your part of the universe. You became the "talk of the town" as every entity knew about your decision and it was celebrated. Your decision not only affected you but had a major significance for the entire universe as your energy is applied to the creation of other tests in other places.

We told you that energetically you are linked to all that is and what you do reverberates and resounds in the universe. That is why we tell you that what you do matters and how you think matters. This is why we repeat over and over that you are beautiful and powerful and you changed your future by changing your "now." Your existence and experience is in your hands and you can manifest that which you wish for. As we hug you we tell you that you have changed that which was scheduled for you and it is time for you to make the additional leap and bring this planet up to a higher vibration where peace on earth can be manifested. It is up to you. You are the bringer of light. Light is channeled through you and manifested in what you now see all around you.

We see so much darkness everywhere, some may say. This darkness would not be exposed if it were not for you. Through the light that you are emitting you are exposing the darkness and that darkness is slowly transforming. You see it as darkness but from where we sit watching you, your planet is being illuminated more than ever before. We are in awe of your progress.

How does it connect to 2012, you may ask?

The year 2012 represents the last reading of the balance of light and dark in this test on earth. It would mark 25 years from the previous reading. The final reading is the end of the experiment. The balance of light and dark will be measured and it will mark the end of time as you know it and a beginning of the cosmic chain of events that we have named the "collision of dimensions." These events will take your planet to a different vibratory level. It is as if you are nearing graduation and your test scores are taken to measure how you did. Based on the balance of light and dark your planet and the angels walking in duality with free choice will begin shifts that are biological, spiritual and dimensional.

What kind of shifts are you speaking of, some may wonder? *Are we sure to pass the test,* others may ask?

We are in love with you and we wish to tell you that your path is honored and you are celebrated just for walking the walk. You are well on your way to pass the test but you are the only ones who have charge of your future. Even spirit does not know how it will end or continue as it is your free choice that is honored and what you do is sacred. We wish to tell you that you, the light workers, are the ones who volunteered to facilitate this cosmic event and channel the light necessary to catapult earth consciousness to a new level, thereby opening its door to other dimensions. Your task is of such proportions that you cannot even imagine it in your 3-D reality. There are multitudes of entities from the universe that are here to facilitate your graduation. Your ascension is being supported by all the masters that ever walked on the planet. You are more enabled than ever before in your current biology. You have all the support and you are doing a magnificent job.

What will happen to us as we approach 2012, you may wonder?

Your planet's magnetic grid has shifted to allow you to shift your vibrations and your abilities have been enhanced. You are coming into a reality where time will warp around itself and dimensions will begin to collide. It may seem very disconcerting to some of you. The dimensional shift will mark the splitting of old and new energies. The new takes hold and the old energy recedes. The battles that we can only describe as light transforming dark will continue for some time but as more light floods your planet the dark will go into hiding or transform. The energy of Gaia that you are part of will go through a cleansing and readjustment period and it will manifest as shaking tremors, bursts and purging of different types. It is appropriate and by design and we wish you to stay balanced throughout this process as it is sacred as well. Gaia is responding to your intent and it is adjusting accordingly. Your mission is to be in a place of love throughout this process. Each one of you who turns on their light can support thousands of "angels." These "angels" will not know your name but they will see light and use your light to navigate their own path.

What do you mean, some of you may ask?

We ask you with all love to see yourself as a lighthouse whose light is showing those who are in the dark the way to safety. Each one of you, when awakened energetically, can make a difference in the life of multitudes of angels. *"How," You may still wonder?* What you do in the moment to moment script of your life is emitting light. Others use your light to see. You will get neither ribbons nor trophies for this. No one will give you money or prizes but your every move is watched and celebrated by us on the other side as you manifest your highest potential in this time of ascension. Not all of you will go all the way and there is never a judgment on how you do and how far you go. We only ask you to wake up to your mission and know that you were meant to be here at this time and that what you do is important. We ask you to celebrate your challenges as they represent the appointments where the light that you potentially create brings more luminosity. The more difficult the test the more light you can potentially create.

What will happen on 2012, some of you may ask?

2012 is just a marker when the new energy will begin to take hold and the shift of consciousness and dimensions will become more apparent. It will mark a shift where the babies that are being born will come with enhanced biology that will enable them to communicate with us more easily. The vortexes to what you call "alien life" that you have been searching for will open up. It will be a grand event when "aliens" will land on your front porch and introduce themselves to you. Many of you will be surprised to discover that they are very much like you. You will then realize that they have been with you observing and interacting with you all along. They will not manifest themselves to you before your vibration reaches a certain level but you are approaching that level. Your year of 2012 is the marker for these changes.

Are we to fear the events that will be forthcoming, some may still wonder?

Fear will be a choice that many of those who are in darkness will select and it will create a further distance between the old energy and the new. Fear will be used by the dark to keep its hold. Those who choose to experience fear could have a challenging time with the upcoming shifts. We ask you to know that there is nothing to fear, as you are masters of your own reality. Nothing that you will undergo can touch you if you choose to keep your light. Furthermore, your light is used as a guide for others who may look to you as an example without even realizing it and take strength from yours in order to move forward. Know that you are built for storms and you have trained for this throughout your lifetimes on this planet as well as on other planets. This is your job description and you are coming to a time when you will need to utilize all you know to catapult the shift that is marked by your year 2012. Know that it is grand. With all love we ask you not to give speeches or march on the street. Your work is through vibration and inner transformation. You are to maintain your inner balance and know that all that is around you is appropriate and by design. Know that your challenges are there to bring you to an elevated place where you can use the knowledge of the master that you are. We wish to impart to you that you are a master and you must wake up to your mission as it is approaching you.

What is our mission again, some may wonder?

As we hug you and sit all around you we whisper in your ear that your mission is to walk in the knowledge that you are a master. Your mission is to know who you are and stay with love, balance, peace and joy inside of you no matter what faces you in your outer experiences. Know that you are loved and supported by legions of us and that you are celebrated daily for your path. Know that it is you who have chosen to bring the new energy. Know that it is you who choose to bring more light. Know that it is you who are here at this time to facilitate the greatest leap in human consciousness this planet have ever experienced. We ask you to celebrate every moment of every day because it is the "now" that you have and that you must build on. Know that you are powerful and walk in the knowledge that the mastery is already inside of you. We ask you to wake up and use the tools that are already in you. Know that you are a divine angel and you are dearly loved, and so be it.

Bond and Bondage

WE HAVE BEEN AROUND you from the beginning. You know who we are because we have been part of you and you have been part of us. We are family and as such we are connected to you all the time. We are excited when you begin to look for us. It is, however, often that you begin your search outside of yourself and although we tap on your shoulder and tell you that we are right here all around you and inside you, many of you do not hear us. We love you and we are very patient. It is part of your journey to discover your divine family and the family that is waiting to be found is always around. Even when you do not believe we exist we are there loving you. Even if you think that all this is just a pile of nonsense we still love you the same. Does it tell you something about your divine family? We never judge you ever. You are honored no matter what you choose. You are celebrated just for choosing to walk the walk. We know that when you come back home, we all get together and laugh at those moments that you insisted that we did not exist. After the celebration and the hugging is over you say to us, "sure I want to go back and this time I will link with you, you will see."

Why are you telling us about our divine family, you may ask?

It is because your path is opening up and you will need to navigate through thick forest at times and you will need to use your senses to walk in the dark and light your path with only your inner flashlight at your side. We ask you to let us in and allow us to walk with you, hand-in-hand, because the meld that is created when you open up to who you really are, is magnificent. We wish you to be in the awareness of your divinity so you'll know where to go when there are no road signs.

Are you telling me that something bad or scary is going to happen?

We wish to tell you that you are living at a time of the initiation of a new reality and many things are changing as we speak. The vibration of the planet is changing and the magnetic grids are changing, your biology is changing, and your physiology is changing. Everything around you is swirling faster and faster as it is appropriate and by design, your design. We ask you to recognize the tools that are at your disposal and use them. In your day-to-day, these tools need to be assimilated and practiced so when you need to use them you will be proficient in the mechanics of the tools.

What should we expect, you may wonder?

We love you so and we tell you that there is nothing to fear from your own journey. Know that you are a master and that which is in front of you is there to guide you to where you asked to be. Know that nothing can touch you without your permission. We wish you to hold the torch high so that many angels will be able to use your light. We ask you to be at your prime in terms of your link to your divine family so that we can walk hand in hand through this together.

It is a grand time indeed and if you choose to use fear you will miss out on the magnificence of this experience. Fear will take you to where it is dark. All the action that we speak of that is now around you is in the realm of light and if you choose to stay in the dark you will not experience any of it. We see those who choose to be on the defensive and say to themselves, "It is going to get worse and I am fearful, let me pile up on some supplies and go to the mountains where it is safe." We wish to tell you with all love that this is precisely where it is dark. Your mission has to do with being that which you are: a lighthouse. Hiding a lighthouse away from the action renders it useless. The place that you were meant to be is where you are: with and around action. Your mission is not to find refuge from all that is around you so you can "rest a little" and "gather yourself." We know who you are. There is never a judgment and your choice is sacred. We wish to impart to you that moving away from your challenge is precisely what lighthouses do when they turn off their light and go to the mountains. Ships do not sail in the mountains so they cannot use your light to navigate. We ask you to link with your divine family and find the tools to light your own path and the path for others because there is no other time and storms will come as it is appropriate. You are needed and your light is needed. We ask you to sit quietly in the middle of the storm. Light a candle and take a deep breath. We ask you to give a hug to yourself and smile knowing that you arrived at the most magnificent time this earth has seen and that you are so blessed to be around. Know that you have all you need and that you are powerful. Congratulate yourself for being at that place and let us hug you as well.

How will I know it is you, you may wonder?

You will know us because you will feel warmth around you and inside of you. You may even sense a faint scent of a perfume you cannot recognize but it smells wonderful. You know it is us because if you allow yourself to feel and open up, you will feel loved.

Why do I need to know all that, you may wonder?

It is a time like no other when the whole premise you were grown and raised on is shifting. It can feel like you are walking on a white water raft and everything seems to be out of control. The only balance you can count on is your inner balance. There will be many tests that will be set for you so you can practice your inner balance. There will be those around you who will show you how a person without inner balance looks and acts. They will mirror to you your potential. They will show you the opposite of what you should be. It is by design as well and is done with love. Those who are out of balance are assisting you in understanding your role, becoming a master. There will be those who are in your close circle, may it be family, friends or co workers, who will come to you unbalanced. They will ask you to be unbalanced with them.

Why would they want me to be imbalanced, you may ask?

It is part of your duality that in order to disperse anxieties and fears you ask those who are around you to be anxious and fearful like you. They are those who, in order to feel that they are okay, ask those around them to feel the same so they will be empowered. You think that together you are stronger in fear. That is why societies and governments often use fear, anger and hate to bond their people together. The energy of fear has been utilized in your history many times to maneuver and exploit situations so as to create bonds and bondage. We wish to impart to you that from our perspective that tendency is moving in the opposite direction of spirit as it uses darkness to create more darkness. When those around you ask you to join them in their darkness we ask you to remain the lighthouse and shine your light. It is seemingly easier to join the dark and appease those whom you love and respect. It is again moving away from your mission as you are to maintain the awareness of the unshakeable master and keep the light illuminated so others can see. We wish to impart to you that in time those who try to move you to their camp so they can feel stronger in fear, will come back to the light if they so choose. You are not responsible for their choices nor can you force them to accept your light. All you can do is what lighthouses do; shine your light. Lighthouses cannot prevent the storms that are surging but they can remain in a place that shows others the path to safety.

What is it that you ask us to do then?

We are your brothers and sisters and your family. We ask you to know who you are and understand that you are eternal and that which you experience is your mission. We wish you to experience the sacredness of the moment by moment of your time on this planet and honor all those who are part of your experience. We ask you to pull yourself above the 3 dimensions of your limited reality and join us in a place that is so beautiful that it feels like a huge cotton ball, all huggy and soft. It is a place in your heart that yearns to open to all that you are. When you are walking in a place of love and you know that you are a master, all the elements and the natural world bow to you when you pass by. They all congratulate you on your discovery. Even the dogs on the street will see it and follow you with their gaze when you pass them by. They can see more than humans can. They see the divinity that each one carries and they honor it as well. Your plants at home will see it and will respond to it. You are part of everything and everything is part of you. We ask you to walk in the knowing that with each breath you are transforming the energy of the planet bringing it to a higher vibration, and so be it.

The Marathon

I T I S O N Y O U to choose your road. You have choices and the roads split all the time. You usually have two choices in each intersection, left or right. There is always a choice that represents your highest potential, and a choice that represents the light. We do not mean that the other represents the dark. We are with you all the time, and your choices are never judged. Whatever you choose is honored and is seen by all of us as sacred.

We wish you to open your senses and allow yourself to feel which road is the one that will lead you to your highest destination.

What is the difference between the high and the low, you may inquire?

The difference is in the way you feel about the moment-by-moment journey you call life. Feeling is the part of you that is a part of spirit as well. When you are walking as a human, your feelings register with your higher part which is spirit. When you feel elevated, acknowledge your divinity and walk in mastery it is as if you activate spirit within you and walk the walk of a master.

Why are you telling us about it?

We wish to tell you as we hug you that we know your challenges. Your challenges come to you seemingly one after the other, and when you solve one you are already preparing for the next one. There is no peace and no vacation. This is your journey as you must change all the time; your biology changes and the circumstances around your life changes. You are connected to a web of angels and each one is undergoing their own shifts and challenges. When you are experiencing your life you are also experiencing the challenges of all those who are connected with you. It is designed that way and it is appropriate. Your journey is about work and transformation.

We wish to impart to you that you can change the way you feel about yourself and your journey when you use the tools of the master and ascend to a higher vibration. From that vibration the vista begins to open in front of your eyes and you see that the challenges are beautiful and magnificent in scope and complexity and you begin to find peace with all that is. When you ascend in vibration, all those challenges that are supposed to shake you, to cause you to feel heavy and to worry become just another piece of the puzzle that when you complete it spells the word *love*. From the higher vantage point, the love of family and of spirit becomes apparent, and you cannot help but smile and feel the warmth flood you. You then realize that you are so dearly loved and that you are fortunate to be here now and to experience that which you have to face. It is no longer outside circumstances that dictate the way you feel. You take the reins of your feelings in your own hands. The way you feel remains balanced no matter what happens outside of you. That is mastery and that is where we wish to hold your hands and lead you to. This is your mission and your goal.

You are to discover that you are a divine being and that those things that present themselves to you throughout your journey are your choices and they are there to teach you about you and to take you to a place that is higher if you so choose. Many of you are under what we call the weight of gravity. We see those of you who carry heavy loads, and your back is all slouched and stooped. We see those of you who say to yourselves, "this is too much. I have been walking on this path with this weight for so long hoping that it will get lighter and it has become heavier. I want to stop and get off this road because it brings me only more weight." We see you and we love you. We know how you feel and we feel your heaviness as we are with you all the time. We would love you to know that when compared to a marathon race you are in the final stretch and there are trillions of us cheering you on. Every step you take gets you closer to where you need to be. We wish to tell you that in this marathon race you are carrying with you the vibration of the planet so your race has high stakes. The completion of your race holds magnificent potential for humanity and the establishment of peace on earth. It feels so difficult because you have been at it for so long and you are tired. You carry with you the knowledge and memory of the whole race and now that you are in the last portion of your journey we wish to tell you: "Do continue." We are all watching you and we wish you to open your ears for just a moment to hear the cheering and the clapping that is coming from the sidelines. You are so dearly loved and we see that your legs are tired, your heart is beating fast and you are not sure if you can make it to the next curve. We ask you to not think of the next turn. Just be in the moment and think of the next step. Your journey is about moving step by step and heartbeat by heartbeat.

We feel that all around us people are happy who seems to be living in darkness and we are supposedly with the light and are so burdened; is this fair, some of you may ask?

You are seeing only part of the journey of so-called "happy people." We wish to tell you that your journey is designed in such a way that you must face certain challenges as you move along your path. You must face your biology, aging, and losing dear ones; you must face loss and you also must face your own mortality. Many of you must face many other challenges besides these. When you say, "I see that others are happy," you see only a small part of the story. "Happy" is something you feel at the moment when something good happens to you, and then a moment later you feel sad because you faced something else which reversed your feeling of happiness. We see many of you who need to put on masks and manipulate your chemistry through alcohol and drugs in order to flow in what you call "happiness." We see those who must hide behind such costumes to feel secure in their "happiness" but when alone in front of the mirror that happiness disappears. We know who you are, and we love you just the way you are without preservatives and chemicals. We wish to tell you that if you removed the masks and the chemicals from the lives of many of the "happy people" around you, it would change their balance.

When we speak of moving upward it is not to a place of happiness but to a place of being in love with yourself and humanity. Happiness is just one side effect of being in that state of awareness. We wish to tell you that it is your contract to bring light to this planet at this time. There are few of you compared to the ones who walk in darkness, and your light is what changes the lives of all those who walk in darkness. You are doing the work for many, and that is why it feels so heavy. You carry the load because you are trained for this race. You have been coming here life after life, running marathons so you can complete the race and know that you have done what you came here to do. Do you wish to quit the race when you have so little to finish what has been in the works for thousands of years? It is the race that you have come this time to finish. Why would you quit just when you can smell the end?

What will happen when we finish, you may ask?

When you finish you will feel that you are at the most glorious place a human can be, and you will be on the victory stand. You will know that this is where you need to be and that you are one of the few who brought about the biggest shift on earth in your history, a shift that is so big that it will catapult the consciousness of humanity to a new dimension.

What dimension will that be, you may wonder?

You are coming into a dimension that can be called a new galactic dimension in which you begin to converse with all that are around you. You will no longer feel that you are alone in the universe. You are coming to a place of vibration that may show you the reality of your divinity and journey. In the process you will get to know some of the players who have been facilitating your journey for eons. A communication will follow in which part of the mystery you call life will be unraveled in front of your eyes, and you will be in awe.

Know that you play a part in bringing that shift. When the marathon is completed, you will know that you were and are at the right place at the right time and those who escorted you throughout this race and who are invisible now will come forward and introduce themselves to you. Would you want to miss such an event?

How are we supposed to run the marathon when we are getting distracted by so many other things?

As we hug you we wish to tell you with all love that the "distractions" are the race. And your running is your moving forward despite the things that try to keep you tied down and constrained. You are continuing to run, and we can only tell you that the secret to a successful completion of the race is in your biology as well as in your intention. You must take care of the vehicle you call your body. You must honor it and love it as without it you cannot run. You must hold your vehicle sacred. With all love we wish to tell you that you also must honor all the challenges that represent your race and thank them for being part of your energy. Your goal is to reach a point where you vibrate higher than ever before and your vibration lights the way to all those with whom you come in contact.

We still feel heavy, you may say.

We wish to impart to you that your journey is about finding peace with all that is and understanding that it is all your creation for the purpose of teaching you about you. It is in your awareness of your reality that transformation takes place. When you find peace and balance within you, your reality will shift to accommodate your new awareness. When enough of you reach the fulcrum point in which you are at balance and peace, you will change the reality on this planet and bring it to its highest point thus far.

Isn't it grand enough for you?

How can we do that when all around us our relationships are trying to hold us back from running the race?

We wish to tell you again that you are in a place of duality. Your relationships are not holding you back from running. Your relationships are the race. You are to transform yourself and move forward as your relationships represent the road, the curves, the hills, the blisters and the pain you feel as you continue the marathon. Honor them as they represent the road to completion.

Know that it is a difficult road and that you can do it as you have trained for it and you have the "know-how."

How do we know that we arrived at the end destination and have completed the race?

You will know because you will feel your entourage waiting for you, cheering you and hugging you. You will know because you will feel bliss and joy and nothing will be able to shake those feelings as they will become you. You will embody the feeling of love, and you will become the one who holds the energy of a master no matter what. You will know because you will have only love in you for those around you and only compassion for those you encounter. You will know because the natural world will greet you wherever you go. You will know because it is as if you become someone else and you will fall in love with yourself. You will know because it will mean that you have discovered your own divinity and it will show on your face. We are asking you for the last time, why would you want to miss such an opportunity? And so be it.

The Ride

HAVE YOU EVER RIDDEN on a merry-go-round? Your answer most probably is, "Yes! Of course we have. Why would you want to know?"

We see where you are heading, and it may feel like a recreation park, at times like a joy ride, and at other times, like a nightmare, so much so that you wish it were over. From where we stand you are about to enter a time in which you will feel much as if you are in an amusement park where you can choose all kind of rides. Some rides will feel very uplifting, and some will feel scary. It is up to you to choose the experience and the ride that you want to be on.

How should we choose, you may ask?

As you enter a period of changes, you must be one with the change. We wish you to be in the awareness that what you are experiencing is an inner process manifested in your outer reality, therefore, you must always seek higher ground of awareness in which you benefit from your experience. We wish you to be in the now so those rides you are on will feel like part of you. It is very disconcerting for humans to go through major changes. We wish to tell you that you are about to experience major changes.

How do we prepare, you may wonder?

Some will stock up on food and water, and some will sell all they have and wait for the change to come. This is your 3D way of preparing as you are built for survival and you wish to make sure you can ride out the storms.

Your response is understandable. We speak, however, of another kind of preparation. We wish to impart to you that for you to benefit most from this journey, you must enter the realm of interdimensionality in which you ride with the changes to a higher consciousness and open yourself up to realms that merge with yours. It is a grand time and a time for celebration. Many of you are accustomed to seeking shelter when storms come. You wait in your shelter until the wind subsides and then you go out and assess the damages. We wish to impart to you that you could be both protected from the changes and experience them at the same time in all their grandeur.

How can we do that, some may ask?

When you are standing on a deck overlooking the ocean while a hurricane approaches, you see the imminent signs of darker clouds, powerful winds, and high surge. You retreat to higher ground, seeking a place that you assume will be safe from the approaching storm. But this storm is different as the "hurricane" will be experienced both in your outside reality and within you. It will be as if you and the storm are one, occupying the same space.

This is what we speak of when we compare it to a joy ride. The seat, which you occupy while going in the "big loop ride," becomes part of you. You and the seat become one as you both experience the same forces of gravity and inertia.

This sounds too scary, some may say. *There is nowhere to hide*, others may surmise.

This is precisely what we speak of. There will be no place to hide and more important, hiding will be an inappropriate reaction from our perspective.

What are we to do then, some may ask?

"You are to stand tall and shine your light," is our answer.

How can we shine our light with such winds and stormy weather, you may wonder? Shouldn't we hide for a while until the storms subsides?

We wish to remind you yet again that you are dearly loved and there is never a judgment as to what you do and how you do it. We are here just to remind you a little so you may recall why you came here at this time. The changes that are coming are your choice and you came here to be part of this ride. You came here to be the lighthouse during the storms. You came here to stand tall when the waves get high so the ships can see where they are going and find refuge from the high waves. You came to be exposed to the elements and lose your fear of survival. That is what your mission is, and you are trained to do it.

Many of you will be seeking shelters to hide, but from where we sit you will not find a space where one can truly hide because the storms are interdimensional, and they are multi-level, both subtle and physical. You will experience changes that are magnetic, electro-magnetic, vibrational and dimensional, and they will shift both your subtle fields as well as your 3D landscape. All humans who walk on earth at this time will be effected and experience the changes. These changes we speak of are not only geographically centered; they are also on all planes of existence. This is why we tell you to be prepared to walk the high ground because there is no sitting this one out.

Should we be fearful of what's to come, some may ask?

Fear is your choice, and fear will be avoiding the experience you have waited for, for so long.

What is coming, you may ask?

We can only see probabilities as the future is in your hands. We see the probability for waves of dimensions merging and colliding, which are indeed magnificent cosmic events. We see the probability for a showdown display of the power of Gaia in all its glory and divinity. If you are in fear you will only think of how to survive this one and miss the awesomeness of the moment. We wish you to remind yourself that you are eternal and you are one of the designers of that which you experience. We wish you to celebrate the moment and understand that you must be in a place of balance allowing your feelings to move through you like a vessel without holding on to anything. Do not hold on to your survival, do not hold on to fear, and do not hold on to your idea of your limited self. This is a time of expansion. You must let go of what you think you need to protect because there is no protection in this scenario. Anything you attempt to protect would only lessen your experience. Metaphorically, it is as if you are the seat on the "joy ride" and as such you are just there without judging and without holding back. You are to allow that which is in front of you to carry you to where it may go, and your task is to stay balanced and peaceful so you can feel it in its entirety. Should you attempt to hold back and protect yourself or use your old method of fear you may miss the opportunity that you now have, moving higher in consciousness.

Do you want us to take risks? Do you wish us to not protect ourselves and risk losing our lives, some may ask?

With all love our answer is no. We wish you to live longer and healthier than ever before. We wish you to stay on this planet so you can be the pioneers of these magnificent changes that you are undergoing. You are less useful to the planet as a baby at this time because you cannot be a lighthouse in a diaper. We wish to tell you that when you keep your fulcrum point in balance you will know where to go when the surge gets high and the winds get strong. You will be protected not because of your being in fear but because you will be aligned with the energy of Gaia, and she will direct you to where it is safe. Using fear and hiding will not necessarily take you to the right place where you are truly protected. Staying balanced and peaceful will allow the communication to flow and for you to be tuned to the "radio station" which is broadcasting in the correct frequency. When you remain with the correct frequency, the information you receive is not only accurate, but also it will guide you to where it is safest and where you can fulfill your mission and help others.

We wish to impart to you that your shift from thinking to feeling is important because the frequency of the messages being transmitted during the period of energetic transformation are sent to your feeling centers. The information may seem illogical at times and even irresponsible, but we urge you to listen to your feelings and allow yourself to follow that which feels right.

When is all that going to happen, some may wonder?

It has been happening and is happening, and it will keep happening in greater frequency and intensity. What you feel all around you, whether you are at a place that has been affected in 3D or not, is pressure and a sense of the greater velocity and intensity of your day to day life. You may have the same routine and not much might have changed, but many of you who are open and vibrating at a higher frequency will feel the changes all around them. The changes are here, and all we ask you to do is wake up to your mission because there is no more sleeping. You must awake whether it is through our bells or through the wind knocking on your window.

There are already many subtle changes taking place all around you that are aligned with these shifts and those of you who are connected to the birds, the plants, the trees, and the dirt under your feet will be observing abnormalities from the way they knew things to be. Anomalies will become the norm as nature is part of you and it is undergoing shifts just like you. There are also observable changes taking place in the planets that occupy your solar system. You will be observing events that your scientists normally consider long-term cosmic processes manifesting in a very short period of time. Your whole reality is shifting in front of you whether you acknowledge it or not.

Do you still feel powerless? You are a master, and you collectively are the one who brought these changes as part of the energy you call God. It is a time of great significance – inside you, on your planet, and on all dimensions in your universe and other universes.

What is it that we need to do with all that information?

As we hug you we ask you to simply understand that all that you can do is be in the awareness of love in all that takes place around you and when interacting with your brothers and sisters. Shine your light, always choosing the highest potential when you reach an intersection. We wish you to give intent to move higher in vibration and to stay peaceful and balanced throughout this transformation. Know that you are a master and all that you witness around you is part of the energy you call love, and it is there to take you with it. We wish you not to resist it but to ride it on the journey of your life to a place of bliss and joy and higher dimensions. Your attitude will determine your destination, and your use of emotions and thoughts will be more crucial during these times. We ask you to be enveloped in the energy of love and create that sacred space within you that knows who you are and what your mission is. As we hug you we wish to tell you that you are fortunate to be here at this time and we are fortunate to be your companions, and so be it.

The Magic Carpet

YOU CAME HERE to discover that which you have lost. Your path of discovery is one of adventure. The task upon you is to choose whether you wish to keep looking for the treasure or settle down and claim that you have found it precluding the need for further searching.

We see many of you who began the search for what you felt you lost. We see you beginning the search and just when it gets interesting and challenging you stop, claiming you have found the treasure. We are in love with you and we are walking with you every day of your life. It is through love that we are connected to you and never through judgment. Although you may never acknowledge that we exist, we still love you just as much. We see you when you are climbing up the mountains through the thick forests, scratched and bruised, feeling as if the journey is impossible. We see you when you are tired, feeling you have no energy for the next step. We know who you are, and we want to tell you that there is a difficult path, and there is a lighter, easier path. Both are sacred, both are divine, and both get you to a higher place. It is your choice, and we wish to speak of the choice of the human to experience suffering in order to ascend or to experience joy and pleasure as she ascends.

We must tell you that it is not a requirement to suffer and bleed as you ascend in vibration. Many of you carry memories of the process and believe that it is through pain and suffering that you become pure and divine. Some of you believe that it is through the life of lack that you get closer to God. There are still those who feel that they somehow satisfy God if they do not take care of themselves, neglecting their passions and doing only those things that benefit others. We see many of you who are committing to a life of service and we want to hug you and ask you, "Who are you serving?" "We are serving God," some may answer. Other may say, "We are helping those in need so the earth will be a better place." With all love we wish to tell you that you are honored for doing that which benefits your brothers and sisters and you are honored as well for searching for God in whatever form you deem appropriate. The journey is about intent, and when you walk with pure intent you walk the elevated path, and it is sacred indeed. With all love we wish to tell you, however, that you must serve yourself first as you are a piece of God, and your divinity is your birth right. Once you have learned self-service and mastered self-love, you are servicing all those who come in contact with you. By being in service for self you are emitting the most powerful beam of light. When we speak of service for self, we do not mean being selfish or self-centered.

What do you mean then, some may wonder?

We ask you to find your truth, be who you are, and love who you are. When you have learned to love yourself and acknowledge your divinity, you become an instrument of love and compassion to all those who come in contact with you. They see you walk in divinity and learn from you. This is what we mean by serving yourself first. From our perspective the geometry of service is embedded in the power of your light, and your light is without filters when you have mastered self-love.

When you neglect the self, inevitably you will emit the geometry of lack rather than abundance. When you take on the role of suffering in order to serve humanity, your geometry will ooze the energy of suffering to those around you. For you to emit the most powerful light without filters of lack, suffering, or self-neglect, you must first conquer self-love, and from there you may do service just by being in that vibration.

We wish to speak with you about an interdimensional journey opening up for all of you. It is a journey that can take you higher than ever before, bypassing many of the attributes of past journeys required for those initiates who wished to ascend. We speak of the long training periods in which you had to be deprived of things and experience suffering and lack so your energy would purify and lighten. You are a vibrating instrument, and like a tuning fork you can be tuned with the resonance of the frequency that is now flooding your planet, or you can be in discord with that resonance. When you are in tune, the new frequency is such that you can ride on it like the "magic carpet" in your myth, taking you to where you need to be through flying and not through climbing. Your physical body is like your modern-day telephone as it transmits to you frequencies of information, directing you towards "your treasure" both internally and physically where it serves you the most. As you receive transmissions you have a few choices that you must make; first, whether to accept the transmission by picking up the phone, second, to intently listen to the transmission, and third, whether to believe the message and follow its lead. Those three choices are the choices standing in front of you in the new energy. It is the choice of the human to fly the magic carpet or to climb the cliffs using ropes and spike shoes. Both ways are sacred and both are honored. In your past you had only one option and now you have two.

Why you may ask? *Why did the number of options change?*

The dimensional vortexes that are now opening to you allow the one who seeks to become interdimensional and fly as if by magic.

How does it work, you may wonder?

The veil that separated you from you is becoming thinner, and the information that was blocked by the veil is now slipping through. You are, therefore, enabled to be, more than before, the recipient of that communication. The information is there, and the pathways are now established. It is up to you to turn your attention to the frequency being emitted so you hear the rings of the "phone." Also, you must have the space and time to hear the message and follow it.

Is it that simple, you may wonder?

We speak to you through metaphors as the physics of such enablement is complicated beyond your ability to grasp at it at this stage of your scientific development. There is much more hidden from you than revealed. You are still communicating in the realm of 3D, and you are able to perceive only those things that are recorded by your instruments which are limited to your sensual reality. Most of the new energy that is coming to your planet and into you through your body is in an interdimensional form and therefore a phantom as far as your reality is concerned.

We wish you to awaken that interdimensional quality hidden within you rather than load your logical minds with details that you may believe in or not and with "facts" that you may be able to confirm or not. From our perspective, this is not necessary as your awakening is related to feelings and not to logic. For us to work with you on the level of logic would mean that we must first have you change your whole system of logic so as to accommodate to the one in tune with the rest of the universe. Your logic is limited to your reality and some of it spills over to our reality but not much. Your journey is about intent and choice. You must, therefore, have leaps of faith every day and at every step. If we had to approach your logical mind, we would get nowhere. With all love we wish to impart to you that we do not try to convince you of anything but to give you an option. We can shine light onto your path, but we cannot make you open your eyes or follow the signs. You must decipher for yourself if it feels truthful and if it works for you. You are the master, and we are the ones who respond to your intent and love you no matter what. You may choose to ignore all the communication in these messages, and we will hug you with as much love. It is your choice and free will that we honor most of all, and we will only take your hand if you ask us to do so. This is our promise to you.

How do we get a ticket to the magic carpet, you may wonder?

We thought you'd never ask.

The answer may surprise you in its simplicity. In order to move into the interdimensional vortex that has opened up for you, you first have to choose the faster track – flying. You then begin to flap your interdimensional wings, and when you feel that the time is right you jump off your perch and fly.

Yeah, right, you may be saying sarcastically. *If it was so simple everyone would do it!*

Everyone can, but you are right, it is not so simple. First you must align your body with the new frequency that is being delivered to you.

How do we do that, you may wonder?

Your Native American tribes on this continent and others have some of the answers hidden in their ancient knowledge. You must become aligned with the natural world. You have to seek a point in which your energy is in tune with nature. At this time in your current reality it may pose a challenge as many of you are living in urban areas and your interaction with nature is limited to walking the dog and watering your plants. More interaction will be necessary to align with the energy of Gaia. Gaia is like a vessel, and when you align with her she transmits the information received from the rays of sun and the universe to you in a form that your biology can interpret and decipher.

What do we need to do, you may wonder?

With all love we wish to tell you that first you must walk in the awareness that you and the natural world are one, and as you walk near a tree or observe the bird flying, allow your attention to take you to its reality. Use your imagination to feel how it experiences its own reality. Try to become the tree and the bird. Enter the reality of the natural world as it will serve you well. This simple exercise will attune you to an aspect of Gaia that you need to connect with. As you begin to open your senses to all the living creatures, plants, animals, and birds that are around you, allow your imagination to become them. You will be guided toward the animals that come to your attention, so be in tune to the "visitors" that come to you from the natural world. Do not dismiss any of them as unworthy. Even the spider has something to teach you, and this is a hint.

You will need to take time and find the space to connect to nature either through taking trips in nature or taking walks in the park. Much of your acceleration lies in your relationships with Gaia. She is your guide, and she has many things to teach you. We ask you to answer the phone when it comes from Mother Gaia because she has your set of instructions to ascension in the "fast track."

How does it make our journey faster or more joyful, some may wonder?

As you walk and interact with the natural world, you are opening vortexes in your body to receive the transmission aligned with the frequency of Gaia. The frequency of Gaia is changing continually as she is on the journey of ascension herself. By staying in tune with Gaia, you are allowing your reception to stay linked with the changing vibration so as not to lose the ongoing communication. These messages are awakening your cells and working with your biology, interacting in an interdimensional space to bring you to a higher vibration; in other words, you are ascending as you are walking in your day-to-day life, in tune with Mother Nature.

Some Native Americans can teach you much about their ways. Study their ways as it can greatly facilitate your journey. Learn the rituals and prayers that they have

h Mother Nature; study their dances as they hold
eys to align your frequency with Gaia.

Give intention, and you will be guided to the source appropriate for you.

We have told you with all love that each and every one of you has her own map. There is no one way to walk this walk. There are as many ways as there are angels walking on earth. Give intention with pure heart, and the road will open up. We ask you to learn to fly, and when you do, allow others to learn from you. Be in the awareness that you are vessels of light and your mission is to channel more light to the planet through love and joy. We ask you to ascend higher than ever before and be in the "now" as it is the greatest "now" you have, and so be it.

The Melody and the Music

WE ARE HERE to celebrate with you a moment in time in which you bring a pure thought into the realm of matter. It is through your intention that one thing through alchemy becomes another. This is what we wish you to become as you move through the greatest shift in the history of your existence as angels disguised as humans on this planet.

The process of manifesting is through intention as what you call "product" is delivered in 3D but carries the messages of multiple "D's." It is that which we wish to discuss with you at this point in time. You play a part as a vessel, and your mission is to become clear and pure as a channel so the message transmitted through you from the other side will be as clear and will hold the vibration without change. It is the integrity of the message that we ask you to hold as sacred and allow it to remain as it was intended. From where we sit there is no waste, and each word holds a vibration that can only be compared to music. The sound vibrations of music are interdimensional as are our messages.

There are a few of you who agreed through contracts to come together and to use your light to bring this information forth. You always have a choice, and you have chosen to do this sacred work. We wish to impart to you that each of you has your role. We know who you are, and we see your strengths and weaknesses. There is never a judgment, and this work is about elevating the vibrations of all those who come in contact with the process. You are the one who was chosen and have agreed to act as a link and a vessel to bring energy and a vibration from the angelic realm which is one dimension to your physical 3D realm, which is another. Metaphorically speaking, there is the one whose role is to receive the melody from the other side and play the music, and then there is the role of your fellow angel who must hear the music and re-transcribe that which he hears to the page, adhering to the rules and requirements of your musical language.

All parts of the process of alchemy are sacred and honored. We are asking that you be in tune with the vibration of the circle and not attempt to translate the circle into your linear perception. You are becoming an interdimensional being, and as you get closer to our reality these messages act as openings or bridges by which one can move to different realities on their own. With all love you are asked at this time not to question the ability of others to understand the messages as you do not ask the audience if they can understand the music. A conductor hears one thing, and a child hears another. A musician who is familiar with the music played will "take" one thing while a person not familiar with that specific type of music will "take" something else.

We wish to tell you that there is never a judgment. It is your intent that allows you to be at a place where you change vibration. The words are just the conveyer that delivers the energy into your biology. The process works on many levels, and the one who decides how much, how far, and how deep is the reader and her intent.

Our reality is devoid of time, and past, present, and future all appear as fluctuations of energy potentials, some manifested and some still in potential even though the timing for manifesting may have already passed. In our reality we greet and hug every single one of you who has the potential to read our messages. Not only can we see you, but we also can also see the circumstances in your life that will be the catalyst for your search. We can see how our messages will facilitate your growth, and we can see your potential for alchemical transformation as a result.

In our reality we speak directly and personally to each one of you. We know who you are, and we know and hug each and every one of you who will ever read these messages. We even hug those who were not born yet and are with us watching you, and they know that they have potential to read these messages. We sit beside you as we lay our invisible arms around your shoulders to let you know how much we love you. We are with those readers who will be reading these messages thirty years from now. From where we sit watching you, thirty years passes as briefly as a minute, and a second lasts forever.

We speak to the one who is transcribing the musical notes editing our messages into the language that you designed for the benefit of recording multidimensional vibration into two-dimensional paper. We congratulate you for your pure intent and honor your part. We ask you to become a pure vessel and translate that which you hear without changing the music.

The process may seem easy, but it is not as we speak to you in a song, and this song must transmit the same rhythm as was intended from our side. With all love know that when we sing to you it is with melody, colors, shapes, and at times scents. When we repeat so often that we love you, it is meant to link to your energy centers or what you call chakras so you will open up to our melody. When we say "there is no judgment" so often, it is to allow you to receive these messages without mixing them with your cellular memory of shame, guilt, and pain. We send you healing through these messages by linking yourself with yourself. Know that we are transmitting love to you from the other side, and as your eyes scan the messages the melody riding on the words is changing your cellular structure, opening your cells allowing love energy to flood into you. The energy coming into you will awaken your cells to their original intention and therefore can avert or clear disease and imbalance that is in your cells now or will be in your potential.

We ask you to go into the circle with us and understand that the words at times may seem redundant, but they light different aspects of the same thing so you may become peaceful with what you see.

We are in love with you and we offer you a light that is without filters; we ask you to not impose your own filters as you direct the light to those who gave intent to receive it. There is a form of how to take a thought and translate it into an object. As an artist you create music through words bringing it from the world of spirit through you. We wish to give you our view of how to structure the object you call book. We wish you to understand that your readers gave intent for these messages to come forth. Therefore, you do not need to "dilute" the message to cater to your readers. They are the ones creating the book in their thoughts from a place that we can only call interdimensional, and in time that is in a quantum state.

From where we sit watching you, we see that the book was meant to be taken like your food buffet. You crave a certain food, and you go to the buffet and pick that which fits your craving. This buffet is in the circle, and your attempts to create a platform which will bring a "linear order" to the circle is like taking a butterfly and trying make it carry a wagon. The messages are in the realm of the subtle delivered through your language which is linear and cumbersome. The order of the chapters may remain the same as they were delivered. We wish you not to place an order of logic on that which is in the circle.

We ask you to understand that in each message there are key words and phrases. It is your mission to find them, highlight them, and index them. These key words or phrases carry a specific melody or tonal frequency. We wish to impart to you that interdimensionally the key words and phrases carry vibration and geometry that will "call out" to those who are searching for answers and wish to learn about the nature of their divinity. It will be as if a chick is calling its mother. There may be many chicks and many mothers, but the one that belongs to the other will recognize each other instantly.

Why can't you just give us the key words, you may wonder?

The work that you do is what we call "light work," and you are facilitating your own growth as well as the growth of others. Finding the key word is the part which will forward your own growth. In order to be in tune with those key words and phrases you must be in a place of high vibration through which you bridge your own reality to ours. It is your mission at this time to bring your vibration to a place that you can see the words highlighted as you read the text – as if they will flash in front of your eyes as you scan the message. Be in the awareness that you are entering the realm of interdimensional space in which some of the rules of your 3D reality will not hold. We ask you not to hold on to your old reality. You are being led to explore your magnificence, and we ask you to be open to the experiences that you face. We wish you to build a bridge to the circle so we can hug you again and celebrate your transformation with you, and so be it

The Tightrope Circus Act

IT IS OUR PLEASURE to see you graduate from one level to the next. We are with you and some of us shed tears of joy as we hug you. It is indeed the time for you to turn the page and to move to the next chapter in the book. You have been serving as a clear vessel and we approve of your work and are delighted with the results thus far. We are with you every step of the way and we wish you to know that you are dearly loved and that which you have allowed through you will reach many souls who have asked for this material. There are many who are searching for Spirit, an energy that is illusive and transparent. Those among you who are searching intuitively know that the information is there as you can feel it in your cells. It is a magnet of sorts that attracts those who are searching for these messages to our messages through the resonance of vibrations so that a particular message can join with the one who seeks that message through attraction and intent. We respond to your intent. When you ask with pure heart to serve as a vessel we celebrate your intent and with joy we begin the process. It is not only your intent which manifests the "messages" as there must be intent from those who are searching for the information, as well. Like the tightrope act in the circus, in order for the rope to be tight, the rope must be pulled from both ends. Only when the rope is tight enough can the balancing circus act take place.

Why circus act? Why tightrope, You may wonder?

The rope symbolizes your willingness to trust and walk on ground that is neither secure nor safe. It also represents your willingness to move forward, defying your instinct for survival. The "circus act" is metaphorically the chapter of your evolution as angels disguised as humans. You are walking and acting in a large tent called earth and each one of you is acting your role as you believe you should be. One is the clown and the other is on the trampoline. Your act is now changing and shifting as the circus is moving to a new destination and you must develop a new set of skills to accommodate the new act.

We wish to impart to you with all love that it is a good time for you to look inside yourself and take notes on your past performance as you are getting ready to move to a new destination. It is with love and without judgment that we present the information from the circle. There will be those who may say, "We do not believe it, this is a hoax." With all love we wish to tell you that you are also dearly loved and whether you agree with what was written or believe it, you are loved just the same. We wish to impart to you that your responsibility is to bring light to your planet of free choice and honor the free choice of angels walking in duality. Hold each and every one's opinion as sacred no matter how uninformed or unenlightened you believe they may be. Love them as you love your brothers and sisters. Love them like you love yourself and allow them to close their eyes when they see the light. The light is there if they choose to open their eyes but you cannot force them to see. Your mission is to make light available. With all love we must impart to you that if you think you need to convince anyone to open their eyes you are missing the point all together. Free choice of an angel walking in duality is sacred above all. The one who you consider "unenlightened" has her journey to make and it is as sacred and as honored as yours. We wish to speak with you about those who choose to close their eyes and ignore the light. We wish to speak with you about angels that are connected with you through the strings of love, may they be family or lovers, and are choosing darkness. We wish to speak with you about their choice and yours. We wish to speak with you about the karma of two angels; one who chooses to transform herself through light and the other who walks blindfolded never even considering removing the cloth covering her eyes, choosing not to see the larger picture.

Yes, tell us what is going on, some may ask?

You are all family and you are all brothers and sisters. You came here for the same reason and from where we sit you are all beautiful. Some of you are at a level where light may be too much for you at your place of lesson. There are those who are walking blindfolded because it serves them at their place of understanding. They do not see the light because they do not believe it serves them. They are at a place where they only know shades of darkness because they are younger on your planet and they have experienced expressions where light was scarce. They are as loved as you are and they like you are moving through a journey of discovery.

We speak to those of you who are on a mission to awaken and transform yourselves and the planet, catapulting it to a new dimension. With all love we wish to impart to you that the vast majority of angels walking on this planet are not at the vibration that you are. Most of humanity at this time is comprised of younger souls who come from other systems to experience this great shift; many of them are not ready to experience light as you do.

Yes, but why am I married to one, some may wonder? Why would we choose a family that is in darkness to block our light, Others may complain?

As we hug you we wish to remind you that light transforms darkness and not vice versa. As you shine your light, the darkness that is trying to block you will transform. There is no one that can ever block your light from shining. Darkness is not active. It is just a lack of light. Darkness does not do things to the light. Light can only do things to darkness.

So why is it so difficult to transform those we love and are connected with?

We wish to hug you one more time and tell you that we know who you are and we can feel your pain. We cry when you cry and we wipe your tears when you sit on your bed at night searching for answers. We wish to hold your hand and tell you that it is not your responsibility to transform those who do not wish to be transformed. The attribute of the light is such that those who wish to be transformed must open their eyes. You cannot force those who you care about to open their eyes. It is not your role and it is not your mission. You are a lighthouse and as one you are to shine your light but you cannot force the ships that are lost at sea to trust your light and use it to navigate back to safety. You can only do so much and your role is the reason you chose those who are in darkness. You are "light workers" and as such you do not rest. Your contract read that you will take under your wings an angel that is in darkness and offer them your light. Your contract does not read that you then shove the flashlight in their eyes and pull open their eyelids. This would be moving away from spirit. You have chosen a mission that is not easy and the ones who are the closest to you are preparing you for a mission that is much greater. They represent the vast majority of humanity at this time. They are your best training ground and you must love them and honor their role as they are bringing you closer to your mission and showing you what obstacles you must face. It is they who volunteered to train you and you can trust that it is not easy for them to be in the darkness and yet in the vicinity of light. They are fearful as they do not wish to transform. They are asking themselves, "How did we end up with light?" Some of them may say; "All I wanted is to be content in my darkness and to be asleep and my partner is ringing the bell in my ears and shining his light projector while I try to sleep and it is driving me mad." And here you are taking their hands and pulling them through hurdles showing them all these things that they do not wish to see. You bring light everywhere you go and they only wish to rest in their darkness. We wish to assure you that they do not have an easy time as well. Honor them for their role and hug them, for their choices are as sacred as yours.

You came to this planet this time around to bring light, information and love as you did in previous expressions. You are old souls. You have been here many times before and you carry with you the scars of many of your past expressions. There are those of you who are healers, shamans, Lemurians, witches and magicians. There are those of you who were the priests, the monks, the rabbis, the sages and the alchemists. You came to shine your light and to act as a vessel so humanity can begin to see. We did not say it will be easy or fast. We do wish to impart to you that those who signed a contract to be with you and act as holders of darkness are your coaches and teachers. They are the one who must show you ways to conquer your own fears and learn about the power of light. We know who you are. There will be those who will threaten you. Know that they do so because they are fearful. Some will tell you that you are hurting them and they will leave you if you continue to shine your light. Know that you must love them and honor their wishes to remain in the dark as you continue to shine your light. We wish you to know who you are and awaken your divinity. You are a master and you must walk in that awareness. Mastery is your mission and it is why you came here at this time. Know that no one can take your light away from you as your divinity is your birth right. Those who wish to take your light away are powerless and they cannot come too close. Keep shining your light and as they come close to you they will lose their darkness. You must walk on a tightrope and know that you have the mastery and the balance, Know that the circus is changing its act and it is your time to be the ring leader. Your time is coming and we ask you to be prepared. We wish you to honor those who are close to you and are in darkness because they are the ones who are rehearsing with you before the new act.

As we preparing to withdraw and say goodbye we wish to remind you that love has no agenda, and it does not need to convince anyone of its existence; the same attribute is true of light. Like love, light just shines. It does not ask anything from anyone or try to sell anyone anything. We ask you to be the light and not try to sell light. We ask you not to evangelize. We ask you to love yourself and honor your journey. It is self-love and self-honoring that allows you to be aware of your divinity. It is through divinity that you develop compassion and radiate love to your fellow angels. It is through love that you are changing the attribute of the earth that you walk on. It is the ground that you walk on that honors your path and gives your journey the sustenance that is needed. You are loved by Gaia and your journey is known to all of us. Know that we are with you now and forever, and so be it.

The Toaster

L IKE FAMILY, WE COME when you call us.

Can you hear us, some may wonder?

We can see your thoughts, is our answer. We can feel your vibration when you set up pure intent to connect to us. We are with you all the time but it is the space that you make for us that allows us to enter your awareness and walk with you, hand in hand.

What does the process of connecting involve, you may wonder?

Like your modern day electrical toaster, it may be occupying a space on your kitchen counter but unless you plug it in to the electrical outlet and push the lever down it will not be activated. We are the toaster of your divinity. We act as a link between you in duality to the part of yourself which is the "I am that I am."

You have a wall and that wall prevents you from seeing who you really are. To begin to see you must activate your toaster. You must acknowledge that there is something else out there beside your 3-D reality and it can only be unveiled to you if you seek it. You must therefore set up intent by taking the plug and finding a place to plug it in. Those who choose to activate their divinity will have the electrical current of divinity flow into them allowing them to become aware of the love radiating from the other side as well as knowledge of their own mastery.

Is it that simple, You may wonder?

Yes it is, but you need to discover the plug and find the outlet. This journey begins with searching.

How do we then find the plug and the outlet, you may wonder?

It is always the intent that organizes the molecules of your 3-D reality into a direction and that direction will lead you to both the plug and the outlet. It is the search that we wish to speak of today. You are all searching for something. Some of you are searching for love, other are searching for fame. There are those of you who search for material wealth and there are those who search for peace. It is a search that usually begins at one point in time and ends when you come back to us. When you come back to us, many of you realize that much of your search was in vain not because you did not want the things you were looking for, but because you had those things all along inside of you. Many of you realize, when you sit with us pondering your previous life journey and examine your lessons, how much of your precious time you wasted feeling that you did not possess that which you had all along. We wish to hug you and whisper in your ears that you do not have to come back home to discover that those things you are searching for are already with you. We wish to take your hands and lead you to see who you are and what you have at this moment in time.

I am surely not wealthy and I have no peace in my life, some of you will claim. Other will say, *I surely am not famous and I have no love to speak of.*

In fact we know some of you who proclaim that no one loves you in the whole world. We know who you are and we know the wall that hides your magnificence and shows you only a biology that is ageing in a struggling reality that is heavy with gravity and karma. Yes, this is one aspect of your journey and it is a sacred aspect that you indeed experience. We wish you to move with us into the circle.

The circle again, some may sigh? *But we live in a line, not in the circle,* others may respond in frustration.

This is the story of your "toaster," we say with a smile. The bread will not be toasted if you do not plug your toaster into the electrical outlet. It is your choice whether to link with the current. Your choices are always honored and never judged. We wish to tell you, however, that you have a toaster and you have electrical current. You also have a plug and an outlet. In fact, you have all you require to "toast your bread." All you need to do is find the different "components" and link them together. It is your spiritual journey that we speak of, and with a smile we wish you to know that your reward will be more than toasted bread.

We wish to speak with you about your journey and some of the misunderstandings you have acquired along the way. We wish to speak with those who seek the outlet and plug outside of themselves and in the process hand their power to someone else. We also wish to speak to those who subscribe to linking with others who you consider more powerful than yourself. Some of you call them all-knowing or powerful teachers or Gurus; some may even name them God. We wish to speak of the process by which an angel is beginning the search into their own mastery by searching for it outside of themselves.

Your need to search is hidden inside your biology. You have an interdimensional "button" embedded in your DNA that is activated at some point in time. This button allows a feeling to flow into you that tells you through yearnings that there is "something" you must look for in order to become whole. Although you do not know what that something looks like you begin the search nevertheless. The search for fame, love, wealth or spiritual knowledge are all part of the same yearning that is activated within you and is part of your cellular dimension as well as your spiritual dimension. It is biological in part and it is activated when you begin to mature. Some direct the energy of the search toward material wealth, others direct it toward finding love or being adored by other humans, and some search for God. With all love we wish to impart to you that your search is sacred and you are so dearly loved for walking blindfolded searching for answers without the ability to see.

The energy of the search is powerful and it is "real". It is a frequency of "passion" or "desire" that is coveted by many in your dimension and other dimensions. This "frequency" is used, in your reality and in other dimensions, to channel this energy, diverting it away from "you" into "others." There is never a judgment and your choices are always honored. To those of you who are told that you must do certain rituals and repeat certain prayers in a certain manner and if you do not "God" will not hear you, know that this is the manner by which your energy may be directed away from you and toward "somewhere else." This is how your frequency is being harvested. Some rituals and prayers are directing your "spiritual frequency" of intent away from you into those who wish to gain your power. Similarly, it is done every day in your 3-D reality on earth. It is done through your media, your governments, your schools and your religious institutions. The search for what you call "truth" is a powerful frequency and there are those who figure out ways to manipulate your reality so that you will begin to believe that the power lies outside of you and not within. It is your structures and institutions that are harvesting the energy both in terms of power and in terms of wealth. Even love-energy can be channeled to serve others. You may direct your love or adoration toward your favorite heroes, be they movie stars or your favorite "sports players". With all love we wish to tell you that much of your frequency that is meant to serve yourself and therefore, your divinity, is channeled to serve others making you weaker and "them" stronger. It is not that "they" represent darkness and you represent light. Darkness simply means that you are not aware of your power and divinity. Light is transparency and self knowledge and darkness is simply lack of light. Even those of you who search life after life for answers outside of themselves and never find them are as loved as those who do. We are here to shine light on your "illusion of reality" so you will begin to see who you are and the power that you possess. You have the power within you at every moment to divert your own energy toward the self and away from others. By doing so, you begin to put together the parts that are missing to activate your "toaster."

We wish to speak with those among you who are angels walking in duality in service to "God." We hug all of you and let you know that your search is sacred and you are so dearly loved. We wish to tell you that from where we sit, connecting to God is connecting to your own divinity. Connecting to your "I am," is the closest link in your physical dimension to that which you call God. When you are being told that God is all merciful, all compassionate, all loving but you must do this and that so God will love you, forgive your sins and absolve you from going to hell, know that it is your energy that is being channeled and diverted to empower "others" and not yourself. The "others" who may be in your reality or on other dimensions, are using interdimensional frequency scrambling pathways to send your thought energy to where they wish, so they can use it for themselves. The universe is magnificent in scope and your energy is coveted by many in the universe. You are powerful and your yearning, when harvested, aids those who wish to ride on your power to empower themselves. We wish to tell you that you also gain benefit from following the so called "God rules" but it is not the rules that get you there but your intent to connect that links you with yourself. You are used to giving power to anyone who asks for it, be it your teacher, your media, your stars , your heroes, your gurus or your Gods. We ask you to examine yourself and see if you feel closer today to finding the answers then you were yesterday. If you are closer, it means that you are linked with your own divinity. If, however, you feel that you are still far away and lost in your search it means, from our perspective, that you have sent your energy to someone or somewhere outside yourself.

How do we know which Gurus or teachings are of the light, some may ask? How do we know if what we are being told is a manipulation or truth?

With all love we wish to impart to you that the answer is simple. You will feel it inside as heavy or light. Your truth will feel light. Your truth may be different than your sister's or brother's truth. If you are being told that you are the master, that you are in control of your journey and the divinity is within you, know that it is coming from the light. When you are told to go outside of yourself and ask "the powerful one", be it a saint, a guru, holy figure or idol, for that which you wish for, know that your energy is being diverted away from you and away from spirit. There is no judgment in us and you may choose either and we will love you the same. It is light that we bring to you and we wish to shine it upon your path so you can see what was hidden from you. We know who you are and we wish to embrace you at every moment.

We know how some of you may feel without your Gods, be they wealth gods, gods of power, or love, or religious gurus and symbols. Without them, you may feel lost and frightened.

You want us to throw away our religions and turn away from our Gurus, you may wonder?

With all love, we do not want you to throw away anything or turn away from anything. On the contrary, we wish you to begin directing your search inside so you can teach your gurus, your institutions and your media how powerful you can be when you are linked to your own divinity. It is then that you shine your light in places that were dark before. From our perspective, your mission is to take part in your day to day activities and participate in your daily rituals but with a different awareness, that of a master. We do not wish you to move away from the darkness. We wish you to shine your light and move closer to the darkness so darkness will be dispelled. This is your mission at this time. Be part of the flow of life and walk in your divinity, sharing the energy of your mastery so the one who is watching you will learn from you the power of light. The energy of the planet is now enabling you more than ever to open your eyes to your multidimensional truth. You are being asked to re-divert the energy that was directed away from you for eons to come back to yourself so you can shine your most powerful light. In doing so you are elevating the vibration of all humanity as well as the planet, catapulting it to the gate of new dimensions where peace on earth can become your reality.

You have yet to tell as about finding love, wealth and fame inside of us, what is the secret, some of you may still ask.

We are in love with humanity and we wish to tell you that all the wealth you ever want is flowing in your veins and is part of your DNA. All the love that you could ever wish for is flowing in your veins and is part of your DNA. All the fame that you could ever wish for, you already have as all the trillions and trillions of us know your name and love you. We wish you to look at yourself in the mirror and see the "I am that I am." And when you do, give yourself a hug and know that it is us who are joining the hug. Know that you are never alone and you are eternal, loved by all of us and known by all of us. We ask you to activate the wealth and love within you and not search for it outside of you. When you do, you direct your energy to those who are in darkness. We ask you to know that you are the master and the most powerful angel in the universe. We wish you to shine your light and share it with all who come in contact with you as this is your mission, and so be it.

The Domino Effect

WHAT A BEAUTIFUL DAY, you may say to yourself as you look out the window.

Indeed it is, we say to you as we hug you.

Is there anything wrong, you ask yourself? Fear begins to crawl up your spine as you take inventory of what is "good" but can turn "bad." *Is my health good,* you ask yourself? Maybe I have something very wrong with me that I am not aware of.

We see some of you who are digging out all the possible scenarios which can turn "bad" and as soon as they have finished their morning tea, turning the day from beautiful to a day full of worries. As you leave your house to do what you do, your mind is in the "what can go wrong" mood. As the day goes by, things seem to be moving smoothly. By the end of the day, you forgot that it was a beautiful day to start with and tell yourself that you are so lucky that nothing bad happened today. Next we see you back home enjoying a moment of introspection at your "good" day, letting your worries start to creep up your spine as you begin to consider all that could go wrong tomorrow. We see many of you say to yourselves, "it is true that today was good but what about tomorrow, I am not getting any younger and there are so many things that I should be worried about." We see many of you living your life in a state of unconsciousness moving from fear to worry to fear, being continuously at the mercy of "luck". We see it in your geometry and in your colors. We see it also in the dim light that is emanating from your beautiful celestial structure. We see you walking in the mind- set of "what can go wrong?" and "how am I going to survive the day just to face the next?" We hug you every day in the morning and at night before you go to sleep and we wish to tell you that when you worry, you actually project your vision of worry into your future reality thereby creating a future where those things may actually manifest in your life. We wish to remind you again that your thoughts create matter and that which you fear is your divine energy inappropriately used to create a reality that is not the "now." It is with love that we wish to remind you that you are the master and the beautiful day that you observed as you woke up in the morning is a choice for you to "see" or not to "see," and so are the "obstacles" that you may or may not face. You may experience your life as beautiful and light or as burdensome and difficult at any point. Your reality is a choice at any given moment and that which you wish for is that which you experience.

What about all the poor people and all those who are suffering, some of you may wonder?

We wish you to honor those who are poor and who are suffering as the same rules apply to them. They are angels just like you and they play their part just like you. You must honor their choice and allow them to learn through their experience. We see many of you wanting to "take away" the experience of the "poor" and turn them more like you: "richer." With all love we wish to tell you that those who are poor and wish to change their path of learning have a choice. As we hug you we wish to whisper in your ears that many of those whom you are trying to "save" from "suffering" or "poverty" do not want to be "saved" and you must honor their wishes. They will find many excuses to be where they are, even when given many opportunities. This is their own choice. It is your choice as well to honor your power and divinity, mastering your path, or being at the "mercy of circumstances." You have a choice at any given moment of how to perceive and interpret your reality. You may be in a place of beauty yet only think of what can go wrong, missing completely the gift of beauty that surrounds you. You may also go through a seemingly difficult situation and choose to see the beauty of what is happening, honoring it and holding it sacred.

We wish to speak of the choice you have and your mission at this time. You are so dearly loved and there is never a judgment as to how you "see" your reality. You are loved whether you see beauty on every corner or see "ugly" at every corner. It is with great consideration that we wish to hand to you a method for you to consider on the path to your mastery. This is a method that was handed from the other side of the veil to change one's reality. There are many realities for you to choose from and the reality that you must choose is the one which serves your highest path and that which supports your divinity and mastery. As we observe you from above, below and all around, we ask you to use this exercise whenever you are facing a situation that seems to overwhelm your senses and may cause you to be thrown off balance.

Are you telling us that we are to expect something "bad" soon, some may ask?

We simply are telling you that we see many of you live your lives as if you expect something "bad" all the time. When indeed something "bad" happens you are surprised. When you are surprised we see your geometry fold up on itself and you stop vibrating all together. Your knees become weak and you stop breathing. We see your light dim and your music stop. It is as if you were playing music on your CD player and someone pulled the plug. It is within a scope of one second that new information enters your awareness and you change reality. When you can change reality in one direction you also have the power to change it to another direction, and that is what we wish to expand on.

You are all moving about in your individual realities and each and every one of you experiences their "reality" differently. We always tell you that you have as many truths as angels walking in duality. No two angels experience the same exact reality. Your reality is a construct of your geometry and each one is unique. However, as you evolved you agreed on certain aspects of reality that all of you share and that is your foundation for action in the physical world. You agree on certain aspects in your three dimensions and you accept them as "truths". From where we sit your 3-D physical "truth" is a limited aspect of your magnificence. You exist on many planes and dimensions simultaneously and you are powerful and eternal, none of which you are aware of as an angel submerged in duality.

What are we to do then, some may ask?

There are many ancient traditions that have shared deep knowledge of techniques for remaining vibrating in the face of a seemingly fearful event. We wish to give you something simple to remember but that is profound when acted on accurately at the correct time. You are asked to breathe deeply and calmly from the bottom of your belly to the top of your lungs. You then must hold the breath for 20-30 seconds. You then exhale the air through your nose as you imagine the air dispersing equally to all part of your body. Do that for a minute or two and then visualize your "pranic tube" which is primarily your spine. This is your link to heaven and earth and also to all the information that we are transmitting. The frequency from our side is absorbed through your pranic tube and not your brain. Breathe in from the top of the pranic tube which is the top of your head into the earth and then from the earth through your base chakra into the top of the pranic tube for 2-3 minutes. Alternate between breathing from earth to heaven and heaven to earth. Then repeat the exercise inhaling from top and bottom alternately hold your breath and exhale through the heart for 2-3 minutes. Your heart can decipher what is it that you are experiencing and by continuing to breathe deeply you allow your life force to circulate in you creating a link between you and us or you and light which is information and love. The information that you need will come to you and will support you staying in balance. Moving away from your fulcrum point at a "difficult time" is moving away from light to darkness. It means that you stop seeing the big picture. Many of you only require a short switch of realities to move away from Balance to fear. You now must remember that it takes the same amount of time to switch back from fear to Balance. As you learn to master "difficult" or "fearful" events in your life, you are coming into your mission prepared to shine your light despite the winds and waves that are swirling all around you.

We wish to speak with you about the game known as Dominos. In your culture you play a game in which you place one cube next to the other and when you place many of them, you enjoy the sight of tipping the first one and seeing all the rest crumbling and folding creating the "domino effect" we wish to use this metaphor at this time. The earth is going through changes and so are you. With all love we wish to tell you that all of you must adjust as there is no one who can stay impervious or unaffected by the events that are unfolding all around you. You chose to change and those changes are upon you now. We see the potential for events that are seemingly "negative or fearful" that may tip the first cube and therefore create the "domino effect" where all those who are standing may lose their ground and miss the opportunity to ascend in vibration. As you are weaved with the same reality as your next door neighbor you may react in the same fashion and just crumble yourself allowing your torch to be turned off. You, the light workers, are the ones who are placed along the "domino chain" and if you remain balanced you may stop the domino effect in its midst. It is enough that some of you will stay balanced to prevent the collapse of the whole. When you stay balanced and do not fold as you are hit by the cube to your side, you help in catapulting humanity to a new dimension. Some of you are placed at locations where your balance may keep all those who come after you standing. So you understand the significance of your staying balanced. It can make a difference for all those who come after you. The dominos are, from our perspective, all of humanity. You are all part of this chain as you are all weaved together in a web of consciousness. All of you will be affected as it is what you have chosen. It is the light warriors, the awakened Lemurians, the renegades, the shamans, healers, "earth Goddesses," the spiritual teachers, the seekers, and the angels who walk the path of mastery who must hold their inner power balanced and remain standing, un- swayed, while everything is shaking all around. Your balance may be the difference between one reality for the whole and another, and between darkness and light. That is why we ask you to wake up as you must stay in a place of balance no matter what your 3-D physical reality is telling you. You must go inside and use your inner resources to stay standing despite all the dominoes that are folding all around you.

How about family, you may wonder? *How can we stay balanced when our family is being affected,* some of you may wonder? Others may say that it is too traumatic to stay unaffected when your loved ones are in peril. You are all angels and you are all eternal. You are built so that you must experience fear and run in the face of danger. You are built to survive and you are built to be attached to your loved one so you will keep your family safe and protect those who are around you. We know who you are and we know your challenges. We ask you to always remember that your loved ones are loved by spirit just as you are and they are divine just like you. They hold their own path which is sacred and honored. You must take care of yourself so you can help those loved ones who are around you. Always remember that your loved ones count on you not to "freeze" when you see the headlight. It is up to you to remain balanced so you can comfort and assist your loved ones in times of challenge. You must always be aware that by staying in balance you are elevating those who are out of balance. If you lose balance you are helping no-one.

We wish to tell you that it is your mission to move from the linear to the circle when the time is right and understand that you are all loved and you are all on a path that is inscribed in gold with the word love on it. You are en route to a magnificent place that none of us predicted.

You are well on your way to ascend in vibration along with Gaia. It is a beautiful and sacred process and changes must take place for you to shift dimensions. You are enabled to know more then you have known ever before and to stay out of harm's way. We ask you to use your tools and wake up to your mission. With all love we wish you to be at a place of elevated awareness so that when the time comes you will be prepared to do that which you came here to do and so be it.

The Gift of Lightning

WHAT HAVE I BEEN *doing*, you may ask?

With a smile, we wish to tell you: plenty. You are walking the walk of an angel who acts and thinks. Those actions and thoughts are what we call your contribution to the consciousness of the whole. Each moment counts. You do not have to "think big" or do "great things." Your actions and thoughts are not measured by size but by quality. It is in the vibration and frequency of your actions and thoughts that your progress is measured.

What is it that you wish us to do, you may ask?

We ask you to live and be the master that you are. We ask you to breathe every moment with awareness knowing that the air you inhale is going into the body of a master. Know that you are a divine being and nothing you say and do may change that. Know that you are an angel walking and acting as a human in a limited 3-dimensional reality but that is just a temporary costume that you wear so you can learn about your Self and add to the magnificence of the whole. We wish you to wake up to your identity and be it rather than think about it. There is a great mystery that you were born into, a great mystery that is part of you. In fact, the mystery is in you. We wish you to stop looking for it in exotic places outside of yourself, and to begin digging inside so you can reveal the treasure and peal away the layers of the mystery that is hidden in you.

We know who you are and we know what you are going through. We are around you all the time as we are part of your energy. We wish you to understand that you are never alone and in those moments where you feel frightened and insecure know that these are also the moments where we hug you and put our invisible arms around you telling you over and over again how much we love you and that you are never ever alone.

There are those of you who come from a place of victimhood and we wish to speak to you. We wish to tell you that when you ask "why me?", when you feel victimized, it is as if you have been sleeping in the classroom. We wish you to be awake and instead of asking why me?, say how fortunate that I am here and now experiencing that which I am experiencing because it is precisely what I need to learn so I can wake up to my divinity. We wish you to be in a place of gratitude so you can take benefit from the journey you call earth cycle.

Please show us where we need to go, some of you may ask.

We do all the time, we reply with a smile. We give you hints every moment and we ask you to be in a place of balance so you can be in tune to our melody and follow the highest path you set up for your Self. As a master you choose your experience and all that you experience therefore is your choice, we ask you to take the reins in your hands and know that you are leading yourself to your own learning. There is a great story that is unfolding in front of you and as you walk the path of the master, every moment counts. You must be in awareness and awake so the walk is joyful no matter how others perceive it to be. Your reality is created by your awareness and not vise-versa. Many of you believe that you have a reality that is forced upon you and you need to deal with whatever comes. We wish to tell you that individually and collectively you are creating all the experiences that cross your path. When you receive a message and the message is overwhelming in size and scope know that it is you who have asked to be shaken so you could move up a step. When for example, lighting hits your house and you experience a loss that is great, know that it is your time to move away from those anchors which hold you chained in the harbor, and sail to the open sea. Know that it is your wishes that are honored so ask not: why me? It is you who have asked for that which you experience and your requests have been honored.

So why am I in pain and suffering? some of you may wonder. *Why would I do such a thing to myself?* you may correctly ask. *I want to be in a place of joy , harmony and balance. I do not wish to be torn, and beaten down to my knees.*

Your place of joy, harmony and balance are always with you. It is your mastery that is part of you and you can never lose it. That is why we wish you to wake up to it sooner rather than later. No one can ever take your joy, harmony and balance from you because it is built in. It is the "reality" of your lesson that is not in a place of joy, harmony and balance. We wish you to learn to use the power of mastery so when the reality you perceive with your senses is out of balance, you maintain your equilibrium. Mastery is not the experience of being in a quiet place, like your peaceful Ashrams, meditating all day long. Mastery is being in life and at times even in the midst of turmoil; awaken so you maintain your power no matter what it is that faces you, knowing fully that you are eternal and loved and that the experience is there to teach you about you. When lightning strikes it is, from where we sit, a delivery of energy that is coming from the tension built between the negative charge and the positive charge in your atmosphere. When the link is created it releases a powerful energy that is carried on as an electric charge. Lightning is light and like you the lighthouse it creates a space for all to see. Lightning penetrates the atmosphere to deliver a message. It is a message that is literal and symbolic at the same time. Within the electric charge of the lightning bolt there is a hidden message which tells the one effected: you are light and it is time for you to show all the power that you carry.

Why does the lightning chooses to hit one place and not another? you may wonder.

It chooses its destination based on the ease with which it can release the electric charge into the ground so it can dissipate and find equilibrium. Everything around you seeks to find equilibrium and this law of nature applies to cosmic law as well. When a master asks for a shift in his life, he asks for a gift to be handed down so he may catapult himself from one place to a higher ground in what we can only call an accelerated leap of consciousness. It is the master who asks for an opportunity to make the pilgrimage to a higher ground. When the gift is handed down from the heavens in a form of a lightning it is the master who must then translate the gift through awareness and the tools of mastery to climb the ladder of ascension. You live in a symbolic reality where everything you experience is connected to everything else. There is no reality that is separated from another reality. You live in a reality that like a spider web is interconnected in multi-layered dimensionality so everything that happens in one dimension affects the whole. When one makes a shift, the whole must reorganize itself to accommodate that shift. That is why we ask you to wake up. Your awakening shifts the whole and reverberates in your own reality and across all realities and universes. All of us know who you are and the steps you take to grow and learn. When you make a giant leap we will have many celebrations in your honor and in a quantum space you will be part of the celebration. When you ask to begin moving, the laws of inertia are utilized so it takes a lot of energy to begin a journey from a point of stillness. However, when you move along your path, much less energy is needed to direct the movement so the faster you move the more subtle the energy used to guide the journey. Lightning is used when an angel asks for a strong push so to greatly accelerate his journey. No one ever asks to be in pain and in loss but the soul is eternal and it holds the vista of the entire journey which is not limited to the moment. When you ask with pure intent to move forward, scores of angels who are responsible for making your wishes come true must carefully orchestrate the reality around you to fulfill your desire. You are the master of your own reality and your wishes are honored. When a storm comes it requires a great effort from the angelic realm to direct a charge to a specific location. It must create a vacuum in that place so the electricity will find it a compelling place to release its charge. In the process it also delivers energy that is sent to the core of the planet and to the crystalline grid, reorganizing atoms and molecules so to create new potentials in your life. The elements of water and fire mixed in such an event signify purging and purifying the old so a new path will open to you. It is in these two natural elements of water and fire as well as the positive and negative charge delivered with the lightning bolt that clues are inserted as to the next phase of your journey. Change and growth are the ultimate landmarks of any spiritual journey.

Why are you telling us about lightning, water and fire, some of you may wonder?

We wish you to celebrate where you are and know that changes are coming to all of you. The earth you occupy is on a spiritual journey and all of you are part of what we call earth consciousness. As the earth spins, you spin with it and as it increases in vibration, you all must shift to adjust to the new earth frequency. You collectively asked for this journey and you are on your way. The elements of water and fire will be prevalent in the lives of many directing and guiding you to the next phase of your evolution as angels in disguise. We ask you to wake up so you can celebrate your graduation and be a teacher and a guide to those who come in contact with you. We ask you to become the master that you are, so you can hold the vibration of peace, love and harmony wherever you go, no matter what is facing you. We are in love with you and we ask you to wake up and feel the love that is all around you and so be it.

The Protocol

HAS IT ALWAYS BEEN *like this*, you may wonder?

Our answer is no; things are changing, and they are always moving from one point to the next. You are on a journey and things that were in your past do not repeat. You exist in a place where your reality does not reflect the "true reality" that a multi-dimensional being experiences. You are moving on a path that is linear where one thing leads to another, whereas in the reality of multi-dimensions all exists at the same time and the movement is not in one line but in all directions at once. You may expand, contract, heat up or cool down and from the perspective of your limited reality it will feel as if you have not moved at all. Your journey in your 3-D physical reality is but a small part of the story your call human life. You are an angel although you are aware of only one reality that you all have agreed to adapt. You operate in fact in many different dimensions. When you sleep in your physical reality you may be hard at work in others. At times when you go to sleep and wake up exhausted it is not because the mattress was uncomfortable but because you were at work all that time facilitating and creating in other dimensions. There is always a bigger story than the one you are aware of. That bigger story is going to begin to unfold in front of your eyes and some of you will be in awe of the scope that will unravel to you. Many of you who are on a path of discovering the bigger story will meet themselves in a quantum place and will become aware of the work that they do in other realities. In essence, you are getting closer to your own magnificence and to the energy that you carry when you are complete and aware of your own divinity.

How can we meet ourselves, some of you may wonder?

Some of you may occupy two bodies and are doing the work in different locations on this earth; others occupy a body on earth but at the same time teach and guide angels on the other side. You are a group and you are singular at the same time.

How can that be? It is a contradiction, many of you will claim!

In your reality something cannot both be one way and its opposite at the same time, but in our reality things often are. There are always many prisms through which to see yourself. You are a large consciousness that is facilitating its many parts in many different realities. All of the different parts belong to the whole but they operate seemingly separated. It is part of your journey and mission to integrate that which is separated and glue the various pieces back together. It is your mission to discover the different jigsaw puzzle pieces and harmonize them into a coherent picture so you can ascend and move beyond your 3-D idea of reality. Your mission is to shine your multidimensional light so others can use your light to wake up to their own divinity.

We are your brothers and sisters and we have been through this journey before. We come from a place you may call your future to help you get to where we see your highest potential manifest. We are your guides and we come here to hold your hands because many of you asked us to be here and to deliver messages through vibrations. All our messages are known to you and our task at this time is to awaken your memory so you will remember. Remembering is the path that allows multidimensional reality to come together and make sense.

What are we supposed to do with this information, many of you will ask in frustration? *It is too abstract and meaningless!*

We ask you to exercise patience.

We have been waiting for so long already, many of you will claim.

Then you can wait a little longer, we answer with a smile, after all, you are eternal. All our messages have energy and at times you do not even remember what you read but the energy you ingest leaves its footprint on your geometric pattern which begins to interact with your larger self, your higher self. As you begin to accommodate and integrate this new energy, awakening will begin to occur without effort. You will be introduced to new kinds of feelings first in your dreams, then in your daydreams, then in your awakened reality. The remembering happens on a cellular level and not with your conscious logical mind. Much of what we speak of does not require effort as much as it requires you to let go of the old idea of who you are and stay open to what is coming. You are about to experience a big shift. It would be considered, from our perspective, the biggest shift humanity has experienced in your collective memory on earth and larger than any mentioned in your history books. You are about to become multidimensional and it was a potential with low probability and now it seems as if you collectively changed that probability to a high one. You are on a path that is beautiful and we are celebrating your progress as we speak. We wish you to awaken to your power and become the divine being that you are.

How do we do that, some may wonder? *Life is hard and we have to worry all the time that we can pay our bills and just stay above water,* others may claim.

You are an angel and you create that which you experience. When you walk knowing that you are loved and when you are remembering and awakening to the love in yourself, all that you face will rearrange itself to accommodate your new awareness as it must. Love links you with spirit and you with all your other "yous". If you think for a moment that there will be no reason to worry, you are missing the point. Reason to worry will always be there but your awareness of your reality and your path will transform the "reasons" to "reasons" for celebration.

You want us to celebrate the things we have to worry about, some may ask in disbelief?

We ask you to celebrate the lessons in your life and to see all that you experience as a creation of love which you chose to teach you about you. When you begin to wear the glasses of a master your reality transforms and you see the colors and shapes through those glasses. Your reality becomes that of a master. The process is grand and we see many of you marching in that direction. We love you so because those of you who walk the path of a master often do not have any idea where they are going and what they are doing. They just surrender and trust that life will present the most appropriate opportunities for their growth. When they encounter opportunity they say, "thank you," and move through it. Many of you believe that the master must be an educated "super-spiritual" being that knows everything about your sacred texts and studies their entire life preparing to become an ascended master. With a hug we must tell you that it does not hurt to study and learn sacred texts and the journeys of other spiritual humans, but from where we seat it has little to do with ascension. Moving upward has to do with surrendering to the highest potential in your life and developing awareness that all comes from love. Surrendering has to do with mostly unlearning what you already know and trust. Trust creates harmonic resonance with spirit which allows you to remember who you are and become the master that you are. Many of the angels who are wearing the roles of leaders sitting at the heads of your spiritual institutions and movements walk the opposite way of ascension by trying to control that which they experience and by attempting to convince others of what they should experience. Many of your establishments which promote spiritual ways of life carry manuals on how to become enlightened. They tell you to get up at this time, and meditate for so long and eat only such food and sleep so many hours and then, you will get there. We are in love with you and we honor all of your choices. If you wish to follow a protocol and it makes you feel better about your life, your choice is honored, if you wish to get up early in the morning and meditate, it is honored as well. With a hug we wish to tell you that in order to become the master you must let go of manuals altogether. You must say goodbye to protocols. You must learn to walk without training wheels and to listen to the one voice which is coming from inside of you. The master is not the one who spends all her time following protocols. The one who walks the path of a master is the one who has no idea what the new day brings. She wakes up and says thank you, and asks for the day to reveal itself in all its glory. The master is the one who asks at night to be in the moment even during sleep. The master is the one who let go of the instructions and let go of dogma. It is the one who develops direct immediate relationship with her divinity within. When you let go you allow the new to come in. Many of you experience great fear when you say goodbye to what you know. You are afraid that you are losing your identity and you no longer have direction and purpose. There is never a judgment and one path is honored the same as the next but from where we sit, not knowing allows deeper knowing to come in.

We ask you to come with us for a brief moment into the circle. You are on an astonishing journey and all that you do makes a difference for the whole. We ask you to celebrate the morning, afternoon and night and thank yourself for coming this time around to shine the light that you carry. We ask you to awaken to the not-knowing and be in wonder for everything that crosses your path knowing that it came to teach you about you. We ask you to be an open book and allow your divinity to be written on the blank pages each moment one second at a time. We wish you to become that which you came here to experience, living as a master and an angel walking the path of a human. You do not need to become famous because you already are, as we all know your name. You do not need to become rich because you already are. You have the richest existence in the universe. You do not need to become anything, because you already are all that you ever need to be. You are the creator and you are powerful. We wish you to remember the beauty that is in you and become a pure vessel to deliver the divine energy of love to all those who are around you. Your ripple will magnify beyond earth as it penetrates all realities and dimensions. That is your true power. We ask you to let go of the idea of who you are and open your palms to your multidimensional self, which is an angel and a part of the energy you call God. We ask you to read the next chapter with the awareness that you are writing it and so be it.

The Helium Balloon

ARE YOU IN A PLACE of balance or are you wobbling along your path being shaken by whatever is happening around you? We are seeing many of you walking the path of a balanced human until such time that something around you changes. It is then that we see your geometry change and the familiar face of fear replaces the one of balance to create imbalance. We see your light dims and your pace slow to a crawl. When you experience fear you walk beside yourself and not inside yourself. We love you and we wish you to walk the walk of a master regardless of the circumstances that surrounds you.

How can we not be affected, when we feel so insecure, some may wonder?

When you experience fear you must go back inside yourself and find "you."

Like a balloon that is inflated with helium gas, you are floating above and when the wind comes from one side, it sweeps you to the left and when the wind comes from the right side it sweeps you to the right. When you are enclosed in a balloon you are separated from all that is around you. We ask you to be aware of air, not helium. We wish you to be aware that you are part of all that is around you and when all moves around you, you are part of it and not separated from it, so you are it. Many of you asked for your balloons to be punctured so the helium will mix with air to become one. This is in simplistic terms what many of you must experience, in order to move away from the walls that you have built and find your true magnificence. Puncturing the balloon is the process we wish to speak of. When it happens it is as if all that you know yourself to be is lost forever and you feel that you are no longer you. Many of you experience fear of death because in effect you let go of the very thin wall of rubber that was holding the gas inside the balloon. You felt protected by this thin rubber layer when in fact it was keeping you from experiencing who you really are. Many of you bunch together to create groups of helium balloons believing that you are stronger this way. We wish to tell you that even as a group when the wind comes, you all shift with it and when you land deflated on the ground the thorns that are part of nature may still puncture your thin layer of rubber. We ask you to let go of your walls and defenses because only then you are truly you. When you walk the walk of a human many of you see yourselves as separated from all that is around you. Many of you even see yourselves separated from your fellow angels. You see yourselves in term of appearance, gender, race, economic background and many other attributes that have very little to do with your divinity. All of those attributes are your choice of course of learning this time around. You are in a school called earth and you are the teacher as well as the student. You choose a balloon outfit before you even begin school. The balloon can be pink, yellow, red or white but it is still a balloon. You wear this outfit as if it is who you really are. When the wind comes and blows you to the side you are surprised and fearful and when over time the helium escapes from your body and your skin ages and you become deflated landing on the ground, then you are fearful of all the thorns that you may encounter on the ground. All of the balloons fly at times and at some point the helium escapes and the body deflates and lands. This is part of the course of study you have chosen in the college you called human life on earth. All of you must experience the journey of a balloon as long as you believe that you are the balloon. Time is changing and the wind is strong. We see many of you being twirled in the air and the geometry of fear is all over your magnificent energetic star.

How can we not be with all that is going around us, some of you may ask?

With all love we wish to tell you that it is your mission this cycle to become one with the air around you. It is your mission to puncture your own balloon in a way that will allow your essence to be mixed with the essence of all that is around you.

We will no longer be who we are then! We may die!? We will not be individuals, some of you may insist.

You are correct that you will no longer be what you have thought yourself to be. You will no longer be a balloon dancing with every little breeze that is twirling around you. You will have to expand and become the consciousness that you are; magnificent and grand. You will become a multidimensional being that is not defined by the outfit of a thin rubber but by the energetic stamp that you have carried before there was time and which you will carry forever. You will become closer to your own being.

It is difficult, too difficult, many of you may say!!

With a hug we promise you that it will not be any easier holding on to your thin layer of protection as all of you must at some point shed your thin layer and become one. We just ask you to become "it" in your awareness so you can experience the joy and the thrill of this time. You have been walking this walk for eons and you have reached a point where the balloon must burst and your angelic essence must come out and meet itself. It is a reunion of sorts. You with you. We see many of you in relationships holding on to your thin layer of who you think you are and the slightest wind makes you question yourself and your companions. From where we sit watching you we can see many balloons in all their different colors, sizes and stages of inflation and deflation. We are in the circle and we can tell you that when all the balloons pop eventually you all mix together to become one and part of the "air" that encompasses all. This "air" is the great consciousness you named God.

What are we suppose to do with this information, some of you may wonder?

It is our intention to hold your hand and lead you down a path that allows you to be part of the whole while walking in your outfit as a balloon. When a balloon is fully inflated and a hole is created, it goes through turmoil of deflation where the pressure of the gas from the inside pushes the balloon body in a hectic dance and in all directions until such time that all the pressure leaves the balloon and it lays on the ground crumbled and empty. With all love we wish to tell you that the process of deflation will face many of you who are anchored in the awareness of separation. This process of deflation is part of a spiritual journey that the earth is undergoing at this

time. You have asked to get closer to your Self and one
of the attributes of this process is allowing equilibrium
to be created between the outside and the inside of you.
You are part of earth-consciousness and all are on a path
of change. It is the time that was prophesied by your an-
cestors as the coming of the New Sun. You are an angel
and you are divine. We ask you to wake up to the process of discovery so you can create joy and balance in the
"now" of your life.

Many of your relationships are being tested at this
time. We wish to speak to the couples who are struggling
to create balance where balance is not available. We wish
to speak to those who are on a path of creating union and
much of the union is tainted by strife and disaccord. We
see many of you trying to become one with yourselves attempting to balance your balloon outfit just to be resisted
and shaken by your partner, lover or close companion.
We ask you to not dismiss so fast the one who teaches
you about you. We ask you to consider that the other is
not the only reason that you cannot ascend. Know that
many of your companions are there by design and they
are the ones who are showing you your own imbalance.
They are mirroring your inner "air pressure" which keeps
you in disharmony with the "outer pressure" of the whole.
We ask you to thank them and hug them. Tell them that
they are greatly loved and give them a hand so they can

join you on this journey. Much of the resistance they put out is your own resistance reflected through them. When you are on a path of discovering your own divinity no one can stop you except your own self. We ask you to take the path that is counter-intuitive and give them a hand asking them to join you. Do not do that by declaring your philosophy about life and love but by being open and not being threatened by their presence. If your partner threatens your conviction it only reflects your own weakness. We ask you to take full responsibility of how you feel and as you become imbalanced imagine yourself as a balloon and allow some of the pressure from the balloon to deflate so you and the outside atmosphere become closer and more in equilibrium. Ask to be shown equilibrium because it is your natural state and no one can ever take it away from you. You are light and you must turn it on so your partner can grow like the seed that is awakened to the sun's rays. Your companion is there to test your conviction, and it is by design, your design. You must hold on to the light as it allows your partner the option to see. If you choose to turn off your light, you are doing disservice to yourself, your partner, your mission and the planet. Even the most resistant companion is there by design and he/she asks you in the angelic form to stay the course.

Know that you are powerful and you are light. The purpose of light is to shine and not hide. Know that no shadow can ever dispel light. We wish you to radiate light and be patient. When you face a circumstance where you are threatened, go inside and hold your candle up high. Shine it and stay still. Know that you are protected and loved. Know that no shadow can ever try to take you over as it cannot. Shadow is just an obscured light; it has no power and no energy of its own. Be patient and know that you are eternal and your mission is ongoing. Do not ask why people change so slowly! With love we must tell you that your mission is not results-based but process- based; to be light all the time, moment by moment, through your thoughts and actions.

We are with you all the time and we know who you are. We also know what you are going through and there is never a judgment from our side only love. Like a pendulum you move from side to side as your emotional body is being affected by outside circumstances. We ask you to sit on the floor and imagine yourself as the air around you. When you are part of the air, even a hurricane storm is not threatening because you are part of it and not separated from it. Know that even during a storm as the air outside is twirling and blowing, the air inside you is still and calm. It is the same air in different states of awareness. We wish you to live in the awareness that you are part of the whole and the whole is part of you. We wish you to awaken to your own divinity and let go of the barriers that keeps you from discovering your own magnificence. We ask you to become an instrument of balance and light. When the time comes and many of the balloons deflate around you and drop in a twirling dance you will know that you are in the right place and at the right time to help them see. We ask you to shine your light because it is what you signed on for. The time to become the lighthouse that you are is here. We wish you to understand that your time is now and your mission has started and so be it.

Crossing the Intersection

YOU ARE A DIVINE BEING. When you feel down and out it does not mean that you have stopped being divine. From where we sit hugging you it means that you have moved further away from yourself. The sun is inside of you and it always shines brightly. When you move away from your inner light, you feel that all is in darkness. The light shines with the same luminosity but you do not feel it.

How can we move further away from ourselves, some of you may wonder?

You do so by moving away from trust and moving away from loving yourself. When you are close to your light, you must be at a place of self-love and trust.

Easier said than done, some of you may complain.

You are on a path of becoming one with your light. Your light is the source of your divinity and when you carry it wherever you go, you walk in your mastery and you are one with everything that is around you.

Some of you may say, "*We try but we do not feel what we are supposed to feel.*"

We hug you all the time and we know of your path and we know of each of your challenges. When you meet a challenge many of you say to *yourself*, "*Not again!! Why me? I wish I was someone else; others do not seem to be going through what I am going through.*" You are unique and you are magnificent in every way imaginable. We wish to wrap you in these words and repeat them over and over again so you understand the esteem in which your journey is held in from this side of things.

There are many of us who are watching your every step and supporting you whenever you ask for support.

You are the one who created the challenges in your life so you can be peaceful with all that is. You asked for the challenges to present themselves at the appropriate time so you could grow and learn. Peace is created by you moving into your own light and shining on these challenges the light of awareness; the awareness that you are so dearly loved and that whatever comes across your path is your free choice. When we speak of free choice we speak of the free choice of the larger "you" and not the limited "you" that is walking on earth in duality and victimhood. You are large and beautiful and it is time to acknowledge it and become one with yourself. Many of you give credit to everything and everyone around you accept to the one who deserves it which is "you."

We hear some of you say to yourself, *"I could not do it without this one or that one, I am really dependent on these people and I am weak on my own."*

As we hug you we wish to impart to you that you are the one who chose who would help you and when to ask for help. Help is being created and the creator of the help is your intent. There is no situation in which you are only "receiving" or only "giving." When you feel that there is imbalance, it is in your awareness and not in the situation. At times the imbalance will be needed for you to realize your inner imbalance and to give you a sign that it is time to find equilibrium within you. All imbalances are first created within and then manifested in your outer reality. When you have pain in the left part of your body, you tend to say," I wish it was like the right side, pain free." We wish to tell you that the pain is your indication that your left and right are not in balance. It is not that the right is good and the left is bad. It is that the two sides are not in equilibrium and it is manifested as pain. Your body is your antenna and it absorbs the subtle signals coming from the larger you and transmits it to you. Often it is experienced as pain. Know that your body "tells" you what it is that you need to work on. Many of you subscribe to "shooting the messenger" or at least

numbing it so it will not bother you when you are doing "more important things." We are around you and we
know who you are. Your imbalances are very important
because your mission is about becoming a balanced human who can stay in balance regardless of the imbalance
projected by your outer reality. When you are not in
balance inside, you add to the imbalance of the planet.
When you are balanced you are one of the balance holders of the planet. This is why we ask you to take care of
yourself. Become balanced and know that your body is
the first indication that you are in balance. It should be
pain free and move with ease. When your body does not
move with ease we ask you to love it and ask it to show
you ways to find balance. Give it attention and do not
ignore it, do not numb it and forget about it. Your body
is conscious and it knows your intention. When you say
to yourself; "Body, I will work with you to find balance
inside," your body responds and directs you to where you
need to go to find this balance. Your body will "tell" you
what you need to do. When you set the intention to find
balance, the ones who can facilitate your intention will
come forward and offer you help.

What it is that you wish us to do at this time, some may
still wonder ?

We wish you to take care of yourself. We wish you
to find ways to be balanced and in harmony with your

body so you can go through the transition of ascending in vibration. When your vibration increases, every atom in your body begins to vibrate faster and the total frequency of your energetic body increases. When you vibrate higher, the electromagnetism in your body must adjust to the new frequency. As the earth vibrates higher the same process happens. All the inhabitants on the planet must adjust to the new frequency. When you are in balance, you will have an easier time staying healthy when the changes take place. The changes are happening now. The electromagnetic frequency of earth's vibration is changing all the time and it is increasing. We ask you to be in balance so you may show the path of balance to others.

There are a few of you who can make a difference for the multitudes. We gave this example before. When the domino effect begins it requires one domino to not fall to stop the domino effect. We ask you to be the one who stops the domino effect when the time comes.

Why do you tell us about all this, some may ask in frustration?

When a mother takes her child by the hand and leads it across a large intersection for the first time, her desire is that the child will learn how to cross this intersection on their own. With love she explains to her child what she needs to watch for as she crosses this large intersection. We act like your mother as we have been where you are. We are not more than you are, but we have been through what you are going through now so we know the challenges you are facing. When you shed your body you are light as we are light and we are all brothers and sisters. It is our mission at this time to support you as you approach this large intersection for the first time. Like your mother, we love you dearly and we wish to hold your hand as you cross but we also wish to teach you so you can do it on your own. It is our desire that you awaken to your power and your divinity. It is our wish that you shine your light so the whole of humanity can learn from you how to cross the intersection for the first time.

With all love we wish to impart to you that our messages are not meant for everyone. There are some of you who will cross this larger intersection without ever noticing it. Some will not care about it and will choose to stay where they are. Others may choose to go home and come back refreshed so they can adjust to the new vibration without the hard work of learning balance. They will come back more equipped, skipping the transition period. You have chosen to be the ones who are the mission carriers and you know inside that you are. We ask you to awaken to your mission because you are the locomotive and your purpose in this cycle is to pull the rest of humanity behind you. Your pulling is done energetically as your work is subtle. We ask you to take care of yourself so you stay balanced.

Is it enough to just stay balanced, some may wonder?

With a smile we impart to you that it is a big first step. Much of your mission will unravel automatically. When you are in balance you will know what to do and where to go. You will intuitively know that you are in the right place at the right time fulfilling your mission and you will not be driven by fear. When you are balanced you translate what is happening around you to others. Through you, many others will begin to see the blessings of this transition and become peaceful with the ongoing transformation. When you are balanced you allow the highest potential to come forward and manifest. With a hug we wish you to take care of yourself and become balanced, and so be it.

You Asked For It

WE LOVE YOU SO and this is just the beginning. We come to you in this form because you have asked us to bring this information to you. Some of you may ask, "But *where is it really coming from?*

Our simple answer is that this information is coming from the circle. Some of you may ask if this is what some call channeling. With all love we wish to tell you that many of you misunderstand the idea behind channeling. You are all channeling all the time. It is your linear perception that keeps you from the awareness that you are many things and are in many places simultaneously.

Channeling, from where we sit, is becoming clear enough to realize the source of the information you are receiving. Like your modern day radio, if you tune into a FM station that transmits Classical music, you will say, "Now I am tuned to that station." When you change the station to Rock, you will know that indeed you have changed the station. The person channeling knows from which station she is receiving the message and can tune to it at will. With all love we wish to tell you that in your day to day life, many of you are exposed to so much noise that you are not walking in the awareness of the circle. It requires you to be in a subtle place to know which music comes from which station.

You are a vessel and that is your mission. It is you who must allow the energy of divinity through so you can become the unlimited multidimensional being that you are. Indeed there are some who channel a particular being from the other side bringing forth specific information. This is not the source of this information. We are angels and we are part of you. You are a group and we are part of your group. You may say to us, *yes but you said that you come from here and there and you do this and that.* Yes, we do and so do you.

You are much larger then you can ever imagine and your group is busy in creating things that you cannot even grasp. This information is coming from a source that is in you.

What if we do not get this information and it does not resonate, some of you may wonder?

With a hug we wish to impart to you that if this information does not resonate with you, know that there is never a judgment, but it is not coming from you and therefore it is not for you. We ask you then to celebrate your diversity and the grandness of your circle and keep searching for your mission. It is never a "one size fits all." You all have missions and they are all perfectly suited for each one of you. The ones who were meant to read these messages will know it immediately and without a doubt.

The simple explanation is that you are linear and this information comes from the circle. It connects to the circular part in you. Those of you who created this information will feel that these words resonate fully with your being. Those who resonate are the creators and the information, although brought through one human, is meant to allow the many to shift vibration. There are many layers to each of the messages. Each message is meant to address an angel at a particular time on their journey. In essence all of the messages combined are just like an alarm clock. They are meant to wake you up on the cellular level to what you already know and remind you that it is time to get out of bed.

You have chosen us to bring this to you and not vice versa. You are the creator and when you go to the store and ask to purchase an alarm clock, the store's clerk hands you one. We are the store's clerk and we follow your request.

But who are you, some of you may persist?

We are part of you, the reader. We wish to take you by the hand and ask you to fly with us into the magical land of the circle. In the circle, there is no time and no space like the one you occupy on earth. All is multilayered and happens simultaneously. The messages must come through one that has achieved harmonious resonance and a high frequency so the messages can flow without much distortion. There are always limitations to the messages as they are being delivered through words, and use the vocabulary of the one who transcribes it.

With a hug we wish to tell you that the real purpose of the message is for you to wake up to your own potential. Many of you may say: *I like this message and I do not like that message. This is from a channel but this is more scientific and it is from the writer's knowledge.* We ask you not to place boxes around the circle. The source is you. You can ascribe it to the author or an entity, or you can attribute it to this being or that but you are the source and you will know it fully when you read the messages. We love you and we wish to tell you that you are the author and you will know it because it will feel as if you could have written it. It will feel so familiar. We also told you with a hug that these messages are not meant for all of you. If you are not the "author" you will know it and there is never a judgment. It does not mean that you are not spiritual enough or divine enough. It only means that you are on a different mission and you may want to keep searching for that which resonates with your mission. You are all angels, all divine, and all on missions. No mission is more honorable or prestigious then the next. You are so dearly loved, we ask you to become that which you are: a master in disguise walking with the knowledge of your own divinity. The writer, editor and publisher of these messages are simply your messengers as they cater to your intent, bringing to you that which you have requested. Do not look at the typeface, the format or the book cover as they are just tools. These messages act as a conveyor of the energy of love which aims to link you with you and to wake you up to your own divinity.

With a hug we wish to impart to you that Love energy acts and harmonizes with your cells facilitating healing in your body when it is appropriate. Again, it is not the tools that heal you but you who heals yourself through intent. We wish to tell you that these messages do not come from an entity or a channel; they come from you, the reader. They come to those of you who requested them. Those who requested them will be guided to these messages and will know instantly that it is for them. Those of you who did not ask for these messages will not be able to finish a single page as it will appear alien or too confusing. You are magnificent and we see you as geometric patterns moving about; these messages correspondence to your geometry and each message links to a moment in time in the cycle you call human life. We ask you to read this book like a recipe book. When you crave a certain type of food, look through the menu and pick the one that seems the most appetizing. Use your feeling and allow the correct message to present itself. Be playful and allow that which comes from the circle to celebrate with you the shifts in you and the planet. You are changing and the planet is changing. Your vibration is increasing and the molecules around you dance differently than they used to. It is the grandest time in your history as humans on this planet and nothing you know will stay the same. All must shift with the shifting of your planet. It is your intent that gave the push for this change and we ask you to become peaceful with all that is around you. We ask you to use love in all your interactions and relationships. We ask you to become the master that you are at every moment that you breathe. There are many who await your awakening. There are trillions of us who support your journey and celebrate every light that shines with its own divinity. We ask you to be in the now and know that there is no other time then the time you are in. With a sweet touch we ask you wake up to your divinity and wear the outfit of the master as it is calling you. And so be it.

Down the River

MANY OF YOU BELIEVE that you are unique in your struggles. Some of you feel that you are walking alone and no one is watching. Many of you feel that you are misunderstood because you are in pain and everyone around you seems to be doing fine. With all love we wish to tell you that we can see all of it. We are going with you to wherever you choose to go and you are honored for just being where you are. It is not the journey that is honored but your willingness to dress up as a human that is clueless of your mission, to come down to a dense world where all thoughts manifest with delay and act and play the game you call life.

Why did we choose to come here, some may wonder?

You came here because this is where things are happening in the universe. This is where excitement is a way of life. You have chosen to come here because it is the ultimate honor. You are not rewarded for how you do; you are honored for jumping in and learning to swim. Part of the journey involves the energy you call karma. Karma does not come back with you to our side. Karma stays where you are and it is recorded in your own library. Karma stays with the planet. Karma is an energy that is part of the consciousness of Gaia, and it is alive and it is changing all the time. Part of Gaia is you and part of you is Gaia. When you shift, your shift is changing the resonance of the crystalline grid and causes the frequency of the crystals to change. You think you are small and alone but you are huge. You are connected all the time to all life and to the large beautiful blue pearl you named Earth. Many of you believe that you are only important when you do something important and other humans recognize it and shower you with honors. We wish to tell you that the most "important" and the most "unimportant" humans on the planet both have the same relationship with Gaia and both are known to trillions of us all across the universe.

How does it make you feel?

When an aborigine native somewhere in the lowland of Australia, transforms through a personal breakthrough and becomes peaceful, all of us know about it and celebrate it. No one in your western world will ever hear about this person but she is celebrated nevertheless and she is as "important" in our theater, as the humans who are known to all of you and are plastered across your media. It is the human and her personal journey that is recognized and celebrated. Your personal evolution is not related to your income, your marital status, your achievement, your fame, what you have or how you look. All these things are outward expressions of your inner path, struggles, and victories which relate to your karmic path of learning. Your physical reality is a dream that is manifested as a 3-D movie allowing your inner world a playground to experiment and grow. You are an actor and your show is now.

If wealth was real you would have been able to take it with you to the other side for eternity. If looks were real, you would have been able to keep "your looks" for all times. If achievements and fame were real you would have been able to rule on the other side as well. With a hug we wish to impart to you that the roles you play come and go very quickly.

You are on a river in a canoe going downstream. Many of you feel that your purpose is to get to the end destination. Many of you can't wait to get to where you need to go so you can rest. We wish to tell you that if you do that you are missing the whole point. Your purpose, from our perspective, is to go through the white water, the rocks and the dangerous parts as well as the calm and beautiful parts, and to be peaceful with all of it. Your purpose has to do with learning to feel love toward the water, the rocks and the calm areas and be in gratitude to the river for teaching you about being in the now and about love.

When we see you going down the river, only thinking of where you are heading, you are not in the now so you are likely not getting the full benefit of your journey. When you are in fear of what is to come or regretting what you believe you missed out on along your journey down the river, again you are not in the now. The now is where you carry the crown of your divinity wearing the cloth of a master.

Why are you telling us about all this? Why do we need to know about a river and a canoe, when we are just trying to make ends meet and have a normal life, we hear you say to yourself?

It is our intention to love you and give you a hand through the times many will consider turbulent. From where we stand, no one will have what you call a "normal life." From where we stand, many of you will have to continuously shift on this portion of your journey down the river. We ask you to understand that waiting for these parts to end and getting back to normal is not an option. It would be as if you wished to go to bed during the most exciting parts of your journey. We ask you to understand that this part of the journey is what so many of you signed up for, this time around. We wish you to be awakened and with the awareness of a master so you can fully benefit from every moment. Your energy, your thoughts and your feelings register with Gaia and the crystalline grids and that, brothers and sisters, *is* the type of wealth that you carry with you for eternity. It is not your currency that is changing in value each time an event changes the perception of worth. Your feelings and thoughts are your treasures. Your vibrations are your name tag and your geometry is what you are known by.

We have told you that many of you will experience the world using vision lenses of fear. Fear is being used by those who are in the dark to limit your vibration so you will stop broadcasting your melody. Like a tuning-fork, you are sending vibrations which communicate with Gaia at all times. When you are fearful it is as if someone places their hand on your tuning-fork silencing your melody.

With all love we wish to tell you that no one can ever silence your melody unless you give them permission to do so. Melody is always part of the light. Dark can never take over light. Dark fills up the space where light moves away. We ask you to not move away. We wish you to stay and hold your light firm as it is your mission. Be in the awareness that all comes from love and your mission is to radiate love. We love you and we wish you to awaken to your mastery now as there is no other time, and so be it.

White Stripe

I F Y O U L O O K U P you will see the sky, if you look down you will see the dirt under your feet. Your vista depends on what you look at. Where you look has everything to do with how you feel. When you look at what you consider negative you may feel depressed and when you aim your vision at the sun, your mood is likely to change.

Why are you telling us about that, it is obvious, some of you may claim?

You are walking the walk of an angel and many of you walk without aim. You walk as if you were guided by what is chasing you from behind. There are those of us who are assigned to hold your hand and lead you to your highest road, the one with the most breathtaking vista. We see you holding on to your ideas of how your world operates and you try to follow the rules. With all love we wish to tell you that the rules are changing and you are about to embark on a road that has not been traveled before. Road signs will not be available and the road map will not be accurate. We wish you to prepare to follow a different set of signs. You are moving into uncharted territory.

Who do you think you are? You are a divine energy and you are beautiful in so many ways, yet, when you cannot pay a bill and you cannot afford what you think you need, you look at the mirror and feel that you are worthless. When something in your life does not flow the way you envisioned, you become depressed. Your light dims and your self-esteem plummet. If you think that your life is all about getting things and paying your bills, then you may be in for a surprise.

Why are you talking about paying bills, you may ask?

Your purpose this time around is to awaken.

Awaken to what? some may ask.

It is time to understand your real power and use it correctly. It is time to realize your divinity and move away from your old ways. It is time to create magic in your life. We wish to tell you that at times the old must be washed away so the new can be established. We wish to speak with you about your path and where are you heading. It is a grand time and the train you are riding is accelerating. You are on the train and from where you sit the train is moving but you are still. From where we sit it is your energy which pushes the train and although you feel you are stationary and all around you the vista is moving fast, the train is actually you. We wish you at this time to expand the idea of who you are and to look at the moving train from above. You and the train are one. You watch the trees pass by you and hills change to mountains and then to desert and ocean but yet you sit in your chair as an observer while your landscape is changing. We observe many of you looking down at their lap top or gadgets and while the train is moving through the vista, your "gaze" is on those things you have yet to accomplish and the bills you have yet to pay and the phone calls you have yet to respond to. When the train finally stops and it is your time to get off, your realize that your journey was comprised of the "things" that you have yet to accomplish and you do not remember anything of the beautiful vista that you have passed by.

Needless to say, when it is your time to step off the train you are shocked at what you find. Your not paying attention to your surroundings when attention was called for is what causes you to be surprised. You were so concerned with what you have yet to do that you have missed what was going on.

We must speak to you with simple metaphors at times so you feel rather than analyze our words. What we ask you to do, as we hug you, is to move beyond your limited understanding of your reality and look around, slow down, smell the scents, take time to connect with yourself and take time to love yourself. The "things" that you have not done will disappear miraculously when your priorities are aligned with your divine purpose.

Is there something in your life you wish to change and you have not gotten to it as of yet? There is a road and the road is marked by a white stripe like your modern day highways. When you drive by at night you only see that stripe and you stay focused on it so you will not miss the road. During the day you can see all that is around and your eyes wander to the view and your surroundings. At night, however, you stay focused on the white stripe that separates your path from the ongoing traffic. This is a metaphor for the journey that some of you are about to experience. We ask you to invoke the light guiding stripe so when the sun sets for a short time and you are lost in darkness, your high beams can light the road in front of you and the white stripe can guide you to stay on the road and not drive into the oncoming traffic or a ditch.

How do I invoke a white stripe, you may wonder, *And why would the road turn dark all of a sudden?*

With all love we wish to use this metaphor to prepare you for what is coming. *Should we be concerned*, some may ask anxiously?

When you know that day comes after the night, and when you drive at night you must turn on your high beams and follow the white stripe to reach your destination, there is never a reason to be worried. However, if you drive like you always have and all of a sudden the light disappears and there are no markers on the road and no light, you may freeze and stop altogether. It is your awareness of the process of change and growth that you are about to experience that will allow you to move about your path with balance and peace and to show the others around you the road so they will not get lost.

We wish to remind you that you are a consciousness, you are a vibration and that you are divine. When your financial markets get filled with the energy of fear they act in the same manner that your body acts. They freeze. Money is energy and you are energy. The movement of money represents the life force of some of your economies. Your institutions, banks and governments require life force to operate and when the vibration of fear is inserted in their reality many of them respond like you, the individual; they freeze.

Your road is beautiful and you must remember at all times the divinity of your path and the fact that all that you know is about to change. We ask you to be prepared not by stocking up on food but by stocking up on balance and peace. Know that when everything freezes around you, it is up to you to stay moving and allowing the flow of life force to move about your surroundings.

Why do you tell us about freezing, some may still wonder?

When you are riding the train, we ask you to not to stare at your laptop but stay focused on your surroundings because they are changing rapidly. We ask you to awaken now because there is no more time to sit pretending that all will return to "normal." Your definition of "normal" is about to change and we ask you to celebrate it and not to fear it.

Can you tell us what is it that we can expect to see, some of you may ask? You are about to shift and all that we have spoken of in previous messages is preparing you to do your mission now on this planet.

Can you be more specific, you may ask?

It is written on the wall that much of the change around you will start in what you consider as invincible institutions and structures. The structures will begin to fracture and disintegrate. There will be time when you will need to rely on your senses, not only the five senses but your new tools which give you access to the circle. We speak of your inner guidance or intuition. The institutions which operate on fear and control will begin to shift and because they resist the change as it threatens their existence, their foundations will begin to crumble. It is a change that you collectively have asked for and it is coming. You have asked to be aligned with Gaia and be in harmony with all that is. You have asked to shift dimensions and for the ability to communicate with the others "yous." You have asked to ascend and grow. All those things that you collectively have asked for are now beginning to manifest and those structures that represent fear, control, greed and imbalance begin to taste their own vibration. It is a time when the light which exposes the dark allows that which was hidden to come to the foreground. When darkness is exposed to light it has no choice but to transform. We ask you at this time to understand that the changes you are seeing all around you are part of the divine plan, your divine plan, so do not try to hold on to the things that make you stay frozen. We ask you to allow the energy of transformation to keep flowing and to be one with it so you will not have to face the growing surge. We ask you to be the shell on the beach rolling with the tide and feeling joyful as the waves are washing it up or down the sandy beach. You have asked to know what is coming, and we reply that your other dimensions are coming to meet with you and before they do, you must transform and Earth must transform with you. You are part of all that is and when a big shift is taking place all must change position regardless if they know it or not. Like your game of musical chairs, the music is playing and before long all your seats will be replaced with new seats. You must get up when the music plays and move around. This is your task and your mission. We ask you to go back to the train and take your seats. As you sit worried about all that is happening to your personal life, we ask you to check in a little deeper and connect to that place in yourself that is eternal and divine. Know that you are loved and that all that is taking place around you has your signature of love on it. With that thought in your heart we ask you to lift your gaze from your laptop or accessories, and look through the window. We ask you to take in the vista and become one with it. Know that you are part of all and all is part of you, and as you vibrate with joy and awareness the whole train will begin to shift as you are the locomotive and what you do affects all that is around you. With a hug we wish to tell you that we are never too far. We hug you often just to let you know how much we love you. We ask you to not fear and know that you are a master, and so be it.

The Aquarium

WE ARE HERE AGAIN to say thank you.

Why thank you, you may ask?

We asked you to be in a place of love when you were walking the walk of a blindfolded human and you have. We asked you to give your hand to spirit when you were lost, and you have. We asked you to trust the journey and you have. You are so dearly loved.

What's next? You may ask.

The turbulence will continue is our answer. There are many tests and trials ahead and they can be easy or they can be perceived as hard. From our perspective they are glorious.

Why glorious? you may ask.

If indeed you choose to see your world as difficult, it will be, and if you choose to experience joy, as all around you people are in fear and despair, know that you are fulfilling your mission. We love you so and we want to show you your contract and it is written on your board and engraved on your akashic record.

What is my contract? some may inquire.

Your contract reads: "I will stay balanced no matter what presents itself to me in the world of manufactured reality." Your contract further reads that you are the master of your own reality and no one and no circumstance can ever shake you from your place of peace. And that you will become the lighthouse when you wake up to your mission no matter what situation you are in and where you are living. Your contract reads that you will emanate love to all the elements even if the elements seem to be angry. It reads that you must find the golden signature of love that weaves through all the circumstances in your life and embrace all of it without judgment.

We wish to ask you whether one could have a more beautiful and divine contract? We are with you and as you walk the walk you are never alone.

I feel alone, some of you may say.

It is your duality that keeps you in that place and we ask you to develop the eyes that see through that duality.

Is it even possible, some may wonder?

It is indeed and we ask you to give intention for your vision to become clear. We have told you before that you are enabled. Your tools are part of your biology and the way to activate them is through intention. We also told you that your 3D reality is becoming more chaotic and confusing and some events may no longer make sense. We asked you to see the divinity of it all with the vision of a master so you will believe in what you are feeling rather than in what you are seeing. We wish you to be in peace and inner joy so you can be in the now even when there is movement all around.

Should we be worried, some may ask?

You should be in joy is our answer and you will know that joy is your only option when your outer reality begins to melt. Institutions and establishments, which you have always perceived as solid, will begin to fracture and change in front of your eyes as they are exposed to the light that is flooding your planet. You will be shown the face that has been hidden from the light for millennia.

Why are you telling us all this, some may inquire?

There is a new energetic component that is coming your way and it is beautiful. It is already observed by your scientists as a new form of radiation that is coming from outer space and penetrating your planet. These particles are very small and they pass through matter easily. It is a deliverance of a love-light frequency from your galactic neighbors as they prepare to contact you, first in your dreams and then in your feeling centers. Eventually they will manifest in your reality though some of you may not see them. Those of you who are in contact with your galactic neighbors and are awakened will know that the ones they are engaged with are "different."

How should we be prepared, some may ask?

You have known about the planned meeting since before you came to this planet and you are already prepared. There is nothing you need to teach yourself that you do not already know. Your mission is the same and your galactic neighbors have been with you, watching and observing you from the time before you walked as a human on earth. They are not new to you and you are not new to them.

So what is the difference now? some may still wonder.

You are ascending and your vibration is moving into a frequency where direct communication will be possible without the use of "tricks." When we speak of "tricks" we refer to your ideas about "abductions" and "alien contact."

What about these stories, Are they real?

We wish to tell you your story in metaphors so you will feel where you are rather than process it with your logical mind. With all love we wish to tell you that from where we sit, you exist in an aquarium of sorts and you are a fish, maybe a golden fish. All around you there are visitors who watch you in your aquarium, studying and admiring you. You, however, from the perspective of the golden fish, can only see to the limit of the glass. You are unable to see what is behind the thin walls that hold your world in the illusion of separation and duality. In fact, from our perch we see that you are in a small aquarium you call earth and that you are surrounded by an infinite ocean. And though you are in the midst of that infinite ocean all you see is your own reflection and limitations inside the glass walls of the aquarium. The aquarium is not your planet but your limited ability to perceive your reality. You can travel to other planets and you will still be in the aquarium. Space and time are not your limits. Your limit is walking your journey blindfolded constricted by the limitations of your senses and perceptions. You are all galactic angels who come from different parts of this universe to act your role in a free-will reality where your true nature is hidden from you. Your mission is to recognize your true nature without having the benefit of a multi-dimensional vision.

The aquarium that you are in is being filled with water and those who move high enough will be able to move out from under the limitations of your reality and swim out of the aquarium to the vast ocean where we, and all of your galactic neighbors, reside. This is glorious and it is the reunion everyone is excited about.

We wish to tell you that you are changing and this change is celebrated by all your neighbors and family on the other side of the aquarium. Imagine that those who love you and have been watching you up close for a very long time, but were prohibited from introducing themselves to you because of the "rules of the Game," can finally meet with you in person. This is huge in galactic terms. It is a reunion of long-lost family. Many of you are reaching the frequency where that kind of communication will become a normal everyday occurrence.

We wish to impart to you that you are the "alien" as you are on the other side of the aquarium observing yourself at times. When you are not experiencing an earth cycle you may be on another system and observing earth, helping from the other side. The other side of the aquarium is in the circle and it is not limited by space-time linear reality. The "alien invasions" you may experience are very different from the version sold to you by your movies. The reunion we speak of is the kind of communication that is transparent and love-based. Now the "rules" are changing and all those who watched you for so long are thrilled to be able to give you a hug and introduce themselves finally.

You have been told many stories about aliens and "ETs." Again the story is about your oneness. Many of you have been sold on the idea that you are to be fearful of aliens who may invade you and take over. It is your linearity and your test that blocks your vision from seeing the galactic life that is around you all the time. It is your existence in the aquarium where all around the aquarium there are many who have come from all over to observe you. They are your brothers and sisters from various systems and dimensions and they are in awe of you. There are those who know much more than they are willing to share about ETs in your institutions and even in your religious establishments. They are holding this information from you because they do not wish you to expand. When you know that you are one with all that is around you, you do not fear. When you are not in fear you are powerful. When you are powerful you do not need religions and governments to protect you because you are protected by your own light from within and your own birthright divinity.

You have a big family and your family loves you without conditions. You are not asked to be part of a certain group or have a membership card. You are a member and you are divine even if you choose not to see it. Those who seek to meet with you know who you are by name. Many of them can see your geometry, your colors and your tonal range. They see your power and beauty and they can see your thoughts that emit a melody. That melody, or song can be heard throughout the universe and those who are tuned-in to you can see you through and through. You are transparent. If we could describe to you the excitement and preparations on the other side it would be of a long lost family member who is about to return after many years away. There are those among you who fear of this reunion. They represent the balance of darkness. You can find them in many of your governments and institutions and they wish you to stay where you are, under their influence. There are many benefits to them from you being weak.

Why would they benefit from us being weak, some may wonder?

It is a game and you are a player. You play with the tools you have and some have used the tools of the dark for many lives and they continue to do so. Light is love and information. Dark is lack of love and blocked information. Without light you are not able to see and therefore you act out of blindness and fear. Those in darkness wish to keep you "not seeing" so they can move you around and channel your energies as they please. You are an easy target when you are not holding on to your own power. In fact you give the authority over yourself to them so they can "protect" you. They first sell you a story that you are weak and in need of protection and only if you stay with them will you be safe. If they told you what they truly knew, you would finally understand that you are powerful and need no one to protect you. They would, therefore, no longer be able to use your energy and resources.

Are they angels like us, some may question?

Yes, they are. They represent a part of the great consciousness in duality.

What should we do with "them," you may wonder?

Love them and honor their role and you balance yourself and love yourself because it is the only way to spread the light so they can see as well. You do not need to talk to them or convince them. You do not need to send them letters or demonstrate on the street. You are light and we are light. To create the bridge of light you must wake up and be the master that you are. When you do, all that is hidden inevitably will become transparent and exposed. You do not need to "do" anything but take care of your own light. Your light joined with others will expose what was hidden.

We love you so and we know that when you see all the injustices around you that you just want to go out there and "fix" the wrongs and make them right. It is honorable and it is sacred. However, we ask you to be in a place of peace and love before you go anywhere to correct the "wrongs" that you see. Your outer reality is just a reflection of your inner reality. When enough of you transform your internal reality, the external will transform as it must. You are manufacturing all the injustices and darkness by free-choice and the power to correct them and dispel darkness is within you.

Many of you who work tirelessly for just causes, and try to correct the "wrongs" and bring light, discover that your efforts are often frustrated by a seemingly powerful dark side. From beyond the veil we can hear you say, *I want to change the situation but the stronger the light becomes, the stronger the dark grows, as well.* With all love, we wish to impart to you that the dark will be moving out as your insides match your intent. When you work on your own darkness, your outer reality will reflect the same and without a struggle. Your struggle reflects you and you must change yourself in order to bring peace on earth.

We are your brothers and sisters. We are waiting to reunite with you. There is so much excitement around your aquarium and with all love we ask you to wake up so you will not sleep through this reunion. You and the "aliens" are one and the same. It is your choice to be born as a visitor/ alien or an angel playing a role of duality on Earth. Many of your "alien" visitors are on a path of their own. Some are technologically more advanced then you, but they lack other properties that you posses so they are here to learn about you. They also have karma and at times they will violate cosmic laws and will need to balance those actions as part of their individual path. We wish to hold your hand and remind you that you are a part of one beautiful consciousness exploring its own magnificence. You are so powerful that not one of your brothers and sisters on the other side of the aquarium will come to you before you are ready. Moreover, no one can ever do anything to you without your permission. They are long "lost" family and they would love to give you a hug. We wish you to light up your own divinity and move forward toward loving yourself. When you do, you connect to and change all those around you.

With a final hug we wish to tell you to not fear anything, and to use love in all you do. Hug yourself often and love yourself all the time. Your true nature is hidden from you and we ask you to open your eyes so you can see your own beauty. With all the darkness that is around you, all the turmoil that you see and the pain of people, the most powerful thing you can do to transform it is to hug and love yourself. You will not need protection when you truly in love with your own divinity. We ask you not to fear outside reality. Even if it is your "enemies" or "aliens" from outside your galactic system, it is all one and all within you. Become peaceful, joyful and loving and your world will change to accommodate the new masterpiece that you are. We shed energetic tears when one of you begins to love yourself. We party all night when one of you builds a bridge of light and wakes up. We ask you to enjoy the most glorious time in your history and to become aware of every heartbeat and every breath knowing that heartbeat by heartbeat and breath by breath you are transforming your now, and creating the bridge of light, and so be it.

END OF VOLUME II

Epilogue from the Angels

WE HUG YOU with tears of joy, and we say hello. We have been waiting for this meeting for a long, long time. With a smile we say that it only feels like a minute. We wish to remind you as you finish reading our messages that you are never alone and always loved. You already know everything that we spoke of in the messages but we are here to gently remind you who you are, why you came here and what your journey is about. We will continue to deliver energy of love to support you on your path and we ask you to open yourself up to that energy as it is your true essence.

We are always near you.

We ask you to understand the sacredness of your journey and the magnificence of your power. You have in you the tools to change the world by reclaiming your mastery. Begin by loving yourself and when you feel lost ask for our hands and know that we are already here with you holding your hands. We come from light and so do you. When our light merge with yours it is like sun to flowers. You are so dearly loved and so be it.

Continuing the Conversation

❧

I N A P R I L I was invited to a meeting at the United Nations' UNICEF House in New York City. The participants were members of the spiritual caucuses of the United Nations and members of the Society of Enlightenment and Transformation within the UN organization. The messages in the *Conversation with Angels* book resonated with one person in particular at the UN who wanted to introduce me to her colleagues. I left Woodstock at about 2pm and arrived in New York City at 4pm. As I was getting closer to the United Nations building on 48th Street, a disturbing thought entered my mind: "Why am I doing this?" I felt great insecurity and my trust and clarity was just about gone. I thought, maybe making this trip to the city and even writing the book was a big mistake. At that moment, my car stalled right in the middle of the street. I tried to restart it but nothing happened, not even a cranking sound. I looked at the gas gauge and it was half full. I tried and tried to start the car but it was DEAD. Very quickly, a traffic jam formed behind me and impatient yellow cab drivers tried to squeeze by me, honking their horns in frustration.

My car never stalled before. The pressure built up in my head as I tried to figure out what was going on and what to do. I considered my options. I could call AAA or push the car to the side. Then I remembered my previous doubtful thoughts and started laughing. I felt that the stalled car somehow was connected to the meeting at the UN and to my journey. It was as if the angels were demonstrating in a harmless, almost humorous way that this is what happens when you lose trust. Everything stops and you get stuck right where you are. I smiled to myself. Taking a deep breath, I went into a quick meditation saying to my angels that I understood the message and thanked them for their love and guidance. Next, I tried the car again and it started immediately. I was smiling all the way to the meeting knowing that all was perfect. The meeting brought me great joy and what I believe will be lifelong friendships with some participants.

After the book; *Conversation With Angels* was printed I shared it with a few friends and asked for help in getting the messages out. Without the backbone of the publishing industry or a commercial appeal this book may not reach those who can benefit from it, I thought. However, the few responses I did received from those who found their way to the book, (see below a sample of emails I received) gave me the courage and sustenance that I needed.

I felt that my mission was making this information available. If it was meant to reach you, the Angels will take care of that and I needn't worry.

I received numerous responses from readers across the country who resonated with the messages. Their encouraging words always came at the right time.

I am grateful for the support and love I received since starting this work, and I am humbled by this journey as I continue to write the messages. It is you, the reader, who made this work possible and I wish you to know that you are so dearly loved, and so be it.

Readers' Responses

One wrote ...... "wow!! I read as soon as I opened the email!!! I finished and stood up, hugged myself, cried, invited the angels to be in my every moment of this life and physically took that step forward as an act of faith to move there." JH 4/12/09

Others wrote:

   ~ "I remain completely blown away by your book, feeling that all who read it and can take it deeply will surely find enlightenment swiftly, regardless if they can believe in the coming shift in dimensions. Every time I read part of it, I end up in tears, it touches me so deeply. But the angels are right; it is probably not for everyone." AP 1/28/09

   ~ "These (messages) are so very powerful._ I had a hard time staying awake as I read them. The messages spoke to me very directly. I am still overwhelmed by their clarity and their embrace. They made so many things,_ experiences in my life,- transparent, and allowed me to recognize them for what they were." LL Phd. 1/29/09

   ~ "Since I was introduced to the book my life has changed completely... I keep reading the book and I am amazed. I feel so privileged to be one the first of receiving these messages." Dr. MD 4/23/09

❧ "I am speechless over "Conversation With Angels". Nothing that I say would even come close to the experience that I am having while reading , All I can say is Thank You" Rev. JH 5/3/2009

❧ "So many thanks to you… and the angels! Your book is the most important book I've ever read, just what I needed exactly when I needed it. It is tying everything together that I already knew somehow and clarifying so much.." JS 5/13/2009

❧ "Dear Dror, thank you so much, you can't imagine how I need this kind of support. I've got no one to talk to here and it feels so lonely at times I think I'm losing it.

Now sitting here in an internet place in Camocim, a little town in the North of Brazil and I almost started to cry while reading your messages. Thanks a million again and a big hug with much love" AK 5/25/09

❧

Dear readers,

If you have a powerful reaction to these messages, please share your experiences with me and I will share them with others by posting them on the book website. I am inspired by your heartfelt reactions and I know others will be, too.

WWW.ANDSOBEIT.COM

DROR B. ASHUAH

Acknowledgments

SINCE THE PUBLICATION OF the first book I have met some amazing people who further encouraged me to follow my path and offered their support. You know who you are and I am forever grateful to you.

My gratitude is flowing to the angels. I can feel you all of the time, and your love and teachings are a gift I will cherish and hold to guide my life.

I thank the many authors, healers and light houses who do the light work for the planet, sharing information about love and our true nature, because without you the planet would not be as bright.

With love and appreciation, I thank my dear friends with whom I shared this material in its early stages and throughout the process. Your encouragement, support, guidance, and love cannot be measured.

I had the privilege to work with some wonderful angels on manifesting the 2nd book to light and I am eternally grateful for your contribution.

I wish to thank my editor Jeff Davis from Center to Page, LLC, who shared his wisdom and sensitivity. I am grateful to Luise Light who has been a tremendous source of light and support both in spirit and in deeds. Her editorial sensitivity made this material more accessible. To my publicist Michael Schwager from Worldlink Media Consultants Inc., who shares his wisdom, passion and love to create a venue which supports our human potential to manifest. I am thankful for your kindness, support and dedication.

I wish to acknowledge a special group with whom I met after publishing the first book and who have been a wonderful source of encouragement. I wish to acknowledge Ichinory M. Tsumagari, Exec. Director of The International Relief Friendship Foundation "IRFF" an organization dedicated to finding solutions to the global problems of poverty, suffering and disease while promoting opportunities for long term, sustainable development for people in need.

I am grateful for the terrific support of Rev. Susana Bastarica organizer of the Peace Vigil in New York City's Central Park. I wish to the acknowledge the heart felt support of Maria Luisa Vargas, Executive Director, Universal Peace Federation "UPF" USA, Office for the Coordination of Hispanic Affairs, and President, Sun International Peace Federation. You have shown me the face of those who keep the light shining at the tall light-houses standing amidst storms and I am grateful for your friendship.

I extend my deep appreciation to my publisher Paul Cohen and the designer Georgia Dent from Epigraph /Monkfish Publishing for their wonderful direction, knowledge, expertise, and overall outstanding support and sensitivity in manifesting this book.

I thank my parents for their love and support and for allowing me to grow up in an environment where anything is possible.

I especially wish to extend my deepest gratitude and love to my family. You have taken me on a journey of living and exploring love on all possible levels, beyond form towards the unlimited. You both have taught me that love has no limits or conditions.

WWW.ANDSOBEIT.COM

Message Guide

VOLUME II

This book is meant to be read like a recipe book. Flip through this Message Guide, scan it and whatever paragraph seems to draw your attention, go to that page and read the message from the beginning of the chapter.

1. The Blind

What you do for yourself is what is changing the planet. You are not asked to evangelize or bring information to those who walk in darkness. You are asked to take care of yourself. You are the one who activates yourself. Your activation is what transforms your reality. When you are transformed, you radiate energy that goes into the soil of the planet. That energy is what circulates and becomes light. This is the light that becomes available to those who walk in the dark. (page 1)

2. The Fishing Boat

It is as if you are on a fishing boat at sea and you have a radio which can warn you when a storm is coming. Your radio, however, is tuned to the old station and no communication is coming through. When your radio is not tuned to the new station, you do not get the advance warning about upcoming events in your life. You have no idea what direction the storms are coming from and where to hide to avoid them. You have no idea when the surf will start to surge and when it will end. You do not know the best places to seek shelter while the storm is creating havoc all around you. You are constantly surprised and you are standing around, waiting for whatever comes, without the knowledge or guidance to know what to do to protect yourself. (p. 10)

3. The Spinning Wheel

The faster you run the faster the wheel spins. We wish to tell you in all love that even when you spin very fast you are still at the same place you were when you spun slow. Only when you get off the spinning wheel and walk beside it, do you know that you are progressing. (p. 20)

4. The Dance

What does it mean to have a relationship with your angels? Who they are? What do they look like?

There are those of you who say *do we have proof that indeed we are not crazy?*

We know who you are and we know what some of you think to yourselves before going to sleep. You look at the mirror and say *I am talking to invisible angels and I hear invisible angels talking to me without sound. I can hear their melody without music, and I can hear their laugh although it is totally quiet. I have probably gone mad and should check myself into a clinic.* (p. 29)

5. Snow Flakes

The universe is vast and it is teaming with life. Conscious life is everywhere whether your scientists see it or not. Life in all systems is fueled and created by consciousness. We wish to tell you that you are part of that consciousness which created all the universes in all dimensions and realities. We know who you are, and to many of you, from your place of duality, it is unfathomable that you are the creator, but you are. Not only are you the creator, but you are part of the one system. This system would not be complete even with one of you not a part of it. This is why you are eternal. You are part of this great puzzle and the picture is incomplete without your piece. (p. 38)

6. Transparency

We wish to impart to you that spirit speaks to you through transparency. Transparency is the language by which information is delivered to you and is one of the forces that you cannot see, but it shapes your life. To many, a traumatic event that comes seemingly from nowhere is tagged as "bad luck" or an "accident." Many of you do not see the transparent threads of karmic settlements which create a shift in your lives. You find reasons for disease, and you find reasons for accidents. You form an investigation to look into why this happened and that happened. Then you find out that the brakes were to blame, or the other vehicle was to blame. We wish to tell you that as you are searching for the mechanics of your life, the real forces that shape your life are not mechanical, they are spirit based. (p. 46)

7. The Drama Class

You may say, "The pain that I suffered cannot be coming from love, and the pitfall that I experienced could only come from the darkness." We wish to tell you that the only darkness that is falling upon you is that which is already inside of you. There is no evil anything that is trying to hurt you for the sake of hurting you. There is no evil mastermind that is lurking at the corner to toy with angels on this planet. There is you and your karma. There are choices that you made and contracts that you signed in order to bring you closer to your true divinity. You choose to put plus or minus signs on your experiences. You choose to attach labels such as negative or positive. From the perspective of spirit, there is no negative. (p. 54)

8. Your Radio Station

We wish to tell you that it is not necessary to connect with spirit through any given text or ritual. You do not even need to speak. You do not need a temple, a book, an icon, a prayer shawl, or beads. In fact all you need to connect is your intention. Your intention can be expressed in one thought: "Dear Spirit, I wish to connect to the divinity inside me." That's who spirit is. It is not outside of you and you do not need tools to connect to yourself. All you are doing is tuning into a radio station that is playing the frequency of divinity inside of you. Many of you believe that spirit comes from above or from some entity that carries a special energy which facilitates their life. With all love, we wish to tell you that spirit is in your biology. It is part of you. It is embedded in every single cell of your body. (p. 62)

9. Walk in the Park

We wish to tell you that you are coming into a time when the truth will be exposed both in its ugliness and splendor. As the light shines brighter, more and more of what was hidden will be transformed. Before it can be transformed it must be exposed. We ask you to be prepared and know who you are and what your purpose is when you hear in the news things which may be most disturbing to you. There are many who are trying to manipulate you into fear. They know that by incorporating fear into your daily life you will be weaker and more easily manipulated. Your reality is built on layers. There is no reality per se that is one for all. Your reality is created by angels walking in duality. Your combined thoughts create the general reality which you live by in your daily lives. Each of you creates their own individual reality based on their personal idea of who they are. There are those who benefit from you being in a reality where you experience fear and control. They benefit because they channel your emotional energy in a way that feeds their greed and power. (p. 70)

10. Golden Bridge

You are coming into a time that is different than any other time humanity has seen and experienced before. You are actually changing the molecules and atoms which create your physical world. You are manifesting interdimensional DNA that has been dormant for eons. You are creating links in the neurons of your brain that have been inactive since the time of Lemuria. We wish to tell you with love that you are becoming the golden bridge and your biology is responding to your intent. We ask you to honor what is unfolding and not resist it. As you create the bridge, you begin to experience new vistas that are not in your dictionaries and encyclopedias. (p. 78)

11. Universal Symphony

When we see you moving about, we see a magnificent display of light, colors, and melody swirling and moving. Your emotions are the most powerful tools you carry and as you experience your emotions, your whole form, and melody and colors change. When you experience love your colors intensify and harmonize with the pulse of the universe. As you vibrate with love, you become a member of the universal symphony. When you feel anger or hate, jealousy or fear, your vibration and melody moves away from the universal frequency of love and you are in discord with the universal vibration. There is never a judgment on how you feel. You are built having the capacity to experience heaven and hell, light and darkness, joy and anger. They are all in you as potentials. It is your choice to play the tune in line with the universal accord or play the tune of discord. You are the musician and your musical tools are neutral. Each one of you comes with the capacity to play the tunes of the entire spectrum. (p. 85)

12. Your Children

Your children in their early years are a pure conduit to spirit and through them you may link to spirit as well. They represent a key doorway to the vibration of love out of the many doorways open for you on your journey. You must however be connected to them. When you really listen to their messages, you have one of the most profound fountains of wisdom on earth coming out of a seemingly blabbering mouth of a three year old. Your children are your teachers and they chose you so they could teach you about you. They teach you by asking you to teach them. When you teach them you learn about you. Again it is the circle. That is how spirit works and the dynamic of your interaction with your child is one of the most sacred contracts that you carry. Your children are angels like you, but they are in a costume of a young body. Many of them at this time have been on earth for millennia and are from the "old soul's tribe." They were here when earth was formed and they have come back to see it through graduation. Your children are the ones who carry the burden of teaching you about you. Many of them get frustrated with you because you do not listen. (p. 94)

13. Child Name Ego

Ego has its own geometry and its own melody as it is a part of you that is the physical manifestation of your expression on earth. When we tell you that you are a group, we mean that part of you is your ego and another part is what you named your soul. When we tell you that you are one we mean that the soul and the ego are part of the foundation of who you are and therefore they both need to take part in your journey. Like flavored water, although it is made out of hydrogen, oxygen, maybe some sugar, coloring and other ingredients you experience it as flavored water. You do not experience the separate components. It is the same with you and your ego. Ego can never be destroyed as some of your ancient traditions ask you to believe. Ego tells you about you when you look at the mirror. It reflects back to you your face which is not your eternal face but your physical face, in this expression, at this time, on earth. If you wish to destroy that which is your physical expression you must also destroy the physical vehicle which carries the ego. (p. 101)

14. Black Hole

We wish to tell you that fear has been used since the beginnings of humanity to control its progress. It was the fearless ones who allowed humanity to progress on the spiritual path.

We wish to tell you that fear is the most effective of all methods to absorb light- energy and dim it. Fear can be compared to what your scientists call a black hole.

Although their understanding of black holes is incomplete, one of its attributes is that it absorbs light, swallowing and trapping it. It emits practically no light as the gravity of the black hole pulls all energy into itself. With love we wish to tell you that the system of fear was developed to control and channel the energy of humanity so those in power can benefit. (p. 109)

15. Favorite Song

None of your religions have an actual physical story that is truer than the other. They are all colored and tainted and brought to you from a frequency that is connected to the human spiritual journey on this planet. Certain religions began when it was time for a certain tune to be played out so humans could climb the next step towards their understanding of themselves and their relationship to God.

We love you and we wish to impart to you that your journey represents one consciousness exploring its own multi-faceted aspects. Your religions are one way to help you discover who you are. Each religion or faith represents a new frequency introduced to the physical plane at a specific point in time, which answers a need for growth or diversity in the human psyche and its quest for answers. When you say that your religion is truer than another religion it is as if you claimed that the song you like is more beautiful than the song that your brother or sister likes. (p. 118)

16. Brush Strokes

When you create your reality it is the gratitude which is the signature on the canvas of your creation. Many of you attach a negative or positive symbol to the various brush strokes that make your painting. From the perspective of spirit, your different brush strokes represent different phases of you and different aspects of your development. None is more valued then the other. The value that is placed on your creation is based on your attitude. When you are in an attitude of gratitude your creation is priceless. When you are in the attitude of victimhood your creation is worthless. It is worthless because you have not put the pieces together so the lesson was not digested. It is as if you went to class but slept through the whole thing. (p. 130)

17. The Disco Ball

Many of you seekers have been advocates of the truth throughout your many expressions and at times you got in trouble for seeking the truth. In your history on this planet, religious institutions, governments and your society has brought much darkness by coercing their constituents to accept their doctrine in the name of truth. There are those of you who pushed the envelope of what you call reality and redefined it in the name of truth. Truth is something many of you are concerned with as you follow the highest spiritual path. We wish to tell you as we hug you that truth is like a disco ball. It is, metaphorically speaking, like a round object with mirrors glued on to it. The disco ball has small mirrors which reflect light or truth from all sides. As you shine the light from one side it reflects to you one truth and as you shine your light from the other side it reflects another truth, both valid and appropriate. (p. 137)

18. The Fashion Designer

What does it mean to love oneself, some may ask?

We thought you would never ask. Loving yourself means to hold sacred all that you are from all directions. Loving yourself is to accept you and to truly honor the gift of life and all that it entails. To love yourself is to love your body as it is a divine instrument that you have been given to hold your energy while on earth. To love yourself means to not love only your head and to negate the rest of the body. You must be in peace and harmony with all your parts. You must become peaceful with your sexuality and your sex organs and honor those parts that give you pleasure and hold no guilt or shame about your body. Your body is a vibrating instrument and when you hold the energy of shame or guilt it is as if you are trying to play a concerto with a damaged instrument. You must learn to love all that you are. You must learn to forgive yourself for the things that you have done that you deem "negative". Loving yourself is the most powerful attribute of a light warrior. You cannot have compassion for others before you master compassion for the self. You cannot learn to love another before you have learned to love yourself.

This whole aim of this journey is to teach "you" about "you." All that you experience is here to teach you about yourself. When you go out of yourself to give to others while neglecting to clear out the self first, it is as if you were a fashion designer who tried to market their designs while walking dressed up in rugs—neither very convincing nor effective. (p. 147)

19. Welcome Home

You fear the transition of death, but this transition from our perspective is the same transition that you experience every night when you go to sleep. You are surrendering your consciousness so it is free to wander in other dimensions and realities, and when you wake up you pick up your consciousness where you left off. Death is very much the same process as going to sleep. Are you fearful of going to sleep? When you go to sleep, you do so in the awareness that another morning is coming where you will be awakened and continue the journey you call life. It is the same with death. When you go to sleep you know that even though you leave your body it is only so that you can wake up in a new body and continue the journey you call life. It is not a fearful event. (p. 156)

20. Hot and Cold

As you move to a place of higher vibration, you will feel the additional enhancement of energy as heat or inner vibration. It is as if your body acts as a heated tuning-fork. The energy feels like bubbles moving outwardly from within. We wish to impart to you that when you choose to connect and sense coldness, this sensation means from our perspective that you are not connecting to the realm of spirit. When you sense fear or imbalance of any sort, you may be connecting to energy, but that energy may be depleting you rather then enhancing you. Your intent is your direct dial to the realm of spirit, and when you set up that area code you will reach the right place. The higher part of you which is also a part of God is a place of peace and balance. Its attribute of heat is nurturing and never threatening. It is never cold as it has balance and love emanating from it. (p. 167)

21. The Sleeping Conductor

There are those in the universe who search for those who do not occupy their body fully and "volunteer" to "help" by filling up the vacancy. It is as if they were driving a car and handed over the steering wheel and the pedals to another so they could drive the car for them. Then they moved to the back seat and faded into the background observing the scenery. From our perspective, although they have made the choice to let go steering their vessel, it is still their ultimate responsibility.

Why would we give up the driving of our vehicle, some may ask?

Some of you feel that giving up the driving frees you from responsibility and difficulty. From our perspective you are not moving forward and you are just delaying your learning. If you choose to not take responsibility for your circumstances you will face similar ones in future expressions.

There is no way to avoid your lessons; you can only delay them as your free choice is honored. (p. 175)

22. The Joy Ride

We wish to impart to you that you are on a grand joyride, and in the amusement park you call life you face many scary visions. We wish you to find the place in you that is always in equilibrium and which holds the intention for the highest potential in your life. Intention is your light as it illuminates the path that you intend. Intention must be set with your heart and not with your mind. Intention is the key as it creates the reality that you experience and the rest falls into place. Once you set up an intention you must trust that you will be guided.

It is not helpful to go all the way just to turn around at the end, not trusting that you were led correctly. We wish you to climb the train in this amusement park and tell yourself that you want the track that will lead you to the highest spiritual path, then trust the path and enjoy the ride. (p. 185)

23. The Chicks

With all love we wish to tell you that a chick flaps its wings and the air acts in resistance to the movement of the wings so the "resistance" actually pushes the body of the chick up thereby assisting it defying the forces of gravity. So it is with you, your close circle acts as the air and their resistance is what helps you to learn to fly. You must use their resistance so you can learn to defy the forces of gravity and take flight. Again it is counter intuitive but it is the way it works. When a chick flaps its wings it is for the purpose of learning the force of the air resistance. It must learn to use the resistance so it can soar above it. This is precisely what we ask you to practice. If you choose to move yourself from relationships because of resistance and seeming incompatibility you are wasting precious time. It is part of your process. (p. 193)

24. Fame and Fortune

Your actions are not measured by the amount of people who know about them or whether it was reported in the news. The importance of your actions and thoughts are never measured from the human-impact perspective. You are an angel and as such your actions are measured in the realm of heaven not earth. Earth is your stage and heaven is your home. You are an angel who volunteered to come down to play a part that is grand. Part of the role you play is forgetting who you are and trying to rediscover your true identity. We see many of you trying to gain fame and fortune in order to feel more significant and important. We wish to tell you with all love that you do not have to work hard to gain these things. In our realm everyone knows who you are and you are part of the most glorious and grand energy in the universe. Your effort is not only redundant but it is often misdirected. (p. 200)

25. Angel in Designer Shoes and Tuxedo

We wish to tell you from our perspective how one angel dressed up in designer shoes and a tuxedo falls in love with another angel who wears a long dress at the prom. We wish to speak with you about the mechanics of humans who pair in order to learn about themselves. Each one of you has a pair who is your polarity and it is magnetic, biological, and spiritual combined. You were built to look for a mate as you carry either a masculine or feminine polarity and to find balance you seek the one who balances you and it is by design and appropriate. You may seek the same gender but the polarity still exists. One will represent the male and the other the female. As in your magnets the attraction stems from the tension that is created by each side carrying the opposite charge which then creates electromagnetic polarity. Where there is no polarity the attraction will be weak. Your biology and science tells you that you are attracted to the one who best represents the continuation of your genetic pool and you seek the one who will be most suited to produce babies that will survive and strive. You are told by your scientists that you are like animals looking for a certain set criteria to hook with the one who can continue you gene pool, protect and support you. The lioness will pair with the lion that defeats the other lions, and the female gorilla will pair with the largest and most powerful gorilla that pushes away the competitors and claims its territory. From our perspective this is just a small part of the story. (p. 207)

26. 2012 Time Warp

2012 is just a marker when the new energy will begin to take hold and the shift of consciousness and dimensions will become more apparent. It will mark a shift where the babies that are being born will come with enhanced biology that will enable them to communicate with us more easily. The vortexes to what you call "alien life" that you have been searching for will open up. It will be a grand event when "aliens" will land on your front porch and introduce themselves to you. Many of you will be surprised to discover that they are very much like you. You will then realize that they have been with you observing and interacting with you all along. They will not manifest themselves to you before your vibration reaches a certain level but you are approaching that level. Your year of 2012 is the marker for these changes.

Are we to fear the events that will be forthcoming, some may still wonder?

Fear will be a choice that many of those who are in darkness will select and it will create a further distance between the old energy and the new. Fear will be used by the dark to keep its hold. Those who choose to experience fear could have a challenging time with the upcoming shifts. We ask you to know that there is nothing to fear, as you are masters of your own reality. Nothing that you will undergo can touch you if you choose to keep your light. (p. 223)

27. Bond and Bondage

It is part of your duality that in order to disperse anxieties and fears you ask those who are around you to be anxious and fearful like you. They are those who, in order to feel that they are okay, ask those around them to feel the same so they will be empowered. You think that together you are stronger in fear. That is why societies and governments often use fear, anger and hate to bond their people together. The energy of fear has been utilized in your history many times to maneuver and exploit situations so as to create bonds and bondage. We wish to impart to you that from our perspective that tendency is moving in the opposite direction of spirit as it uses darkness to create more darkness. When those around you ask you to join them in their darkness we ask you to remain the lighthouse and shine your light. (p. 234)

28. The Marathon

We would love you to know that when compared to a marathon race you are in the final stretch and there are trillions of us cheering you on. Every step you take gets you closer to where you need to be. We wish to tell you that in this marathon race you are carrying with you the vibration of the planet so your race has high stakes. The completion of your race holds magnificent potential for humanity and the establishment of peace on earth. It feels so difficult because you have been at it for so long and you are tired. You carry with you the knowledge and memory of the whole race and now that you are in the last portion of your journey we wish to tell you: "Do continue." We are all watching you and we wish you to open your ears for just a moment to hear the cheering and the clapping that is coming from the sidelines. You are so dearly loved and we see that your legs are tired, your heart is beating fast and you are not sure if you can make it to the next curve. We ask you to not think of the next turn. Just be in the moment and think of the next step. Your journey is about moving step by step and heartbeat by heartbeat. (p. 241)

29. The Ride

We see where you are heading, and it may feel like a recreation park, at times like a joy ride, and at other times, like a nightmare, so much so that you wish it were over. From where we stand you are about to enter a time in which you will feel much as if you are in an amusement park where you can choose all kind of rides. Some rides will feel very uplifting, and some will feel scary. It is up to you to choose the experience and the ride that you want to be on.

How should we choose, you may ask?

As you enter a period of changes, you must be one with the change. We wish you to be in the awareness that what you are experiencing is an inner process manifested in your outer reality, therefore, you must always seek higher ground of awareness in which you benefit from your experience. We wish you to be in the now so those rides you are on will feel like part of you. It is very disconcerting for humans to go through major changes. We wish to tell you that you are about to experience major changes. (p. 250)

30. The Magic Carpet

When you neglect the self, inevitably you will emit the geometry of lack rather than abundance. When you take on the role of suffering in order to serve humanity, your geometry will ooze the energy of suffering to those around you. For you to emit the most powerful light without filters of lack, suffering, or self-neglect, you must first conquer self-love, and from there you may do service just by being in that vibration.

We wish to speak with you about an interdimensional journey opening up for all of you. It is a journey that can take you higher than ever before, bypassing many of the attributes of past journeys required for those initiates who wished to ascend. We speak of the long training periods in which you had to be deprived of things and experience suffering and lack so your energy would purify and lighten. You are a vibrating instrument, and like a tuning fork you can be tuned with the resonance of the frequency that is now flooding your planet, or you can be in discord with that resonance. When you are in tune, the new frequency is such that you can ride on it like the "magic carpet" in your myth, taking you to where you need to be through flying and not through climbing. (p. 257)

31. The Melody and the Music

Our reality is devoid of time, and past, present, and future all appear as fluctuations of energy potentials, some manifested and some still in potential even though the timing for manifesting may have already passed. In our reality we greet and hug every single one of you who has the potential to read our messages. Not only can we see you, but we also can also see the circumstances in your life that will be the catalyst for your search. We can see how our messages will facilitate your growth, and we can see your potential for alchemical transformation as a result.

In our reality we speak directly and personally to each one of you. We know who you are, and we know and hug each and every one of you who will ever read these messages. We even hug those who were not born yet and are with us watching you, and they know that they have potential to read these messages. We sit beside you as we lay our invisible arms around your shoulders to let you know how much we love you. (p. 269)

32. The Tightrope Circus Act

Like the tightrope act in the circus, in order for the rope to be tight, the rope must be pulled from both ends. Only when the rope is tight enough can the balancing circus act take place.

Why circus act? Why tightrope, You may wonder?

The rope symbolizes your willingness to trust and walk on ground that is neither secure nor safe. It also represents your willingness to move forward, defying your instinct for survival. The "circus act" is metaphorically the chapter of your evolution as angels disguised as humans. You are walking and acting in a large tent called earth and each one of you is acting your role as you believe you should be. One is the clown and the other is on the trampoline. Your act is now changing and shifting as the circus is moving to a new destination and you must develop a new set of skills to accommodate the new act.

We wish to impart to you with all love that it is a good time for you to look inside yourself and take notes on your past performance as you are getting ready to move to a new destination. It is with love and without judgment that we present the information from the circle. There will be those who may say, "We do not believe it, this is a hoax." With all love we wish to tell you that you are also dearly loved and whether you agree with what was written or believe it, you are loved just the same. (p. 276)

33. The Toaster

Like your modern day electrical toaster, it may be occupying a space on your kitchen counter but unless you plug it in to the electrical outlet and push the lever down it will not be activated. We are the toaster of your divinity. We act as a link between you in duality to the part of yourself which is the "I am that I am."

You have a wall and that wall prevents you from seeing who you really are. To begin to see you must activate your toaster. You must acknowledge that there is something else out there beside your 3-D reality and it can only be unveiled to you if you seek it. You must therefore set up intent by taking the plug and finding a place to plug it in. Those who choose to activate their divinity will have the electrical current of divinity flow into them allowing them to become aware of the love radiating from the other side as well as knowledge of their own mastery. (p. 284)

34. The Domino Effect

We wish to speak with you about the game known as Dominos. In your culture you play a game in which you place one cube next to the other and when you place many of them, you enjoy the sight of tipping the first one and seeing all the rest crumbling and folding creating the "domino effect" we wish to use this metaphor at this time. The earth is going through changes and so are you. With all love we wish to tell you that all of you must adjust as there is no one who can stay impervious or unaffected by the events that are unfolding all around you. You chose to change and those changes are upon you now. We see the potential for events that are seemingly "negative or fearful" that may tip the first cube and therefore create the "domino effect" where all those who are standing may lose their ground and miss the opportunity to ascend in vibration. As you are weaved with the same reality as your next door neighbor you may react in the same fashion and just crumble yourself allowing your torch to be turned off. You, the light workers, are the ones who are placed along the "domino chain" and if you remain balanced you may stop the domino effect in its midst. It is enough that some of you will stay balanced to prevent the collapse of the whole. (p. 294)

35. The Gift of Lightening

As a master you choose your experience and all that you experience therefore is your choice, we ask you to take the reins in your hands and know that you are leading yourself to your own learning. There is a great story that is unfolding in front of you and as you walk the path of the master, every moment counts. You must be in awareness and awake so the walk is joyful no matter how others perceive it to be. Your reality is created by your awareness and not vise-versa. Many of you believe that you have a reality that is forced upon you and you need to deal with whatever comes. We wish to tell you that individually and collectively you are creating all the experiences that cross your path. When you receive a message and the message is overwhelming in size and scope know that it is you who have asked to be shaken so you could move up a step. When for example, lighting hits your house and you experience a loss that is great, know that it is your time to move away from those anchors which hold you chained in the harbor, and sail to the open sea. (p. 304)

36. The Protocol

Moving upward has to do with surrendering to the highest potential in your life and developing awareness that all comes from love. Surrendering has to do with mostly unlearning what you already know and trust. Trust creates harmonic resonance with spirit which allows you to remember who you are and become the master that you are. Many of the angels who are wearing the roles of leaders sitting at the heads of your spiritual institutions and movements walk the opposite way of ascension by trying to control that which they experience and by attempting to convince others of what they should experience. Many of your establishments which promote spiritual ways of life carry manuals on how to become enlightened. They tell you to get up at this time, and meditate for so long and eat only such food and sleep so many hours and then, you will get there. We are in love with you and we honor all of your choices. If you wish to follow a protocol and it makes you feel better about your life, your choice is honored, if you wish to get up early in the morning and meditate, it is honored as well. With a hug we wish to tell you that in order to become the master you must let go of manuals altogether. You must say goodbye to protocols. You must learn to walk without training wheels and to listen to the one voice which is coming from inside of you. (p. 312)

37. The Helium Balloon

Many of you bunch together to create groups of helium balloons believing that you are stronger this way. We wish to tell you that even as a group when the wind comes, you all shift with it and when you land deflated on the ground the thorns that are part of nature may still puncture your thin layer of rubber. We ask you to let go of your walls and defenses because only then you are truly you. When you walk the walk of a human many of you see yourselves as separated from all that is around you. Many of you even see yourselves separated from your fellow angels. You see yourselves in term of appearance, gender, race, economic background and many other attributes that have very little to do with your divinity. All of those attributes are your choice of course of learning this time around. You are in a school called earth and you are the teacher as well as the student. You choose a balloon outfit before you even begin school. The balloon can be pink, yellow, red or white but it is still a balloon. You wear this outfit as if it is who you really are. When the wind comes and blows you to the side you are surprised and fearful and when over time the helium escapes from your body and your skin ages and you become deflated landing on the ground, then you are fearful of all the thorns that you may encounter on the ground. All of the balloons fly at times and at some point the helium escapes and the body deflates and lands. (p. 320)

38. Crossing the Intersection

When a mother takes her child by the hand and leads it across a large intersection for the first time, her desire is that the child will learn how to cross this intersection on their own. With love she explains to her child what she needs to watch for as she crosses this large intersection. We act like your mother as we have been where you are. We are not more than you are, but we have been through what you are going through now so we know the challenges you are facing. When you shed your body you are light as we are light and we are all brothers and sisters. It is our mission at this time to support you as you approach this large intersection for the first time. Like your mother, we love you dearly and we wish to hold your hand as you cross but we also wish to teach you so you can do it on your own. It is our desire that you awaken to your power and your divinity. It is our wish that you shine your light so the whole of humanity can learn from you how to cross the intersection for the first time. (p. 329)

39. You Asked For It

These messages act as a conveyor of the energy of love which aims to link you with you and to wake you up to your own divinity.

With a hug we wish to impart to you that Love energy acts and harmonizes with your cells facilitating healing in your body when it is appropriate. Again, it is not the tools that heal you but you who heals yourself through intent. We wish to tell you that these messages do not come from an entity or a channel; they come from you, the reader. They come to those of you who requested them. Those who requested them will be guided to these messages and will know instantly that it is for them. Those of you who did not ask for these messages will not be able to finish a single page as it will appear alien or too confusing. You are magnificent and we see you as geometric patterns moving about; these messages correspondence to your geometry and each message links to a moment in time in the cycle you call human life. (p. 336)

40. Down The River

You are on a river in a canoe going downstream. Many of you feel that your purpose is to get to the end destination. Many of you can't wait to get to where you need to go so you can rest. We wish to tell you that if you do that you are missing the whole point. Your purpose, from our perspective, is to go through the white water, the rocks and the dangerous parts as well as the calm and beautiful parts, and to be peaceful with all of it. Your purpose has to do with learning to feel love toward the water, the rocks and the calm areas and be in gratitude to the river for teaching you about being in the now and about love. When we see you going down the river, only thinking of where you are heading, you are not in the now so you are likely not getting the full benefit of your journey. When you are in fear of what is to come or regretting what you believe you missed out on along your journey down the river, again you are not in the now. The now is where you carry the crown of your divinity wearing the cloth of a master.

Why are you telling us about all this? Why do we need to know about a river and a canoe, when we are just trying to make ends meet and have a normal life, we hear you say to yourself?

It is our intention to love you and give you a hand through the times many will consider turbulent. From where we stand, no one will have what you call a "normal life." From where we stand, many of you will have to continuously shift on this portion of your journey down the river. We ask you to understand that waiting for these parts to end and getting back to normal is not an option. It would be as if you wished to go to bed during the most exciting parts of your journey. We ask you to understand that this part of the journey is what so many of you signed up for, this time around. We wish you to be awakened and with the awareness of a master so you can fully benefit from every moment. (p. 342)

41. White Stripe

There is a road and the road is marked by a white stripe like your modern day highways. When you drive by at night you only see that stripe and you stay focused on it so you will not miss the road. During the day you can see all that is around and your eyes wander to the view and your surroundings. At night, however, you stay focused on the white stripe that separates your path from the ongoing traffic. This is a metaphor for the journey that some of you are about to experience. We ask you to invoke the light guiding stripe so when the sun sets for a short time and you are lost in darkness, your high beams can light the road in front of you and the white stripe can guide you to stay on the road and not drive into the oncoming traffic or a ditch. (p. 347)

42. The Aquarium

We wish to tell you your story in metaphors so you will feel where you are rather than process it with your logical mind. With all love we wish to tell you that from where we sit, you exist in an aquarium of sorts and you are a fish, maybe a golden fish. All around you there are visitors who watch you in your aquarium, studying and admiring you. You, however, from the perspective of the golden fish, can only see to the limit of the glass. You are unable to see what is behind the thin walls that hold your world in the illusion of separation and duality. In fact, from our perch we see that you are in a small aquarium you call earth and that you are surrounded by an infinite ocean. And though you are in the midst of that infinite ocean all you see is your own reflection and limitations inside the glass walls of the aquarium. The aquarium is not your planet but your limited ability to perceive your reality. You can travel to other planets and you will still be in the aquarium. Space and time are not your limits. Your limit is walking your journey blindfolded constricted by the limitations of your senses and perceptions. You are all galactic angels who come from different parts of this universe to act your role in a free-will reality where your true nature is hidden from you. (p. 355)

THE END

Breinigsville, PA USA
17 November 2009
227722BV00001B/1/P